MW00775341

Wisdom and Work

Wisdom and Work

Theological Reflections on Human Labor
from Ecclesiastes

J. Daryl Charles

CASCADE *Books* · Eugene, Oregon

WISDOM AND WORK
Theological Reflections on Human Labor from Ecclesiastes

Cascade Books
An Imprint of Wipf and Stock Publishers
199 W. 8th Ave., Suite 3
Eugene, OR 97401

www.wipfandstock.com

PAPERBACK ISBN: 978-1-7252-6537-0
HARDCOVER ISBN: 978-1-7252-6536-3
EBOOK ISBN: 978-1-7252-6538-7

Cataloguing-in-Publication data:

Names: Charles, J. Daryl, author.

Title: Wisdom and work : theological reflections on human labor from Ecclesiastes / by J. Daryl Charles.

Description: Eugene, OR: Cascade Books, 2021 | Includes bibliographical references and index.

Identifiers: ISBN 978-1-7252-6537-0 (paperback) | ISBN 978-1-7252-6536-3 (hardcover) | ISBN 978-1-7252-6538-7 (ebook)

Subjects: LCSH: Bible. Ecclesiastes—Criticism, interpretation, etc. | Work—Biblical teaching.

Classification: BS1475 .C50 2021 (print) | BS1475 (ebook)

06/07/21

Contents

Abbreviations

AB	Anchor Bible
ACW	Ancient Christian Writers
ANETS	Ancient Near Eastern Texts and Studies
AOTC	Abingdon Old Testament Commentary Series
AOTC	Apollos Old Testament Commentary Series
BASOR	*Bulletin of the American Schools of Oriental Research*
BETL	Bibliotheca Ephemeridum Theologicarum Lovaniensium
BHHB	Baylor Handbook on the Hebrew Bible
BibSac	*Bibliotheca Sacra*
BKAT	Biblischer Kommentar: Altes Testament
BST	The Bible Speaks Today
BThB	*Biblical Theology Bulletin*
BWANT	Beiträge zur Wissenschaft vom Alten und Neuen Testament
BZAW	Beihefte zur Zeitschrift für die alttestamentliche Wissenschaft
CBQ	*Catholic Biblical Quarterly*
CBQMS	Catholic Biblical Quarterly Monograph Series
CBS	Core Biblical Series
CC	Communicator's Commentary
CEB	Contemporary English Bible

CSR	*Christian Scholars Review*
ESV	English Standard Version
EvQ	*Evangelical Quarterly*
FOTL	The Forms of the Old Testament Literature
FT	*First Things*
HeyJ	*Heythrop Journal*
HAT	Handbuch zum Alten Testament
HUCA	*Hebrew Union College Annual*
JANES	*Journal of Ancient Near Eastern Studies*
JBL	*Journal of Biblical Literature*
JBQ	*Jewish Bible Quarterly*
JCHE	*Journal of Christian Higher Education*
JEA	*Journal of Egyptian Archaeology*
JMM	*Journal of Markets and Morality*
JNES	*Journal of Near Eastern Studies*
JSOT	*Journal for the Study of the Old Testament*
JSOTSS	Journal for the Study of the Old Testament Supplemental Series
MBPS	Mellen Biblical Press Series
MEV	Modern English Version
NASB	New American Standard Bible
NEB	Die Neue Echter Bibel
NIBC	New International Biblical Commentary
NICOT	New International Commentary on the Old Testament
NIV	New International Version
NIVAC	New International Version Application Commentary
NRSV	New Revised Standard Version
NSBT	New Studies in Biblical Theology
OTG	Old Testament Guides

OTL   Old Testament Library

RSV   Revised Standard Version

SBJTh   *Southern Baptist Journal of Theology*

SHBC   Smyth & Helwys Bible Commentary

Them   *Themelios*

ThSt   *Theological Studies*

TB   *Tyndale Bulletin*

TJ   *Trinity Journal*

THOTC   Two Horizons Old Testament Commentary

TOTC   Tyndale Old Testament Commentary Series

TTC   Teach the Text Commentary Series

VT   *Vetus Testamentum*

VTSup   Supplements to Vetus Testamentum

UBSHHT   United Bible Society Handbooks Helps for Translators

ZAW   *Zeitschrift für die alttestamentliche Wissenschaft*

— 1 —

Introduction

A person can find nothing more rewarding than to eat and drink and find satisfaction in his work. This clearly is from the hand of God.

That everyone may eat and drink and find satisfaction in his work— this is a gift of God.

So I saw that there is nothing better for a man than to enjoy his work, because that is his portion.

Moreover, when God gives anyone wealth and possessions and enables him to enjoy them, to accept his portion and be happy in his work— this is a gift of God . . . because God keeps him occupied with gladness of heart.

Then joy will accompany him in his work all the days of the life that God has given him under the sun.

Whatever your hand finds to do, do it with all your might.[1]

The Challenge of Ecclesiastes

ECCLESIASTES REPRESENTS ONE OF the most—if not *the* most—intriguing and misunderstood books in all of the biblical canon. It has captured the fascination of readers everywhere for over two millennia with its mix of poetry and personal reflection, its probing of the human experience and its piercing assessment of human activity "under the sun." None would deny its status as a literary masterpiece. In fact, one might argue that, along with the book of Job, Ecclesiastes is virtually inexhaustible as a lit-

---

1. Eccl 2:24; 3:13; 3:22; 5:19; 8:15; and 9:10 (my translation).

erary work,[2] both in substance and in style. Moreover, the person who studies this book will likely find it impossible to be dispassionate about its contents. For a host of reasons it will always be relevant, particularly given its preoccupation with the human condition, which tends toward despair without further qualification.

At the same time, Ecclesiastes is "a mystery still to be solved,"[3] in the words of one thoughtful commentator. Among the Old Testament "wisdom" documents with which it is classified, it lacks, in the words of one esteemed Old Testament scholar, the "passion of Job," the "desperate complaints" and "noble outpourings of praise" contained in the Psalms, as well as the "laconic dogmatism" of Proverbs.[4] In addition, virtually everything about Ecclesiastes—from its language and message to its structure, its seeming internal contradictions, and its purported lack of orthodoxy—has long puzzled students of the Old Testament. For many, it is quite simply "the black sheep of the Bible,"[5] the "problem child" of the biblical canon.[6]

It is surely no exaggeration to say that Ecclesiastes is the most marginalized book of the Old Testament canon.[7] In the words of one senior Old Testament scholar, "No book of the Bible has been so maligned yet so misunderstood."[8] The book has been described as heretical, heterodox, blasphemous, wrongheaded, revolutionary, relevant, despairing, frustrating, postmodern, enigmatic, ambiguous, and more, while its author has been called an atheist, an agnostic, a materialist, a pragmatist, a skeptic, a doubter, a determinist, a cynic, a hedonist, a Stoic, a pessimist, a free-thinker, a rebel, a deconstructionist, an early existentialist, and, of course, unorthodox; on occasion, he has been called God-fearing and orthodox. In the words of one commentator, "Two thousand years of interpretation . . . have utterly failed to

2. So Kreeft, *Three Philosophies of Life*, 7.

3. Gutridge, "Wisdom, Anti-Wisdom, and the Ethical Function of Uncertainty," 1.

4. Whybray, *Ecclesiastes*, 11.

5. So Wright, "The Interpretation of Ecclesiastes," 18.

6. So Borgman, "Redeeming the 'Problem Child.'" Borgman considers Ecclesiastes a "problem child" to the extent that it causes "intrigue and frustration" resulting from professional scholars' many and diverse interpretations. This, he worries, undermines the book's authority and does a "disservice" to the church (62–63). It is difficult to disagree, although the precise reasons for the book's "diverse" interpretations will need thorough unpacking in the following chapters.

7. Almost a century ago, Knopf, "The Optimism of Koheleth," 195, could lament that Ecclesiastes had been "much abused" due to neglect and certain interpretative tendencies.

8. Kaiser, *Ecclesiastes*, 11. Literary critic Leland Ryken describes Ecclesiastes as "one of the greatest masterpieces in all of literature and also one of the least understood books in the Bible" (*Words of Delight*, 319).

solve the enigma" of Ecclesiastes.[9] Few writings have generated more diverse interpretive approaches, and none has resulted in more diverse understandings than this remarkable piece of literature, even among professional scholars.[10] This diversity at the technical level has not served the average lay reader very well; nor has it assisted us in terms of the church's and the synagogue's teaching and equipping responsibilities.

A partial confession here is in order. Doubtless the reader of the present volume will sense in my writing a measure of dissatisfaction with some of the consensus conclusions of mainstream biblical scholarship, whose reading and interpretation of Ecclesiastes, in my view, have been stuck in the book's presumed "pessimistic resignation," "dangerous theology," and "deconstruction of traditional religion." Several generations of academic scholarship, which have poorly informed the teaching and preaching functions in our churches, parishes, and synagogues, have helped to inoculate us against some of the most valuable insights emerging from this member of the biblical canon. Broadly unnoticed along the way is the fact that we may have missed—if we have not *dis*missed—the book's main teaching and its contribution to theology. And given the dominant interpretive trends among Old Testament scholars as they approach Ecclesiastes, the book's purported message would be more likely to *undermine* rather than strengthen the believer's faith.[11] This unfortunate state of affairs notwithstanding, given the wisdom that is resident within this literary work of genius, the neglect of its insights results in great loss to any generation, and especially ours, for it addresses questions of a universal nature—questions

---

9. Whybray, *Ecclesiastes*, 12.

10. Disputed by the rabbinic schools of Hillel and Shammai in the first century, Ecclesiastes was allegorized for much of Christian history—that is, up to the Lutheran revolt in the sixteenth century. Allegorizing had the effect of "rescuing" the book by blunting its "contradictions" and supposed non-orthodox statements and by reinforcing its emphasis on "vanity." Modern interpretation, far removed from a "Reformational" reading of the book, has moved in the opposite direction, generally casting doubt and suspicion on the book's very "worthiness" and place in the biblical canon.

11. Ellul, *Reason for Being*, 10–12, is one of the few to challenge scholarly examination of Ecclesiastes by calling into question certain historical, theological, and exegetical tendencies among commentators that strike him as erroneous—among these: (1) distorting the book's message by an inability to discern the literary-rhetorical strategy at work; (2) a related inability to properly reconcile seeming internal contradictions; (3) the assumption that the writer is an iconoclast and deconstructor of traditional wisdom and Jewish religion; and (4) the assumption that a pious editor (or two) needed to adjust the main writer due to embarrassing, non-orthodox—or outright mistaken—statements. Ellul's view is that all together the above biases undermine Ecclesiastes's place in the biblical canon. I am inclined to agree.

that transcend time, culture, and social location. Hence, it behooves us to recover some of that wisdom.

The Virtually Unexamined Thesis in Ecclesiastes

The present volume seeks to explore a *Leitmotif*[12] in Ecclesiastes—human labor—which is roundly ignored, when it is not misinterpreted, by scholars, theologians, teachers, and preachers. It does so against the backdrop of the "wisdom" perspective as found in Old Testament "wisdom literature," of which Ecclesiastes is a part and which is the focus of chapter 2. Although wisdom literature has experienced something of a renaissance in biblical scholarship during recent decades and although Ecclesiastes has received a significant—and perhaps surprising—amount of attention in the scholarly literature, the book remains the "strangest" and most "enigmatic" treatise in the Bible—for biblical scholars, for clergy, for teachers, and for the average lay person. As evidence thereof, it is supremely rare to hear standard teaching or preaching from Ecclesiastes in our day. And the chances of hearing insights from Ecclesiastes's wisdom perspective that bear on a most significant aspect of human activity—namely, work—are virtually non-existent.[13] "Where shall wisdom be found?" cried Job in the presence of his three "friends" (Job 28:12).[14] In our generation, we are surely justified in asking, *Where indeed will it be found?* Are our universities, our divinity schools, and our great centers of learning making us "wise"? Have our faith communities made us wise? Where, or to whom, do we look?

The inattention to wisdom literature generally and to Ecclesiastes in particular in the church's teaching and preaching—not to mention to perspectives on human work that are found in the book—should not surprise us, however. Despite a surprising degree of attention devoted by biblical scholarship to specific commentary on Ecclesiastes, there exists virtually no consensus as to matters of form, structure, style, theology, and purpose of the book. Where there *does* exist consensus, it is a widespread agreement that Ecclesiastes (1)

---

12. *Leitmotif* may be understood, quite simply, as a word or word-group that is recurring in a literary work, with its repetition facilitating a better grasp of meaning and thereby illuminating a work's basic structure.

13. My own experience with Ecclesiastes, while by no means exhaustive, is nevertheless probably representative of that of most people. In forty-five years of serious interest in the biblical text, I cannot remember ever hearing—in *any* context—either (1) an exposition of the book of Ecclesiastes as a whole, (2) an exposition of the enjoyment theme that is laced throughout the book, or (3) any teaching on work/human labor as presented in the book. Surely that experience is instructive.

14. Job's answer, as that of Ecclesiastes, locates itself in the fear of the Lord (28:28).

is "unorthodox" and (2) challenges (if not rejects) traditional Hebrew notions of theology and ethics. In contemporary or "postmodern" terms, the book is deemed a form of "protest literature."[15] If Ecclesiastes is generally deemed problematic for scholars, it is no wonder that pastors and priests, teachers and preachers (let alone, thoughtful lay persons!) are at a loss to interpret the book and *make application in practical and meaningful ways.*

The present volume represents a modest attempt to address this state of affairs. It is not, however, simply another standard commentary on Ecclesiastes (of which, as already noted, there is a surprising number). Rather, it is an attempt to plumb the riches of this neglected "book of wisdom" with a view not only to make sense of its overall message but also to highlight what is an important theme in the book. Even among professional scholars of the Old Testament who have written extensively on the wisdom literary genre or Ecclesiastes, *not a single volume* of which I am aware has attempted to address the matter of *work in Ecclesiastes* as a self-standing theme.[16] "There is nothing," wrote one Old Testament commentator a century ago, "that has had such scant justice at the hands of . . . [Ecclesiastes's] interpreters" as the book's "gospel of work."[17] That unfortunate state of affairs remains every bit as true today. Where work *is* addressed in most commentaries, it tends to be relegated to the status of a "footnote," receiving very little attention. Hence, it is my hope to draw attention to a significant theme in the book that has received scant attention, even among professional Old Testament scholars devoted to the study of Ecclesiastes.[18] This attempt, of course, will require that we address some long-standing and relatively unchallenged assumptions about the text itself.

15. This assumption, namely, that Ecclesiastes represents something of a "crisis" in the wisdom perspective, is examined in chapter 2.

16. The lone possible exception is Tyler Atkinson's *Singing at the Winepress* (2015). The subtitle to this volume—*Ecclesiastes and the Ethics of Work*—is, however, somewhat misleading, for in actuality the volume does not address "the ethics of work in Ecclesiastes" so much as it focuses on the hermeneutic of two Christian exegetes: St. Bonaventure and Martin Luther. The next closest examination of the theme is an unpublished Masters-level paper, written forty-eight years ago, under the title "The Concept of Work in Ecclesiastes," by Albertus L. DeLoach.

17. Genung, *Words of Koheleth*, 84.

18. As an illustration of this remarkable state of affairs, in my research I have come across three essays by Old Testament scholars on the topic of work in Ecclesiastes written *in the last century*. H. G. T. Mitchell's 1913 essay "'Work' in Ecclesiastes" examines the writer's usage of three terms in the book that are translated "work" or "labor." Mitchell concludes that enjoyment "offsets" the wearisome nature of labor, serving at best as "solace" rather than expressing satisfaction *in* and *through* our work. Stephan de Jong's 1992 essay "A Book of Labour" devotes itself to "structuring principles" in Ecclesiastes that are thought to highlight the theme of work. Despite the essay's title, de Jong strangely never gets around to actually examining and interpreting the various passages

An important caveat needs to be offered at the outset. The present volume does not concern itself with questions of authorship, dating, social setting, and canonicity. Nor will it devote itself chiefly to matters of literary genre and language, even when it is true that genre-related and lexical discussions offer important insights into a book's message. As it is, all of the aforementioned questions are sufficiently addressed in standard critical commentaries of our day. The design of this volume, rather, is to highlight in a pastorally relevant manner the value of wisdom as it informs an important—though supremely neglected—subtheme in Ecclesiastes: *the meaning-fulness or meaninglessness of human labor.* The value of work in particular needs an accounting, if for no other reason, because *all human activity* "under the sun" is depicted throughout Ecclesiastes as "meaningless" or "futile" (*hebel*)[19]—a declaration that not only forms the bookends of the treatise (1:2 and 12:8[20]) but finds repeated emphasis throughout.[21] And at the theological level the value of work needs an accounting inasmuch as human beings are created in the image of God and hence made to flourish.

How to Read Ecclesiastes

Here, then, we are confronted with the need for a bit of hermeneutical as well as theological reckoning. Although "meaninglessness" in Ecclesiastes is

in Ecclesiastes that highlight enjoyment and satisfaction in work. Finally, William H. U. Anderson's 1998 essay "The Curse of Work in Qoheleth" bears the character of its title: work itself—rather than *the ground* as pronounced in Genesis 3—is "cursed"; therefore, any joy that appears in Ecclesiastes cannot be reasonably or rationally expected as the norm, especially in our labors. Also absent from Anderson's essay is any interaction with the six "enjoyment" refrains in the book that explicitly commend satisfaction in and through our work.

19. At the most basic level, one of the central elements of Ecclesiastes interpretation that eludes consensus is how to translate the Hebrew *hebel*. A quick perusal of commentaries establishes immediately that scholars disagree wildly on how to render this term. The variations range from "vanity," "meaninglessness," "futility," "deception," "profitlessness," and "pointlessness" to "absurdity," "emptiness," "frailty," and "nothingness" to "enigma," "mystery," and "incomprehensibleness" to "transience," "temporality," and "fleetingness" to the term's literal meaning—"vapor" or "breath." Although Bible translations vary, most opt for a reading of "vanity," "futility," or "meaninglessness." My own position is that the term is multivalent and can have different inflections in Ecclesiastes, depending on the context; however, unless otherwise noted, I adopt the rendering of "vanity" or "meaninglessness" throughout. For further discussion of translating *hebel* and its significance for the interpretation of Ecclesiastes, see chapter 3.

20. "Vanity of vanities . . . Everything is vanity."

21. The term *hebel* ("meaningless," "vanity") occurs thirty-eight times in the book, while the declaration "Everything is vanity/meaningless" occurs in 1:2, 1:14, 2:11, 2:17, 3:19, and 12:8.

applied to all human activity "under the sun"—i.e., to wealth and possessions, health and prosperity, sensual pleasure, honor and privilege, the acquisition of wisdom and knowledge, the pursuit of justice, as well as human labor—it is *not* applied to human work intrinsically or categorically. It applies, rather, to anything that represents *human striving* and stands apart from a theocentric outlook on human existence. Ecclesiastes is not "a resigned lament over life's perplexities and disappointments,"[22] as is commonly thought; nor is its message that the world is irrational and disordered. Rather, it is that human perception of the world is limited, with the book's entire argument building on the opening salvo that "God has laid on men a heavy burden" (1:13).[23] This "burden," however, needs to be identified with some precision and is qualified in 1:14: "I have seen all the things that are done under the sun; all of them are meaningless, a chasing after the wind."[24]

A further hint of the precise nature of the burden placed by God on all human beings is found in 3:9–11, where the pronouncement of 1:13 is repeated (3:10). Here the "burden" is clarified against the backdrop of divine sovereignty and inscrutability and in the comparison of the temporal and the transcendent.[25] It is the burden or the business of *finding meaning*—true happiness and fulfillment—in life.[26] The problem, however, is that none are wise enough on their own, as the main body of the writer's argument will argue in excruciating detail.

There are essentially three ways to read Ecclesiastes: (a) one can understand it as mirroring cynicism, pessimism, resignation, and a sort of (resultant) quasi-hedonism[27]; (b) one can understand it as advancing God-fearing faith and grateful receptivity to all of life while offering a blistering

---

22. Contra Brown, "Book of Ecclesiastes," 278. Brown's view is representative.

23. My translation.

24. NIV.

25. Some versions of Eccl 3:10, such as the RSV, read: "I have seen the business that God has given to everyone to be busy with."

26. It is the tendency of most commentators to depict the "burden" placed on humankind by God in rather harsh, severe terms, often giving the impression that God intends to tease, torment, and torture his creation. But this interpretation fails both textually and theologically; in all likelihood, it issues out of commentators' own personal biases or personal disappointments in life and theological deficiencies. As noted above, this "burden" or task of every human being is to *make sense of the world*, and our ability to do so is linked to our ability to be cognizant of our limitations, acknowledge the transcendent (3:11), and fear God (3:14). This operating assumption, which informs my approach to the text of Ecclesiastes and the book's theology and which is not shared by all who study Ecclesiastes, will need further examination and testing in chapters 3, 4, and 5.

27. The consequence of this approach is that, even without being aware of it, we end up distrusting the book, reading it negatively, and hence minimizing its worth.

critique of contemporary thinking[28]; or (c) one can attempt to "split the difference" between (a) and (b) through a "synthetic" but incoherent attempt to meld resignation and moments of pleasure. This third interpretation treats Ecclesiastes as a sort of tossed salad with no identifiable structure and no consistently clear message—or, with other words, a sort of "sweet-and-sour" mix, if you will.[29]

Disillusionment is undeniably present in the book, as the bookends, 1:2 and 12:8, and the periodic "All is meaningless" statements clearly indicate. However, that is only *half* of the book's contents—an emphatic half, to be sure, which represents the spirit of the age in which the writer lives but which is *not* his own position, as shall be argued in the following chapters. "All is meaningless" is true "under the sun," but it is not the *whole* truth.[30] Stated with different words, "All is meaningless" is true—i.e., very real—in an existential or anthropological sense, but it is not metaphysically true. A closer reading of the text yields compelling evidence that this generally negative reading of Ecclesiastes and subsequent wider consensus are "rebutted" by the writer, and that an unexpected and strangely positive message is intended. To make this distinction—a distinction that observes two antithetical metaphysical outlooks on display in the book[31]—is to go against the mainstream of conventional biblical scholarship. This distinction, with its crucial interpretive results, is taken up in greater detail in chapter 3.

Consistent with a standard technique found in wisdom literature, the wider strategy of the writer of Ecclesiastes is to contrast and juxtapose. All interpreters of Ecclesiastes—whether past or present, ancient or modern—acknowledge that Ecclesiastes is a book of contradictions. That is, the book seems simultaneously to hold perspectives on life that are diametrically opposed. Precisely how these "contradictions" are explained and reconciled determines how the reader understands the book's basic structure as well as

28. Or, as expressed by Maltby, "The Book of Ecclesiastes and the After-Life," 39, we can come under the fascinating spell of its peculiar literary charm and value it.

29. Michael Fox, considered one of the more authoritative voices in Ecclesiastes interpretation, is representative of the confusion surrounding the book's message and meaning; he asserts that the writer's counsels "are not solutions"; they "are only *accommodations*," and any hints at joy are "little meanings" lodged "within the great absurd" ("The Inner-Structure of Qohelet's Thought," 232 [his emphasis]). In the same vein, Murphy, "The 'Thoughts' of Coheleth," 102, summarizes the message of Ecclesiastes: "life is vanity, but it can be enjoyed." But to argue that Ecclesiastes's message is *both* "meaningless" *yet* "enjoyable" should strike the average reader as nonsensical and schizophrenic.

30. So, properly, Eaton, *Ecclesiastes*, 57.

31. Ryken, *Words of Delight*, 320–23, describes these two outlooks in terms of the book's "double theme": a life lived apart from faith and a life lived by faith.

its intended message. Contradictions in Ecclesiastes are allowed to stand side by side, with the writer moving back and forth throughout the treatise seamlessly without telling the reader along the way, "Now pay attention; here is a radical shift," or, "Here is the grim alternative." The argument of the present volume proceeds on the assumption that the writer's seeming disillusionment emanates from his very aim: he wishes to meet his readers *on their own ground*, in order to convict them of the inherent vanity and futility of their materialistic outlook on all of life—an outlook that denies the transcendent. A key in interpreting both the form and content of Ecclesiastes is to grasp the dialectical method undergirding the entire work. Contrast and contradiction constitute the organizing principle, and moving back and forth between these two competing perspectives functions to "keep the reader alert," which is the function of dialectic.[32] While the writer's strategy is to keep despair in the foreground, there are periodic hints—shifts in perspective—that punctuate his argument. Attending these typically unannounced shifts in the writer's presentation is reference to God the Creator—reference that is rhetorically significant and explored in chapter 4.[33]

The wider aim of the book of Ecclesiastes is to probe the question of life's meaning and purpose—an aim that is implied in the opening rhetorical question of 1:3: *What do people gain from all their labors at which they toil under the sun?*[34] The writer's response to "Where can lasting profit be found?" may be summarized as follows: "Happy is the person who can accept his or her limits set in place by a sovereign Creator." The writer is engaging contemporary debates on the meaning of life in wholesale fashion, and he does so with a view to lay waste to a prevailing outlook. A careful reading of Ecclesiastes reveals "a thread of brilliant rebuttal" to the "wisdom of the world."[35] Ecclesiastes weaves two strands, two outlooks, together in contrast, demolishing the one while affirming the other. The reason for this demolition is that life for the materialist/non-theist is a "zero-sum game."[36] Here, then, we are confronted with one of the most highly contested elements in Ecclesiastes, namely, the matter of structure. As it happens, a great literary work has a structure, whether or not the reader—or even the writer,

32. Ryken, *Words of Delight*, 320.

33. Without these shifts or interpretive signals, Ecclesiastes would simply be advocating resignation and despair.

34. This rhetorical question can be interpreted more broadly—i.e., "What do people gain through *any of their efforts in any sphere* of human existence?"—or more narrowly—i.e., "What do people gain through *their work* in this life?" The implied answer is *nothing*, as 1:4–2:23 will painfully set forth.

35. Knopf, "The Optimism of Koheleth," 199.

36. Jones, "The Values and Limits of Qoheleth's Sub-Celestial Economy," 26.

for that matter—is conscious of it. And that structure conveys meaning.[37] In Ecclesiastes, the structure, as argued in the following chapters, indicates that there is more than what appears "under the sun."[38]

The rhetorical question "What profit is there . . . ?" is intended to discourage a false view of "success" or "wisdom." At play throughout the treatise is a contrasting of two perspectives on life: one issues from what might be called an "under-the-sun" secular or materialist outlook, while the other might be termed an "under-the-heavens" theistic outlook.[39] Two interpretations of reality, two understandings as to what is meaningless or meaningful, two competing teleologies or ultimate ways of viewing human existence. Those things that appear meaningless when viewed "under the sun," in the end, have meaning if they are viewed as "gifts" of a God whose ways and works are inscrutable.[40] The argument being presented in the present volume is that Ecclesiastes possesses a double theme; that is, it contrasts two outlooks on ultimate reality: one anchored in human striving *without* acknowledgment of the transcendent and one *with* that confession.[41]

One particularly conspicuous recurring shift in the book concerns the value of human work. Viewed from the perspective of human striving "under the sun," work is burdensome toil that has no lasting "gain" (*yitrôn*) or benefit and value (1:3; 2:11; 3:9; 5:15); it is "wearisome, more than one can express" (1:8) and a mere "chasing after the wind" (1:12 and 2:11).[42] Viewed theocentrically, in stark contrast, work is the source of a level of satisfaction and

37. So, properly, Viviano, "The Book of Ecclesiastes."

38. Arguing for a reasonably identifiable, when not air-tight, structure in Ecclesiastes is Steele, "Enjoying the Righteousness of Faith in Ecclesiastes," 225–42.

39. While the present reader may react and view my use of the term *secular* as anachronistic and inappropriate, I am using it in the widest—and non-modernistic—sense to signify a metaphysical outlook that is either indifferent to or rejecting of theism and which is essentially materialistic in its conception.

40. Part of the writer's literary-rhetorical strategy is to be stark, thorough, and relentless in his critique of a "materialist" approach to reality; the reader is allowed to *feel* the pain, futility, and hopelessness of its end.

41. To argue that Ecclesiastes possesses a "double theme" is, however, *not* to argue that "meaninglessness" and "contentment" co-exist, as if the writer is arguing for a type of "sweet-and-sour" approach to life. This line of inconsistent thinking, unfortunately, typifies a great number of commentaries on—and interpretations of—the book. Rather, it is to argue that two philosophies of life, two metaphysical outlooks, are being contrasted. Nor does this contrast *require* that the writer is being autobiographical (which may or may not be the case); contrast and juxtaposition may be a *literary-rhetorical device* that engages the reader (more on which, see chapter 3).

42. As a catchword in Ecclesiastes, *yitrôn* ("gain," "profit," "return") occurs nine times (1:13; 2:11, 13; 3:9; 5:9, 16; 7:12; 10:10, 11) and thus figures prominently in the writer's overall argument.

contentment that is part of life's "enjoyment," and this enjoyment is a "gift" of God.[43] Eight "refrains" occur throughout Ecclesiastes in which admonitions toward enjoyment are variously highlighted (2:24–26; 3:12–13; 3:22; 5:18–19; 7:14; 8:15; 9:7–10; and 11:7–12:1). Several of these highlight the connection between the gift of God and satisfaction in our work—for example:

> There is nothing better for a man than to eat and drink, and find enjoyment in his labor. This also, I saw, is from the hand of God. (2:24)

> I know that there's nothing better for them but to enjoy themselves and do what's good while they live. Moreover, this is the gift of God: that all people should eat, drink, and enjoy the results of their hard work. (3:12–13)

> So I saw that there is nothing better than that all should enjoy their work, for that is their lot . . . (3:22)

> Behold, what I have seen to be good and fitting is to eat and drink and find enjoyment in all the toil with which one toils under the sun the few days of his life that God has given him, for this is his lot. Everyone also to whom God has given wealth and possessions and power to enjoy them, and to accept his lot and rejoice in his toil—this is the gift of God. For he will not much remember the days of his life because God keeps him occupied with joy in his heart. (5:18–20)

> So I commend enjoyment because there's nothing better for people to do under the sun but to eat, drink, and be glad. This is what will accompany them in their hard work, during the lifetime that God gives under the sun. (8:15)

> Whatever your hand finds to do, do it with all your might . . . (9:10)[44]

These statements, along with two other refrains, are the focus of chapter 5. As part of the writer's literary-rhetorical strategy, they are intended

---

43. The failure to see the writer's literary-rhetorical strategy in play here—namely, back-and-forth contrast between two diametrically opposed outlooks—leads the reader to interpret work as "meaningless" and merely the result of human striving—something "wearisome, more than one can express" (1:8). W. Sibley Towner's interpretation is representative: "For all their claims of unique creativity, human beings cannot escape this universal futility." See Towner, "The Book of Ecclesiastes," 292.

44. My translation based on several versions.

to stand in utter contrast to the despair and futility of human activity "under the sun" that has been described in the surrounding material.[45] In the six above-noted refrains, the connection between joy or contentment and work is made explicit. Together these indicators suggest a picture that departs radically from conventional thinking about Ecclesiastes: there is *indeed* meaning, purpose, and satisfaction in human existence, *if* life—from a metaphysical standpoint—is viewed properly. Moreover, that satisfaction is conveyed in and through our work. The admonitions in Ecclesiastes to enjoy life and work, it needs emphasizing, are contextualized in another important sub-theme, namely, the fear of God.[46] As the final *carpe diem* piece of advice (11:7–10; cf. 9:10) indicates, human beings are to pursue a joy that is tempered with sobriety. After all, hedonists, gluttons, and workaholics tend not to reflect on God's wisdom and his good gifts, and no one acquires the gifts of God by his or her own efforts. Hence, no one can claim to have acquired these gifts as personal gain or "profit," which is the implied answer to the opening rhetorical question in Ecclesiastes (1:3)—a rhetorical question that will be repeated.[47]

In the final analysis, Ecclesiastes addresses everything that constitutes normative human activity, inclusive of human labor. The writer does not despise or devalue work; rather, through contrast he is recontextualizing— and sanctifying—it. Specifically within a theocentric context, work is not portrayed as "meaningless toil" but rather as (a) satisfying and (b) a gift of God. The argument presented in the present volume is not that human existence is without toil and hardship; it is that due to a fundamental misreading of Ecclesiastes the theme of enjoyment manifesting itself in satisfying work has been all but ignored—when not denied or misconstrued—by commentators,[48] and hence by the Christian church more broadly. Expe-

45. Utterly intriguing is the extent to which commentators tend to deny or minimize the "enjoyment" theme in Ecclesiastes (on which, see chapter 5).

46. See 3:14; 5:7; 7:18; 8:12 (twice), 13; and 12:13.

47. It will be posed again in 3:9 and 5:16. This underlying premise—*gifts* cannot be "gained"—is stated explicitly and clearly in the very first "enjoyment" refrain of 2:24–26 and is implicit in the comparison found in 2:10–11.

48. Representative is Longman, *The Book of Ecclesiastes*, 106, who writes: "If there is no ultimate meaning in wisdom or one's work, then one must look to enjoy life as the opportunities present themselves . . . In a darkness of a life that has no ultimate meaning, seize upon the temporal pleasures that lighten the burden." But this sort of quasi-Epicurean cynicism is *not* the message of Ecclesiastes; in truth, no book was ever *less* "Epicurean" than Ecclesiastes. Neither is such a tendency found anywhere in the Old Testament. Moreover, the failure to discern the writer's literary-rhetorical strategy of *juxtaposition*, a matter taken up in chapter 3, results in an interpretation that attempts to "reconcile" the absurd and the despairing in the book with a so-called "wisdom" perspective—an interpretation that, alas, itself is absurd and self-contradicting. Life

riencing joy and contentment in one's work is neither the stuff of divine determinism, nor is it cancelled out by drudgery and oppression, nor is it a periodic respite in the form of a veiled hedonism with some anesthetic effect from a harsh, distant, and arbitrary God, as many interpreters and readers of Ecclesiastes would suppose. Rather, it is a part of the wisdom perspective based on metaphysical realities—a perspective anchored in a sturdy doctrine of creation that is roundly neglected yet very much needed in our own day. The world, in the end, is not so much a theater of the absurd[49] as it is the arena of God's unfathomable glory.[50]

The Abiding Relevance of Ecclesiastes

Perhaps Ecclesiastes is consigned to neglect—in the past and in the present—because we have not properly understood its message. And perhaps, as part of the "wisdom" perspective, because it confronts us as readers with our own ills and what we fear the most.[51] It is withering in its exposure of life's absurdity and nakedness when bleached of an acknowledgement of the Creator, whose ways, at bottom, are inscrutable. Regardless of the reasons for our dullness, Ecclesiastes, in its own unique way, is an invaluable guide to living faithfully in a world and culture that are agnostic or hostile to the Creator, sustainer, and judge of *all things*.

In its argument, then, the present volume is unique because of the supremely neglected topic at hand: the theme of work as a satisfying and gracious gift of God as presented in Ecclesiastes. And it is unique for one

cannot be both "meaningless" and a "gift of God." As chapters 3 and 5 of the present volume argue, the writer's *own* position is not that there is "no ultimate meaning"; it is that there is no ultimate meaning for the person *who refuses to revere God* and *who refuses to accept life as a gift* from God.

49. Or, "a theater of continuing frustration and illusion," in the words of Alter, *The Wisdom Books*, 341.

50. That God's ways and works are "unfathomable" or inscrutable to human beings—the major theological undergirding of Ecclesiastes—is a stumbling block for many commentators. Not infrequently, the interpreter brings his or her own theological biases and deficiencies to the text of Ecclesiastes, with the result that the book is thought to teach pessimistic resignation in the light of life's perversions and disappointments (an interpretation that is critiqued in chapter 3). This, however, is not the book's message. Divine sovereignty and human fallibility—two sides of the same coin, theologically speaking—are parallel doctrines that stand at the center of biblical theology. And, in this regard, Ecclesiastes is orthodox at its core.

51. In this respect, Ecclesiastes bears some resemblance to the New Testament epistle of James, a work which strikes the contemporary reader, both in substance and style, as utterly unique, given its appropriation of "wisdom" sayings, perspectives, and devices.

other reason as well. While a secularist-materialist perspective strips life and life's vocation of its inherently religious meaning, vocation properly understood infuses mundane secular life—the "ordinary"—with meaning and significance.[52] Such renewed understanding of the ordinary occurred in significant ways 500 years ago in Western history. One of the breakthroughs of early sixteenth-century Protestant reform, the focus of chapter 6, was to recover a deeper understanding of the notion of *vocatio*, following over a millennium of the church's devaluing of human work aside from a "calling" to the priesthood and the monastery.[53]

In Martin Luther's reaction to this long-standing devaluation, which is taken up in chapter 6, we find that the book of Ecclesiastes played no small role in helping shape his thinking on human labor and *vocatio*. In his introduction to *Notes on Ecclesiastes*, published in 1532, Luther laments the enormously powerful (and, to his way of thinking, destructive) influence that "saintly and illustrious theologians in the church" have had on the church's wider understanding of the book. He believes this influence to be detrimental because these theologians thought that Ecclesiastes was teaching what they call *contemptus mundi* ("the contempt for the world").[54]

Luther is at pains to counter the long-standing tradition of ascetic monasticism and isolation from the world. In his view, this was counter to a proper understanding—and acknowledgement—of creation's essential *goodness* (Gen 1:31). Monks, however, were *dis*engaged, which caused Luther to polemicize against the world-fleeing monastic tendency. In his attempts to make sense of Ecclesiastes, Luther observes that "it is almost a bigger job to purify and defend the author" from mistaken ideas that have been "smuggled in" by the church.[55] Two priorities, he believes, have been obscured: one is the author's purpose, and the other is the author's unique style. The author's aim, then, is clarified by Luther: "to put us at peace and to give us a quiet mind in the everyday affairs and business of this life, so that we live contentedly in the present . . ."[56] In the end, Luther asserts, what

---

52. Ryken, *Words of Delight*, 321, views Ecclesiastes as addressing "the acquisitive and commercial spirit" of human life, whether ancient or modern, and therefore, ever relevant.

53. At the council of Jamnia in the late first century, the schools of Shammai and Hillel disagreed over Ecclesiastes's canonical suitability, although its presumed Solomonic linkage and orthodox affirmations, despite perceived internal contradictions, tipped the scale. In subsequent centuries a chiefly allegorical interpretation prevailed—until the sixteenth century.

54. Luther, *Notes on Ecclesiastes*, 4.

55. Luther, *Notes on Ecclesiastes*, 4.

56. Luther, *Notes on Ecclesiastes*, 7.

Ecclesiastes condemns is not "creation or the created order" but rather "depraved affections" and a "lack of contentment."[57] One might argue that, in his reading of the book, Luther was contending for the "recovery of Eden," to the extent that theologically he envisioned the true church recovering "some small resemblance to what we were made for."[58] And, in fact, the writer of Ecclesiastes observes that "God created mankind upright, but they have gone in search of many schemes" (7:29[59]). Luther's theology seems to have been anchored in a sturdy doctrine of creation,[60] as is that of Ecclesiastes in particular and the Old Testament's wisdom literature in general.

On occasion throughout its history, as in the sixteenth century, the Christian church is permitted to gain renewed insight into its "apologetic" mission in the world. Part of that mission entails rediscovering the meaning and purpose of neglected domains of social life—for example, in the arts or sciences, in language and linguistics, or in the study of history, literature, philosophy, and the social sciences. And not infrequently, as we shall argue in the final two chapters, those breakthroughs—as they did in the early sixteenth century—adjust our views of the marketplace as we grasp a deeper understanding of the concept of "vocation." Vocation properly understood– the focus of chapter 7—has the effect of "recalibrating" our sense of duties and obligations within the larger ethical framework of God's providential care and purpose. Work, then, even when it does not represent the totality of our calling, is perhaps the most significant element of the believer's vocational calling because of how it utilizes the skills, talents, and gifts that have been given to us by God. Stewarding these precious commodities, for the believer, becomes an exhilarating exercise in service to God and to others. Thus, when Ecclesiastes commends work as a "satisfying gift" and the yet the believer's day-to-day experience at work is *neither* satisfying *nor* viewed as a gracious gift, theological recalibration is in order. Anything less is a failure to live in harmony with our Creator and to flourish.

Regardless of its interpretive difficulties, Ecclesiastes, as most readers intuit, is strangely relevant to any age—particularly ours. Because the book is intended to probe the meaning of life, it addresses misguided attempts at pursuing happiness, materialist orientation, conventional wisdom, promises

---

57. Luther, *Notes on Ecclesiastes*, 8.

58. Eswine, *Recovering Eden*, 15.

59. NIV.

60. As created beings, we are recipients of what the Creator gives, and he gives good gifts. The brunt of the message of Ecclesiastes would seem to be that there are "counterfeit gifts," "forged advantages," and "illusory pleasures" that result in madness, vain striving, and meaninglessness (*hebel*); so, correctly in my view, Eswine, *Recovering Eden*, 16.

of success, idolizing pleasure, pursuing reputation and worldly esteem, and living as if we don't die. None of these—inclusive of the realm of work—are left unscathed; all broadly accepted cultural attitudes are subjected to withering—indeed devastating—critique by the writer. The parameters of this critique, however, are to be found (and properly understood) in the context of "wisdom literature," to which we shall initially turn for guidance.

— 2 —

Wisdom Literature and the Wisdom Perspective

The Wisdom Perspective: Its Character, Content, and Value

ECCLESIASTES IS PART OF a literary corpus called "wisdom literature." Significantly, the wisdom perspective was common to wider ancient Near Eastern culture and not merely to Israel, even when Hebrew wisdom, canonized in the text of the Old Testament, has remained with us more than its ancient counterparts.[1] Hebrew wisdom (*hokmah*) was part of a prevailing "culture-pattern" that enveloped Egypt, Babylon, Syria, and Palestine during the second and first millennium BCE.[2] The earliest forms of wisdom literature are to be found in Egyptian culture, dating as earlier as the third millennium BCE. Hence, Hebrew wisdom did not arise in a vacuum. It was part of a deposit that was universally accessible. Old Testament texts such as 1 Kgs 4:30–31, Prov 30:1–31:9, and Jer 49:7 suggest that ancient Near Eastern

1. The wisdom literature of the Old Testament includes the books of Job, Proverbs, and Ecclesiastes, with a number of Psalms—for example, 1, 37, 49, 73, 78, 91, and 126—falling into this category. Roman Catholics and Orthodox include *Ben Sira* (*Ecclesiasticus*) and the *Wisdom of Solomon* (*Wisdom*) in this corpus and in the canon of Scripture.

2. Gordis, *Koheleth—The Man and His World*, 9. To Mesopotamian, Egyptian, and Hebrew sources we might even add Canaanite and Phoenician influences. Hereon see Dahood, "Canaanite-Phoenician Influence in Qoheleth," and Albright, "Canaanite Phoenician Sources of Hebrew Wisdom." On the presence of wisdom literature in wider ancient Near Eastern culture, see Westermann, *Roots of Wisdom*; Smothers, "Biblical Wisdom in Its Ancient Middle Eastern Context"; Troxel et al., eds., *Seeking Out the Wisdom of the Ancients*; and Clifford, ed., *Wisdom Literature in Mesopotamia and Israel*. An unusually concise and accessible summary of ancient Near Eastern wisdom literature as it bears upon Ecclesiastes is found in Eaton, *Ecclesiastes*, 28–36. Even when scholars may be prone to overstate the influence of non-Israelite wisdom *directly* on ancient Israel, its presence in ancient Near Eastern culture is not to be denied.

sources of wisdom were well established in Israel's day. This, in turn, suggests the importance of wisdom as a form of general revelation.

Wisdom, as human beings perceive it, is a human trait, an element that is part of our createdness and thus to be found among all peoples. While it is true that people are not wise by virtue of having been brought into this world, they are created with the potential of thinking, speaking, and acting wisely; this capacity, hence, cannot be denied any human being *per se*. One student of the wisdom genre describes its universality in this way: "Wisdom is something that unites people, rather than dividing them. Religious wars persist to this day, yet wars have never been conducted for the sake of wisdom and never will be. Wherever there is any discussion of wisdom, its value is recognized."[3] And, indeed, it would be difficult to find cultures—past or present—in which wisdom is devalued or not even acknowledged.

The wisdom perspective, which we may accurately call a *tradition* and hence an outlook on reality,[4] concerns itself chiefly with how to live. It is thus universal and enduring in its character, applicable to ancient as well as modern life, irrespective of social-cultural milieu. Diverse nations and cultures have had a share in the deposit of truth.[5] Because of this universal quality, wisdom serves as a bridge and means of dialogue with the world. Wisdom seeks to probe what is elemental in the human experience. What is truth? How is it known and pursued? Wherein are meaning and purpose in life found? And how are human relations and spheres of human existence ordered in light of this reality?[6] Job's question posed to the three "friends"—"Where is wisdom to be found, and where does understanding dwell?" (Job 28:12)—rings out in an abiding way, and sadly his observation holds true in an abiding way as well: "Humankind does not comprehend its worth" (23:13a).

The point needing emphasis is that wisdom serves as an important bridge between people. This was true of ancient cultures, it was true of the Davidic-Solomonic era, it was true of the post-exilic Hellenistic era, it was true of the first century, and it is true of our own day. In theological terms,

3. Westermann, *Roots of Wisdom*, 1.

4. So Hill, *Wisdom's Many Faces*, 6.

5. Whether Israel's wisdom was sharpened or strengthened—and to what extent—by either ancient Near Eastern sources or later by Hellenism has been a lively debate for several generations of scholars—a debate that lies beyond the scope of this volume.

6. It should not be at all surprising that in a "post-consensus," post-everything cultural climate such as ours such questions are deemed offensive. To ask in the public sphere today "What is truth?" or "Wherein is truth and meaning found?" or even "What is wise?" is to meet with ridicule, perhaps even mild persecution. Hence, when we ask the question "Where is wisdom to be found?" (Job 28:12) it is little wonder that we search in vain.

"special revelation" and "general revelation" stand alongside each other.[7] Wisdom permits an appeal to what is shared in common.

Wisdom, which has been described as "the art of steering" and "an attitude of prudence,"[8] is to be discerned both practically—in human skills, talents, and aptitudes—and theoretically—in sensing, for example, that there is order and purpose in the cosmos.[9] While defining wisdom may elude precision, it often appears alongside such terms as "understanding," "prudence," "insight," "skill," or "instruction." At the "macro" level, wisdom can be said to have framed all of creation.[10] Creation teaches us and prods us in the direction of wisdom. And if wisdom is revealed in and through creation, it is accessible to all people. As stressed in Israel's wisdom tradition, its beginning and its essence is the fear of the Lord.[11] Therefore, its value is supreme, surpassing that of gold or silver and all things deemed precious in the material world.[12] To be wise is to possess the practical capacity for life's responsibilities.

The fact that wisdom is a central biblical concept, encompassing both Old and New Testaments, is anchored in the fact that it inheres in the order of divine creation. That order is framed in natural law and basis on divine law. God the Creator bestowed on human beings the capacity for making moral judgments, for discerning, and for distinguishing between what is beneficial and destructive, good and evil, just and unjust. Because wisdom is related to humans' ability to function according to their nature and design, wisdom can grow as it accompanies and indwells the human person; hence, the admonition in Proverbs: "Get wisdom, get insight . . . Do not forsake her, and she will preserve you; love her, and she will keep you" (Prov 4:5). For this reason, it is customary to speak generally of older persons as "wise," since they are "ripe in years" and thus ripe in experience (Prov 20:29). This, of course, is not to say that older persons always are "wise"; after all, it is possible for them to be "foolish" if they have not cultivated a pattern of wisdom through the years. Nevertheless, there are good reasons for associating "wisdom" with age and life experience (Prov 20:29: "The glory of young

7. We observe the Apostle Paul utilizing both as he testifies before the esteemed Areopagus Council in Athens (Acts 17:16–34); hereon see chapter 4.

8. Zimmerli, "The Place and Limit of the Wisdom," 317.

9. So, for example, Job 28:23–27 as well as the epilogue to Job; see also Ps 19:1; 104:24; and Prov 8:22–31.

10. Ps 104:24; Prov 3:19; 8:22–31; Jer 10:12; Col 1:17; 2:3; and Heb 1:2.

11. For example, Job 28:28; Prov 1:7, 29; 2:5; 3:7; 9:10; Ps 33:8; 67:7; 86:11; 102:15; 112:1; and 119:63. In fact, the fear of God may be viewed as both the beginning or root of wisdom as well as its end or crown (so Eichrodt, *Theology of the Old Testament—Vol. 2*, 92).

12. Prov 2:4; 3:14–15; and 8:10.

men is their strength, but the splendor of old men is their gray hair."[13]), the
tragic life of Solomon notwithstanding.

In the Old Testament, in addition to counseling and instructing human
beings along life's journey,[14] wisdom is depicted as the mark of a soldier,[15]
a quality that informs technical skill and craftsmanship,[16] and the guide of
leaders and kings as well as judges.[17] Applied to Israel of old, it allowed the
"chosen" to live as a nation whose God is the Lord.[18] Without wisdom, peoples and cultures are consigned to volatility and folly.[19] In the grand scheme
of things, then, wisdom may be rightly described as "the fundamental principle of the universe and the guide of human life"[20]; in truth, the context
of wisdom is to be found in the streets and the marketplace (cf. Prov 1:20;
8:1–4; and 9:3). It is the fruit of creation and providence, accessible to all,
and may be understood theologically, as we have noted, as a central aspect of
"general revelation" or "common grace."[21]

Both Job and Ecclesiastes, significantly, can be seen to oppose presumptuous ways in which even *religious conviction* falls short of divine wisdom. One sees this most clearly in the attitudes and speech of Job's three
"friends"—material that constitutes the largest part of the book.[22] And in

13. ESV; cf. Job 15:10.

14. Prov 1:1–9:18 and 14:1–35.

15. Prov 21:22 and Eccl 9:18.

16. Exod 28:3; 35:25–26; 1 Kgs 7:14; Isa 10:13; 40:20; Ezek 27:8; and 28:5.

17. Gen 41:33, 39; Exod 7:11; Deut 1:13; 1 Kgs 3:28; 1 Chr 27:32; and Prov 8:15–16.
In fact, the importance of wisdom and counselors in supporting kingship is on display
frequently in the Old Testament—for example, in 2 Sam 15:12; 16:20; 17:14; Esth 1:13;
Isa 3:3; 16:3; Jer 50:35; 51:57; Dan 5:7–16; and Obad 8.

18. Deut 6:1–5.

19. Thus Isa 33:6 and numerous sayings in the book of Proverbs.

20. Paterson, *The Book That Is Alive*, 80.

21. In Calvinist theological terms, "common grace" is distinct from "particular
grace." By the former, all of creation is understood to be maintained and preserved
through God's providential care; by the latter, that is, what we call special revelation,
we enter into communion with God by means of atonement, cleansing from sin, and
walking in newness of spiritual life.

22. That self-righteousness and presumption characterize the three "friends"
is noteworthy. In a similar vein, Eccl 7:16 reads, "Do not be overrighteous—neither
be overwise . . ." (NIV). These words baffle a great many interpreters, who insist on
understanding them as the golden mean between extreme positions (i.e., "virtue" in
an Aristotelian sense). A more accurate interpretation, consistent with Old Testament
wisdom literature, is to understand "overly righteous" as *self-righteous*. One cannot be
"overly wise"; such is an impossibility. But one *can* presume to be overly "righteous" by
trusting in one's own merits or one's own knowledge. This both fits the context—i.e.,
"the person who fears God" (7:18)—and agrees with another wisdom saying: "There

Ecclesiastes the writer's argument, from beginning to end, unfolds against the theological backdrop of divine sovereignty and inscrutability. Humans can only plumb wisdom in a superficial way; much remains hidden behind a veil, so that in the end wisdom beckons human beings, in their limitations and in awe-struck silence, to adore an all-wise Creator.[23]

Wisdom, then, can be described as "pious sobriety amidst uncertainty," with its acceptance—joyfully and not begrudgingly—of human limitations.[24] The fear of the Lord, so central not only to Israel's wisdom literature but to the entirety of the biblical canon, is predicated on God's holiness, his otherness, his unapproachable nature. This guiding motivation suggests that discernment and wisdom are at odds with—and oppose—the hubris and false confidence that characterizes human nature. Not a few biblical commentators, in their reading of Ecclesiastes, wrongly assume and conclude that this "fear" amounts to dread and terror. This false caricature, however, proceeds from a theological deficiency in commentators themselves that is then imported into the text itself. Inhering in the fear of God is an element of confidence, trust, self-surrender, and indeed wonder as well.[25] And, in Ecclesiastes, as we shall observe, it also expresses itself in joy and gratitude—precisely what we find in recurring refrains (see chapter 5) that reach a crescendo in 9:7–10 and 11:7–10. One theologian is justified in identifying the "wedge" of Ecclesiastes' message: the writer seeks the "dethroning of all autonomous wisdom."[26] Failure to distinguish between an "autonomous," anthropocentric (and hence *worldly*) wisdom and *divine* wisdom may be one reason why, in wider Ecclesiastes scholarship, "the positive elements are on the whole too little regarded."[27] And that failure also leads to the tendency among scholars to interpret the fear of God in the book in such utterly negative ways.[28]

To have wisdom is to walk in harmony with the Creator.[29] For this reason, "wisdom literature"—which expresses the "wisdom" perspective on

---

are those who are clean in their own eyes but are not washed of their [own] filth" (Prov 30:12–13, NASB).

23. Notice the effect of silence and awe generated by the divine speeches in Job—Job, in the end, does not speak but rather listens and bows down—as well as the manner in which worship is depicted in Eccl 5:1–7.

24. So, properly, Gutridge, "Wisdom, Anti-Wisdom, and the Ethical Functions of Uncertainty," 20, 166.

25. See, for example, Job 1:8; Prov 3:7; 8:13; 14:2; and 16:6.

26. Eichrodt, *Theology of the Old Testament—Vol. 2*, 88.

27. Eichrodt, *Theology of the Old Testament—Vol. 2*, 89n2.

28. On the significance of the theme of the fear of God, see chapter 4.

29. To depict "wisdom" as "our awareness of the inherent tension between the inner

life—is important for numerous reasons, several of which would seem basic for the day in which we live. At the most basic level, in relative terms we live in a foolish culture—a fact that applies to virtually all modern Western societies. As a consequence, to make claims today in the public sphere that call for virtuous behavior, moral formation, or moral discernment frequently results in charges of being "hate-filled," "bigoted," and "intolerant." Alas, to seek wisdom is decidedly out of step with the times. Second, most formal attempts in the twenty-first century to account for either virtue or vice tend to reduce (at least in Western culture) to biology, neuroscience, or related materialist constructions of the human person and the human brain. Representative of this mind-set, one science writer observes,

> a lot of recent research in neuroeconomics and (in a broader sense) social neuroscience—including related fields like cognitive neuroscience, behavioral psychology, moral philosophy, and the like—strikes me as an immensely fertile area to till for fresh new insights into the nature of wisdom.[30]

Third, and perhaps most importantly, standard Christian teaching and preaching tends to ignore wisdom literature with its invaluable perspectives[31] and is often subservient to the cultural-ecclesial idols of "church growth," "seeker-friendliness," numerical assessments of "success," and the like. We miss valuable insights into living—to our great peril—by ignoring wisdom literature. Among these insights are the importance of virtue and moral formation, lessons from physical nature that bear upon human nature, the "value" of suffering, the reality of divine providence in light of life's mystery, and an anatomy of stewardship.

'I' and the outer world," as one materialist philosopher in our day posits (Hall, *Wisdom*, 9), is insufficient, even when we may grant it to be a starting point. Wisdom entails more—not merely an awareness of this tension but taking practical steps, based on a theistic framework, to live in harmony (1) with others, (2) with the surrounding world, and (most importantly) (3) with the Creator.

30. Hall, *Wisdom*, 16. For Hall, the vocabulary of human virtue reduces to "the eight neural pillars of wisdom" (19, 59). Hall, of course, is merely representative of the great mass of "science" writers and social philosophers today for whom ethics and virtue reduce to a study of neurology and brain science.

31. In all fairness, even the devoted reader of the Bible who jumps from the Old Testament's historical or prophetic books encounters a vastly different world in wisdom literature, where there is little (if any) discourse about God's character, covenant, a chosen people, the Temple cult, the law, priesthood, and the like. The emphasis appears to be anthropological rather than strictly theological, with a focus on human behavior or human experience and with its tendency to draw from both reason and revelation.

Ecclesiastes and the Form of Wisdom

While questions such as what exactly constitutes "wisdom literature" and what the precise origin of this literary genre is are the subject of lively—and in some ways interminable—debate among Old Testament scholars,[32] a number of features are peculiar to the wisdom genre as found in the Old Testament. Among these are:

- its focus on how to live;

- its accent on actions, human labor, and economics;[33]

- its universal outlook and cosmic perspective, given the doctrine of creation;[34]

- its pedagogical use of nature through analogy to reflect lessons for human nature;[35]

- its social concern;

- its ability to utilize many literary forms, including aphorism, repetition,[36] allegorizing, personification, and rhetorical questions;

- its use of quotations, which mirrors an awareness of insights by past wise individuals and hence the recognition of a "wisdom tradition";

32. So, for example, Sneed, ed., *Was There a Wisdom Tradition?* On the matter of the origins of "wisdom literature," strong disagreement can be observed. Some would argue that it was the outgrowth of oral folk wisdom in various ancient cultures, while others would argue that it originated in "wisdom schools." Entering that debate, however, far exceeds the scope of the present volume. For a concise overview of that debate, see Westermann, *Roots of Wisdom*, 3–5.

33. In Ecclesiastes, the "economic" references are many—for example, the references to "profit" or "gain" (1:3; 2:11; 3:9; 5:16), allusions to wealth and possessions (2:4–11; 5:8–17; 6:1–9), and metaphorical allusions to "sowing" and "reaping" (11:1–6). Blenkinsopp, *Wisdom and Law in the Old Testament*, 78, perhaps overstates it when he writes that the writer is "obsessed" with "toil" as the defining characteristic of human activity. We can agree, however, that human labor is *central* to the writer's overall argument.

34. Creation teaches us—we may even say, *prods* us—in the direction of wisdom, to the extent that we share affinities with the natural world of which we are a part for the purpose of stewarding it.

35. Nature supports the theological framework in Ecclesiastes by serving as an analogy to the unpredictability and inscrutability of the divine purpose. Just as we cannot predict the weather or death or guarantee the results of our "sowing" (11:1–12:8), since fortunes change continually, we cannot penetrate God's purposes.

36. Repetition is a—if not *the*—key feature of wisdom literature. In the words of Alter, *The Art of Biblical Narrative*, 111, repetition can be "imposing" to the average reader, even when it initially may strike us as "primitive" due to its schematic simplicity.

- its implicit theology;

- its accent on experience and observation;

- its distinction between truisms and unchangeable truth; and

- its complementary status with Torah/law.[37]

Some comment about the aforementioned features of wisdom literature is in order. First and foremost, in general terms wisdom literature commends a certain way or path of happiness or blessing in terms of human behavior. Here it is important to stress the difference between "truisms" and *inviolable truth* in terms of the human experience. A truism holds true *generally* in human experience yet without guarantee. It is possible, for example, that not all good or righteous behavior will be immediately rewarded or "blessed," and it is possible, in human experience, that injustice and evil "triumph." The seeming "contradiction" or "reversal" of moral reality (as suggested, for example, in Eccl 4: 1–3, 6:1–6, and 8:14) need not, however, result in our concluding that "cause and consequence" or "reward and punishment" are being challenged or negated in Ecclesiastes, as the overwhelming majority of commentators want to insist (on which, see below).[38] Speculative wisdom, such as we encounter in both Job and Ecclesiastes, does not deny the act-consequence principle of practical wisdom. It simply probes, with at times excruciating intensity as we also find in various psalms of lament, when and where the principles of "justice" appear not to apply in the human experience.[39]

Wisdom literature is characterized by a peculiar literary form, often didactic in character, with an emphasis on practical lived experience, as well as a particular language and vocabulary that mirror a focus on the human

---

37. A most helpful summary and discussion of these "wisdom" characteristics can be found in Hill, *Wisdom's Many Faces*, 17–64.

38. Representative of this widespread misperception among Old Testament scholars are, for example, Crüsemann, "The Unchangeable World"; Blenkinsopp, *Wisdom and Law in the Old Testament*, 75–76; Brown, "Character Reconstructed"; Adams, *Wisdom in Transition*; and Balantine, *Wisdom Literature*. Crüsemann, cited above, speaks of the "collapse" of the act-consequence relationship in Ecclesiastes, whereby, he insists, there is "no connection" whatsoever between the writer's personal beliefs and the moral principle of sowing and reaping.

39. Childs, *Introduction to the Old Testament as Scripture*, 588, helpfully in my view, compares the canonical place of Ecclesiastes in Scripture and the book's associated misperceptions with those surrounding the epistle of James in the New Testament. Both writings serve as a corrective to misunderstandings—in James's context, to a misunderstood Paul, and in the case of Ecclesiastes, to misunderstandings of what constitutes true "wisdom."

condition (and hence an epistemological concern).[40] As already noted, wisdom literature possesses an indirect theological orientation, owing to creation and natural theology. In addition to its focus on human destiny, it frequently presents a contrast of justice and injustice or wisdom and folly. Wisdom literature can employ multiple shapes and forms. For example, it can utilize parable, allegory, riddle, proverb, numerical formula, didactic poetry, rhetorical questions, didactic narrative, allegory, the catalogue or list, or oracle. Or it can take the shape of a philosophical treatise or disputation, with the book of Ecclesiastes—in a fascinating way—incorporating several of these forms, even when it fits broadly into the latter category.[41]

Because of its hybrid nature in terms of genre, attempting to interpret Ecclesiastes is difficult,[42] as evidenced by a perusal of most biblical commentaries and the fact of its general neglect in standard teaching and preaching. The following are representative of "mainstream" biblical scholarship's attempts to identify the genre of Ecclesiastes: (1) royal testament;[43] (2) diatribe;[44] (3) philosophical reflection; (4) a collection of sayings;[45] (5) debate or dialogue;[46] and (6) an expanded parable.[47] That works such as Job and Ecclesiastes are more speculative and less "practical" than, say, the book of Proverbs does not, however, detract from their essence as "wisdom literature." In the main, wisdom literature can be categorized according

40. The writer's "theology" stems from an "empirical epistemology," based on his a theology of creation. Hereon see Hayman, "Qohelet and the Book of Creation," 98–102.

41. The abundance of proverbs and rhetorical questions as well as the striking didactic poetry in Ecclesiastes make it clear that the writer was "rooted in the rich soil of common Israelite wisdom" (so Westermann, *Roots of Wisdom*, 100).

42. Thus, for example, Murphy, *Wisdom Literature*, xxi, 129–33, believes that the literary genre of Ecclesiastes "escapes" us. "There is no satisfactory solution to the literary form of the book," he intones. Nevertheless, it is broadly accepted that "wisdom literature" knows a diversity of forms, of which Ecclesiastes is graphic proof.

43. Galling, "Kohelet-Studien."

44. Braun, *Kohelet und die frühhellenistiche Populärphilosophie*, and Lohfink, *Kohelet*.

45. Zimmerli, "Das Buch Kohelet."

46. Perry, *Dialogues with Koheleth*.

47. Klein, *Kohelet und die Weisheit Israels*. More recently a rather novel interpretation has been offered by Douglas in *A Polemical Preacher of Joy*. Douglas argues that Ecclesiastes is arguing against "apocalyptic" thought of its day and thus belongs to the classification of "anti-apocalyptic." This theory, however, seems not to fit the internal evidence. The outlook being opposed in the treatise is materialistic and "secularistic," not "apocalyptic" (whose roots are religious and a later development, ante-dating and post-dating the Christian advent). The *hebel* being decried is induced not by apocalyptic eschatology or apocalyptic "seers" but by self-striving autonomy and attempts to "earn" (*yitrôn*) happiness, as the opening multifaceted lament in 1:3–2:23 illustrates.

to two general types—practical and metaphysical/speculative[48]—with Job and Ecclesiastes belonging to the latter. Part of the wisdom perspective is to wrestle with the problem of suffering and life's mystery, and to search for life's meaning.[49] Yet, despite the "many faces" of wisdom, it still has a distinctly "recognizable complexion."[50]

Because wisdom literature, as we have noted, utilizes a variety of shapes and forms, and given the difficulties in assigning a particular "genre" to Ecclesiastes, the attempt by one Old Testament scholar to classify Ecclesiastes as an extended *māšāl* or "parable"[51] deserves mention.[52] Wisdom can be viewed as an art form, as poetic verse scattered throughout Ecclesiastes well illustrates. Paradigmatic in character, the *māšāl* can function generally in several ways: it can confirm a viewpoint, it can offer advice or counsel, or it can serve to counter a viewpoint.[53] In addition, it can appear in a shorter, concise form (as Jesus often employs it), or it can assume a more extended form and shape (for example, Psalm 49 or the Balaam stories of Numbers 23–24, to note but two examples).[54] Depending on the language and literary-rhetorical design of the author, it can set forth an argument with convincing force. As will be argued in chapter 3, the writer of Ecclesiastes at different places in the treatise appears to be countering a viewpoint (by means of juxtaposing an alternative, theocentric perspective that manifests itself in the recurring theocentric "enjoyment" refrains), as well as offering counsel and then confirming a particular viewpoint. Not only is this confirmation of a particular outlook recurring, it is also stated with force at the conclusion (12:13–14).[55] A strategic part of the

---

48. Gordis, "Quotations as a Literary Usage," speaks of wisdom literature in terms of "lower" (practical) and "higher" (speculative/metaphysical) forms.

49. Wisdom literature—whether Mesopotamian, Egyptian, or Hebrew—is of two general varieties: prudential admonitions and reflective essays that not infrequently are dialogical and pessimistic in nature. Hereon see Rylaarsdam, *Revelation in Jewish Wisdom Literature*, 1–46; and von Rad, *Wisdom in Israel*, 24–50.

50. Hill, *Wisdom's Many Faces*, 3.

51. The term *māšāl* generally corresponds to the English "byword" or "proverb," i.e., a short pithy saying in common use that mirrors reality in the human experience.

52. Klein, *Kohelet und die Weisheit Israels*.

53. Klein, *Kohelet und die Weisheit Israels*, 37.

54. Hereon see Johnson, "Mashal."

55. Against most interpretations of the epilogue in Ecclesiastes, according to which the editor is thought to *restore* the so-called "traditional" wisdom perspective because of supposed "heterodox" statements throughout the treatise. Among those who pit the theology of the epilogue against the theology of the writer of Ecclesiastes are Anderson, *Understanding the Old Testament*, 501; Williams, *Those Who Ponder Proverbs*, 54; Crenshaw, *Ecclesiastes*, 192; Crenshaw, "Unresolved Issues in Wisdom Literature," 222;

writer's literary strategy is the frequent use of the "better than" rhetorical device (on which, see chapter 5), which both serves to counter a viewpoint and confirm an alternative viewpoint.[56] Simply said, these sayings combine *comparison* and a *verdict* by which they seek to convince the reader of something that is contrary to conventional thinking.[57] Significantly, it is the comparative proverb as a group that is employed most frequently in Ecclesiastes, some of which appear original to the writer and some deriving from earlier proverbial wisdom.[58] While the view that Ecclesiastes represents an extended *māšāl* has not garnered a huge following, it serves to highlight several features that aid the interpretive process.

In addition to the comparative proverb, one other significant literary feature is peculiar to Ecclesiastes and thus deserving of some focus. It is the writer's use of the rhetorical question. Understanding and appreciating the function of this fascinating and strategic literary device can aid the reader in discerning the overall structure of the writer's argument and hence the message of Ecclesiastes. Remarkably, one searches in vain to find any full-length study devoted to this feature, which in Ecclesiastes—perhaps more than any other biblical book—plays a crucial interpretive role. Rhetorical questions are used nearly thirty times in the treatise.[59] This in itself is a stunning degree of frequency for a work that is so brief, and yet apart from one doctoral dissertation that appeared thirty-four years ago,[60] no thoroughgoing study of this phenomenon has been done with a view to help elucidate the message and meaning of Ecclesiastes.

In general terms, the rhetorical question functions in several ways: (1) to interrogate on a matter open to dispute; (2) to augment a matter of interrogation; (3) to assert a point of view or offer information in support of that view; and (4) to elicit a response or call for a verdict. As each of these functions suggests, the rhetorical question is at home typically in the context of a dispute, a debate, or a dialogue (on which, see chapter 3). Where the rhetorical question draws particular attention to a particular focus of

---

Dillard and Longman, *An Introduction to the Old Testament*, 255; and Longman, *The Book of Ecclesiastes*, 30–32.

56. As evidenced by the four "nothing better" devices found in the recurring "enjoyment" refrains (see chapter 5), this device is a convention of "wisdom literature"; see, for example, Ps 37:16; Prov 17:1; 21:19; 27:5; and 27:10.

57. As it applies to Ecclesiastes, Klein, *Kohelet und die Weisheit Israels*, 95–105, examines the writer's use of the "better than" rhetorical device, identifying some twenty-five usages throughout the entire work.

58. So, for example, 2:24; 4:6; 4:9–12, 13–16; 6:3, 5, 9; 7:1, 2, 3, 5, 8, 26; 9:4, 16, 18.

59. By my count, twenty-eight rhetorical questions can be identified in the text.

60. Johnson, "The Rhetorical Question as a Literary Device."

dispute in a polemic, it can have several effects in terms of *persuasion*. It might amplify a particular premise that has been spoken or unspoken. It might serve to help build a consensus. Or it might accentuate a polarity, contradiction, or inconsistency that needs acknowledgement. Where a writer employs the rhetorical question to introduce a topic, it serves to "load" the argument up front, in order to guide the listener's response. Where the writer employs it as part of a conclusion, it serves to "seal" the argument. Both of these functions occur in Ecclesiastes.[61]

In addition to its "persuasive" function just noted, the rhetorical question also assists the reader in structural division. Identifying any sort of structure to Ecclesiastes is one of the most—if not *the* most—vexing of matters associated with study of the book. *No* consensus whatsoever is to be found among commentators in this regard. Rhetorical questions, however, can provide us with helpful hints or clues as to the flow, direction, and structure of the writer's argument. So, for example, a rhetorical question may mark a shift in the writer's argument. In Ecclesiastes, as it turns out, there are continual shifts, whereby the writer moves back and forth, without announcing that a shift is occurring, between two outlooks—one that is "meaningless" and one that is God-inspired—a tactic that is examined in some detail in the following chapter and demonstrated in chapter 5.

In its effect, the rhetorical question often—though not always—is intended to produce a negative response of interpretation on the part of the reader/listener.[62] That is, where an argument is designed to counter or negate a particular position, it serves to call into question the very premises of that faulty position. In Ecclesiastes, the writer in a cyclical manner is demolishing a particular philosophical outlook on life—one that assumes that happiness and meaning in life can be "gained" or "earned" (Eccl 1:3) and pursued apart from the hand of the Creator God. The effect of the writer's "demolition" through his "Everything is meaningless" lament is so intense, so thorough, and so forceful, that most commentators, whether past or present, assume that the writer is a pessimist and resigned to a strange mix ("synthesis") of despair mingled with quasi-hedonism until death. As the present volume argues, this traditional line of interpretation, in many ways almost universal, is misguided and in the end fails to discern the book's message. One of the reasons for this interpretive confusion is an inability to discern the work's structure, and informing the work's structure are

---

61. On the function and effect of the rhetorical question, see Johnson, *The Rhetorical Question as a Literary Device*, xiii–xiv, 209–26.

62. Johnson, "The Rhetorical Question as a Literary Device," 249–50.

literary-rhetorical devices such as repetition and refrain, strategic use of catchwords and catchphrases, and the use of rhetorical questions.

Above it was noted that the rhetorical question has the effect of accentuating or magnifying a polarity or contradiction. This function is particularly important to the writer of Ecclesiastes, who is utilizing juxtaposition—i.e., setting in opposition two competing viewpoints—constantly throughout the treatise. These "polar opposite" positions might take the form of human versus divine, human striving versus dependence on God, seeking gain versus receiving from God's hand, human limitations versus divine sovereignty, worldly wisdom versus divine wisdom, oppressive labor versus satisfying work, and meaninglessness versus joy and contentment. Following are representative rhetorical questions posed in Ecclesiastes that bear upon the "polarity" of thought that weaves its way continually throughout the treatise:

- 1:2–2:26

    - 1:3—What profit is found from all man's labor?

    - 2:2—What does pleasure accomplish?

    - 2:12—What more can be done than has already been done?

    - 2:15—What do I gain by being wise?

    - 2:19—Who knows whether the next person will be a wise man or a fool?

    - 2:22—What profit does man get from all his labor and anxious striving?

    - 2:25—Apart from God, who can eat or find enjoyment?

- 3:1–22

    - 3:9—What does the worker gain from his toils?

    - 3:21—Who knows what occurs beyond death?

    - 3:22—Who can see what will occur next?

- 4:1–5:8

    - 4:8—For whom am I laboring? Why am I depriving myself of enjoyment?

    - 5:6—Why should God become angry at you and destroy the work of your hands?

- 5:9–6:12

    - 5:11—What benefit are increased goods except to stare at them?

- 5:16—What does a man gain in toiling for the wind?

- 6:6—Don't all go to the same place?

- 6:8 (twice)—What advantage does a wise man have over a fool? What does a poor man gain in knowing how to conduct himself in public?

- 6:11—How do many words profit anyone?

- 6:12 (twice)—Who really knows what is good if life is meaningless? Who can tell him what the future holds?

- 7:1–8:17

  - 7:10—Why were the old days better than these?

  - 7:13—Who is able to straighten what God has made crooked?

  - 7:16—Why destroy yourself?

  - 7:17—Why die prematurely?

  - 7:24—Whatever wisdom is, who can discover it?

  - 8:1 (twice)—Who is like the wise man? Who can explain things?

  - 8:7—Who can predict the future?

The Morality of Wisdom

Earlier in this chapter it was observed that speculative wisdom of the type that we encounter in Job and Ecclesiastes does not deny the act-consequence principle of practical wisdom. Rather, its burden is to probe—and often with painful severity (such as one also encounters in the psalms of lament)—the pathos of human experience when and where people seem *not* to "reap" what they "sow" in terms of behavior. And while the sentiment expressed by one commentator is understandable—"What traditional wisdom inextricably tied together, namely right character and prosperity, Qoheleh, like Job, has split asunder"[63]—it needs to be challenged. The reason for this is that it wrongly assumes Ecclesiastes to be attempting to undermine or negate the "traditional" wisdom perspective (on which see below). Two problems with this way of thinking need identifying.

First of all, proverbial maxims that typify "traditional wisdom" are not *guarantees*; rather, they mirror *tendencies or truisms*, as noted above. That is to say, the fear of the Lord and obedience *do* generally tend toward

---

63. Brown, "Character Reconstructed," 134.

reward or divine "blessing," even when they do not *guarantee* such in our experience (or our *perception* thereof in our experience). The problem with Job's three "friends" is not that humans do not reap what they sow; *usually* they *do*. However, the wisdom perspective also takes account of righteous or unjust suffering. The lesson of both Job and Ecclesiastes (as well as the psalms of lament) is that humans cannot know the *why* behind suffering; God's ways and purposes are inscrutable.

Second, Ecclesiastes *does* affirm the link between character and ethics, as 2:26 and 8:12–13 make quite clear and as do the assorted proverbs in chapters 6, 7, and 10. And if this were *not* the case, the book's concluding admonition to "fear God and *keep his commandments*"[64] (12:13, emphasis added)—which, we are told, is "the whole duty of man"—would be utterly absurd and self-contradictory. Character *does* count, even when God is inscrutable and wrongdoing, injustice, and evil seem to abound. Simply because we "cannot be sure of what God does" and simply because "injustice reigns," it does not follow that there is no cause and effect or that people ultimately do not "reap what they sow." In fact, precisely this seems to be the rationale behind 11:1, 2, and 6: "sow-give-sow" is the admonition, which is another way of saying, "There *is* profit in our labor/virtuous acts"—when and where, that is, our motivation is correct" (cf. 1:3; 2:11, 22; 3:9; and 4:9)—and even when we cannot guarantee or perceive the outcome. Thus, those writers and commentators who deny the "act-consequence" principle of human behavior and the relationship between character and virtue end up embedded in a sort of interpreter's schizophrenia, as the following assertion by one commentator suggests: "Although Qoheleth espouses certain virtues, he does it in recognition that *there are limitations, even dangers, to living the virtuous life.*"[65] If this line of thinking—namely, that there are limitations and dangers in being virtuous—truly represents the "moral philosophy" being espoused by Ecclesiastes, then it stands in contradiction to the rest of the biblical canon. One can only imagine its effect when and where it is preached from the pulpits of our churches, parishes, and synagogues or taught to our children and our students.[66]

In this regard, basic biblical theology is to be our guide, which serves as the thread uniting the Law, the prophets, and the writings of the Old

64. "Keeping the commandments" is not only central to the Torah (see, for example, Deut 4:1, 2, 40; 5:28–29, 32–33; 6:1, 6–9; 8:1, 2; 11:26–28 30:15–18), it is central to wisdom literature as well (in addition to Eccl 8:5 and 12:13, see, for example, Ps 19:8; virtually all of Ps 119; Prov 2:1; 3:1; 4:4; 6:20, 23; 7:1, 2; 10:8; 13:18; and 19:16).

65. Brown, "Character Reconstructed," 140 (emphasis added).

66. Such a line of interpretation—"Fear God but know that it is unwise to be too virtuous"—renders the book nonsensical.

Testament. According to the wisdom perspective, the cosmos operates by an order that is framed by natural law and based on divine law. Hence, wisdom, in the words of one astute observer, is "the *second moral focal point* in the Old Testament"[67]—a fact that would astound the average reader of Scripture yet which reflects its supreme significance to Scripture and biblical revelation. As observed in Deut 32:28–29, to neglect the law is folly. For this reason, the Psalmist, in uniting the law and wisdom, can exclaim:

> Oh, how I love your law!
>
> I mediate on it all day long.
>
> Your commands make me wiser than my enemies,
>
> For they are ever with me.
>
> Righteous are you, O Lord,
>
> And your laws are right.
>
> The statutes you have laid down are righteous;
>
> They are fully trustworthy. (Ps 119:97–98, 137–38, NIV)

The divine law has been revealed through both creation and con-science—a moral reality confirmed in the New Covenant when it speaks of the law "written on the heart" (Rom 2:14–15)—and is thus not hidden. Thereby it expresses divine wisdom—a wisdom that is revealed to human beings who seek after her (Prov 2:4; 3:13–15; and 28:22–31). The Genesis narrative of creation and the fall does not present an "arbitrary" view of human motivation and action. The language by which wisdom literature depicts the fruit of human decisions tends to use "wise" for the righteous or good and "foolish" or "sinner" for the unbelieving or wicked. In ad-dition, on occasion wisdom literature will make comparisons between physical nature and human nature (so, for example, Prov 30:18–19, 24–28, 29–31; and Eccl 11:1–6), inferring lessons for pedagogical purposes and laying claim to both reason and revelation. The reason for this is that wis-dom's perspective is anchored in the reality of the created order.[68] And because that order is in fact *created*, wisdom begins with the fear of God, the Creator himself. It is surely accurate to say that we have lost the won-der of creation, with its many important lessons.[69] Re-engaging wisdom literature can help restore some of that wonder.

67. Fredericks and Estes, *Ecclesiastes and the Song of Songs*, 36 (emphasis added).

68. After all, in theological terms the doctrine of redemption expresses creation *restored*.

69. Consider, for example, the four-part proverbs recorded in Prov 30:24–28 and

Ecclesiastes and the Theology of Wisdom: Reconciling
Divine Sovereignty and Human Limitation

"Theology" as it is typically understood is not advanced explicitly in wisdom literature. It is at best inferred or implicit in nature. Where wisdom literature does speak of God, it is not specifically theological discourse of a more comprehensive nature. At the same time, because of the universal character of wisdom, its basis—as we have emphasized—is a "theology of creation," wherein the natural world is—and remains—pedagogical in its function. For this reason, wisdom literature speaks of "God" in generic terms—*Elohim*, the God of creation—and not as *Yahweh*, the God of Israel.[70]

"Wisdom theology," unfortunately, has generally not been well integrated into biblical theology as a whole,[71] causing one Old Testament scholar to describe "wisdom theology" as "an orphan in the biblical household."[72] A past generation of Old Testament scholars tended to see a "canon within the canon," placing wisdom literature at the canonical periphery. One consequence of that placement up to the present day is that wisdom literature has received comparatively little attention in terms of its contribution to theology. To illustrate, one of the most celebrated Old Testament theologians of a previous generation describes Ecclesiastes as standing "at the farthest frontier" of Jewish religion,[73] while a highly esteemed wisdom scholar speaks of Ecclesiastes as "theology from below." Another example will suffice for our purposes. Volume one of the magisterial *Theology of the Old Testament* contains not *a single* reference to the book of Ecclesiastes in 542 pages; volume two of the same devotes a mere thirteen out of 573 pages to "The Wisdom of God."[74] Virtually the exact same thing applies to the two volumes of the equally authoritative *Old Testament Theology*, wherein only about thirty pages of volume one

---

30:29–31.

70. Zimmerli's assertion that wisdom "has no relation to the history between God and Israel" ("The Place and Limit of the Wisdom," 315), may be viewed as an overstatement. It is true that the purpose of wisdom literature concerns the practical—i.e., how to live—but it is not true that wisdom literature bears "no relation to the history between God and Israel"; rather, it is more accurate to argue that as a genre *its focus differs* from that of the Law and the Prophets.

71. In general terms, it can be argued that the Christian church has not appreciated and articulated a *theology of creation* as it should. The result is not only that we have lost the insights of wisdom but also that our doctrine of redemption becomes weakened, inasmuch as redemption is a *restoration* of the creation order.

72. Crenshaw, ed., *Studies in Ancient Israelite Wisdom*, 1.

73. Rad, *Old Testament Theology—Vol. 1*, 458.

74. Eichrodt, *Theology of the Old Testament* (2 vols.).

are devoted to "Israel's wisdom."[75] If Ecclesiastes is considered the "black sheep" of the Old Testament canon, then surely wisdom literature may be considered the *step-child* of Old Testament theology.[76]

The abiding contribution of the "wisdom" perspective is that it is neither "sacred" nor "secular"; it entails all of life, based on the order of creation. This creational "order" can be seen, for example, in (1) the reality of physical and moral "laws" in the universe; (2) correlatively, the reality of the "law written on the heart"[77] (i.e., the natural moral law); (3) the need for justice to govern all human relationships; and (4) the need for self-governance in light of #1–3. Because wisdom literature conveys this multifaceted "order" in continual and compelling ways, it is able to speak to all people everywhere and at all times; God is active in creation, in nature, in the cosmos, and in human community. The "wisdom" perspective, consequently, confronts us in unmistakable—and irreplaceable—ways with the "big questions," i.e., questions of theodicy, cosmology, anthropology, and ethics.[78] Surely Job goes to the heart of biblical wisdom in posing the question "Where shall wisdom be found?" (Job 28:12). It is a question that gnaws at *every* generation.

Although from a human vantage-point divine wisdom is impenetrable, wisdom as it enters the human experience nevertheless sheds partial light on the mystery of providence—light that will allow human beings to practice discernment, persist in the midst of suffering, put divine mystery and inscrutability in its proper perspective, and walk in harmony with their Creator. Coming to terms with divine mystery through a serious reading of Ecclesiastes will confront the reader with an important aspect of wisdom; at bottom, Ecclesiastes serves as a useful—indeed *requisite*—antidote to shallow self-righteousness and unreflective belief. As will be argued in the following chapter, two approaches to ultimate reality—one that fails to reckon with divine providence and inscrutability and one that humbly embraces them—are in "dialogue." The former leads to an outlook that is despairing and marked by resignation; the latter receives life, with its fleeting moments, and everything in it—inclusive of human labor—as a "gift" of God.

Scholarly treatment of Ecclesiastes has tended overwhelmingly to interpret the treatise as promoting an outlook of pessimism and resignation.

75. Rad, *Old Testament Theology* (2 vols.).

76. One searches in vain to locate a work devoted to a "biblical theology of Ecclesiastes"—in fact, *any* "theology of Ecclesiastes." The only such study I have located is an unpublished ThD dissertation by Neal Williams, "A Biblical Theology of Ecclesiastes" (1984).

77. Rom 1:19–20 and 2:14–15.

78. Hill, *Wisdom's Many Faces*, 94, has pressed this point quite effectively.

This interpretation is anchored in certain presuppositions about the literary and philosophical character of the book. Two general trains of thought inform this interpretive reasoning. On the one hand, we find ancient Near Eastern texts, dating from the second and first millennia BCE, which serve as a helpful comparison to Israel's wisdom literature. Take, for example, a Sumerian composition entitled "The Sumerian Job," dated in early second millennium BCE, which—like Job of the Old Testament—describes a man's affliction with sickness and disaster. He prays and repents and experiences joy, although, unlike Job, he does not question divine justice. Or, similarly, take the "Dispute over Suicide"[79] and the "Tale of the Eloquent Peasant"—both Egyptian texts—or the "Dialogue between a Man and His God" and "Dialogue of Pessimism"—Mesopotamian texts from the first millennium BCE, the latter of which has been compared by Old Testament scholars with the book of Ecclesiastes.[80]

Ecclesiastes, writes one Old Testament student of "wisdom literature," "may seem shockingly pessimistic and even nihilistic . . . It reminds us that ancient wisdom literature had a bleak and cynical strain."[81] Whether or not non-Israelite versions of "wisdom literature" were "bleak and cynical" is not our concern here, only that such presuppositions are not infrequently imported into Old Testament interpretation. Comparative ancient Near Eastern literature, it is quite true, provides fascinating parallels to Old Testament "wisdom" writings—parallels, however, which must not set aside the baseline differences between Hebrew monotheism and pagan polytheism. Among those things setting Israel's wisdom apart are (a) its basic starting-point, namely, an emphasis on the fear of the Lord (so, for example, Prov 1:7, 29; 8:12–13; 14:26; 15:33; 22:4; Ps 19:9; 34:11; 111:10; Job 6:14; 28:28; Eccl 3:14; 5:7; 7:18; 8:12; and 1:13), as well as (b) its theological framework that rests upon a theology of creation.

A theology of creation can be found to undergird not only wisdom literature in general but the very framework of the book of Ecclesiastes, for it presumes certain "givens"—i.e., certain moral realities—about human nature, even when its shape as a literary genre is vastly different from that of the

---

79. This Egyptian work is otherwise known as "The Man Who Was Tired of Life" and was first published in 1896 under the German title *Gespräch eines Lebensmüden mit seiner Seele*. It consists of a "discussion between a man and his soul" on the matter of suicide. An English translation, with notes and commentary, can be found in Faulkner, "The Man Who Was Tired of Life."

80. For a helpful—and accessible, not overly technical—overview of both Egyptian and Mesopotamian "wisdom" texts, see Smothers, "Biblical Wisdom in Its Ancient Middle Eastern Context."

81. Clifford, *The Wisdom Literature*, 97–98.

Psalms or the book of Proverbs. Wisdom is therefore something that unites the Old and New Testaments. Jesus' own speech demonstrates this continuity. Wisdom was an essential component of his language and proclamation; many of his recorded sayings are in fact "wisdom" sayings. The same can be said of the Pauline epistles and especially the epistle of James.

Within the argument being developed in Ecclesiastes, the writer explicitly anchors his anthropology in the Genesis creation narrative: "God made men upright, but they have sought out many devices" (7:29).[82] And at the heart of the anthropological dilemma, in the words of Genesis, is lodged "the knowledge of good and evil."[83] This element—corruption of human nature through the fall—sets the Old Testament creation narrative apart from its various ancient Near Eastern counterparts. At the same time, it needs emphasizing that to accentuate human limitations is *not* to deny our dignity or the dominion mandate described in Genesis. Given the present "apologetic" need, however, the writer of Ecclesiastes finds it necessary to respond to dominant thinking of his day by emphasizing not humankind's glory and achievements—which typifies the anthropology of his contemporaries—but humankind's limitations and boundaries. Those boundaries are established by a Creator God whose ways and works are inscrutable and whose purposes are eternal (3:1–22). The accent on human limitations, as witnessed by the writer's utter annihilation of human autonomy, represents "the front-guard against *any* form of self-reliance."[84] Reminders throughout Ecclesiastes of those limitations are injustice, oppression, disaster, and death—i.e., effects of the fall—that mirror the writer's implicit debt to Genesis 3.[85] Contrary to the line of thinking of much commentary, the writer is not denying the "wisdom" principle of cause and effect or punishment and retribution; nor has he rejected divine justice.[86] He is simply demonstrating the fruits of a flawed anthropology—one in which human achievements and successes are glorified and injustice is often found.

---

82. NASB.

83. Gen 2:17 and 3:5–6.

84. Eaton, *Ecclesiastes*, 48 (emphasis present).

85. Clemens, "The Law of Sin and Death," argues that Ecclesiastes is "an arresting but thoroughly orthodox exposition of Genesis 1–3."

86. Contra Brown, "Character Reconstructed," 143, God does not "transcend the laws of moral retribution." Rather, those laws inhere in the very divine character itself. Otherwise, God would not hold human beings accountable for their actions (Eccl 3:13; 17; 11:9; and 12:14). To the contrary, the accent in Ecclesiastes on divine judgment shows that the writer *affirms* retribution. Whether human beings *mirror* those moral standards, of course, is a very different question, and whether human beings discern the *timing* of the implementation of divine justice clearly must be answered in the negative.

A primary assumption undergirding the present volume—an assumption developed more fully in the following chapter—is that Ecclesiastes is intended to be an "apologetic" work for its time, hence its "philosophical" and reflective character. Regardless of whether that cultural background is located in the tenth century or the fourth century BCE,[87] the first century AD or the twenty-first century, the wisdom perspective concerns itself with anthropology—a "realist anthropology."[88] It goes without saying that every successive generation believes that it is further along, more advanced, and better off than the previous generation. However, an important part of the argument developed in Ecclesiastes is that all rivers flow to the sea, as it were, that generations come and go but life and human nature do not change (1:4–11); hence, the thoroughgoing and devastating critique on human activity and the accent on everything being "meaningless" or "profitless" (*hebel*). Ecclesiastes distinguishes itself and its view of human nature by its emphasis on human limitations and human uncertainty. A man of his own time, the writer develops his argument with a view to accent humankind's *creaturely* status. Failure to recognize and acknowledge this status constitutes humankind's greatest flaw, insofar as reverence before the sovereign and inscrutable Creator, dependence on that Creator, and obedience (so, for example, Eccl 2:26; 5:1–7; 12:1a; and 12:13–14) are our calling as human beings. To underscore our creaturely status accords with the wisdom perspective more narrowly and the breadth of biblical theology more widely. Hence, against much commentary, Ecclesiastes is to be viewed as "orthodox."[89]

It is impossible to ignore the fact that death is an important theme in Ecclesiastes. Its prominence in the book requires that we understand the role that it plays in the writer's broader "apologetic" argument. The frequency with which it surfaces in the book has led many commentators to conclude that the writer is *obsessed* with death. This conclusion, however, misinterprets the role that it plays in the wider argument. Death is not an "obsession" in the work.[90] Neither is the writer's accent on death

87. Virtually all commentators date Ecclesiastes as a fourth- or third-century BCE document, based on (1) linguistic evidence, (2) assumptions about the work's social setting, and (3) the philosophical tenor of its argument. For an overview of the linguistic evidence, see Seow, *Ecclesiastes*, 11–21; Fredericks, *Qohelet's Language*; and Holmstedt et al., *Qoheleth*, 3–45.

88. Fisch, *Poetry with a Purpose*, 172.

89. Two generations ago Ginsberg, "The Structure and Contents of the Book of Koheleth," 147, famously declared that the writer is "by no means" orthodox in the faith—a matter taken up more fully in chapter 3. Many interpreters since then have adopted this position.

90. Typical of this misinterpretation are Christianson, "Qoheleth and the Existential Legacy of the Holocaust," 43, who insists that the writer of Ecclesiastes has "a fixation

an advancement of "fate" or "resigned hedonism," as one Old Testament scholar proposes.[91] Nor does death constitute "the ultimate reason behind Qoheleth's commendation of simple enjoyment."[92] Nor is the writer denying the afterlife; the fact that "resurrection" *per se* is not found in Ecclesiastes should not strike us as unsettling or "dissonant."[93] Rather, death is a part of his theology of divine inscrutability and human limitation. He merely wishes to assert that death is the great arbiter, the great leveler. And there is an important reason for this depiction. Death bears on our achievements by reminding us not only of life's brevity but *why* we live as we do. It is the major antidote against humankind's tendency toward self-sufficiency, self-exaltation, and self-determinism.[94]

Death, then, has moral and anthropological significance. Being reconciled to death and dying allows us to truly live as we ought, guiding our varied pursuits. Once reconciled to the reality of death, we can relax, as it were, and enjoy the simple things of life, receiving them as a gift from God—something which the materialist is incapable of doing. *This*, then, is the response—the counter-argument—in Ecclesiastes to "meaninglessness." Despite humankind's hubris, one force to which every human being must submit is death. And in this regard humans are no different from animals: all go to their appointed end.[95]

---

with death"; Adams, *Wisdom in Transition*, 10, who writes that in Ecclesiastes "death overwhelms all other topics," and "Qoheleth views all of reality through the darkness of Sheol" (10); and Duncan, *Ecclesiastes*, xvii, who asserts that Ecclesiastes is "more than anything else" about "the human encounter with death." In fact, a serious reading of the text reveals that the "good"/"enjoyment," God's "giving," and "what God does" have a far higher visibility than death in Ecclesiastes. Nevertheless, death *is* portrayed in a manner that, based on God's sovereignty, shows it to be the final arbiter, the great leveler, given human autonomy and self-assertion, which are being countered by the writer.

91. Blenkinsopp, *Wisdom and Law in the Old Testament*, 73. The writer may well have been familiar with Epicurean or Stoic philosophy in his day, but he surely was not an advocate thereof, as the didactic poem (3:1–8) and its interpretation (3:9–22) make abundantly clear.

92. Contra Brown, "Character Reconsidered," 139. Rather, it is the "gift" of God and providence that constitute the true reason for enjoyment. And this, of course, is reinforced by the fear of God. Lo, "Death in Qohelet," essentially adopts the same position as Brown, arguing that the theme of death determines the writer's arguments. But it is more accurate, structurally and thematically, to argue that death is *illustrative* rather than *determinative* of the overall argument.

93. Contra Provan, *Ecclesiastes, Song of Songs*, 23.

94. Secular materialism, after all, is incapable of giving an account of evil and of death.

95. The argument in Ecclesiastes concerning the unity of humans and animals before death (3:18–19, 21) is not intended to deny the fact of human dignity and our creation in the image of God. Rather, it is meant to underscore our creaturely status.

The Universality of Wisdom

When it is contrasted, say, with science, the value of wisdom, at least as it is expressed through "proverbial" wisdom, consists in the fact that it is accessible to *all*; it is found universally. Theologians tend to distinguish between "special" and "general" revelation, with the latter referring to that which is on display everywhere in the universe, open and accessible to all fully apart from the role of faith. The relevance of general revelation to daily life is evidenced in the fact that people representing all cultures, eras, and locations have developed particular insights into living—"proverbial wisdom"—and in many cases enshrined this wisdom in ways that allowed it to be passed on to successive generations. In some cultures this transmission was chiefly oral, in others it assumed written form, and very often both expressions were part of social and cultural life, as evidenced, for example, by the role that wisdom and, over time, "wisdom literature" played in ancient Near Eastern societies. Wisdom proceeds from observations about physical as well as human nature. Wisdom is not confined to one people or culture; it is the possession of all who seek it.

Proverbial wisdom, then, does not admit of a distinction between "sacred" or "secular." In fact, proverbial wisdom arose among farmers, craftsmen, sheepherders, husbandmen, families, etc. and not among priests, scribes, or the like, which in and of itself suggests that work—especially manual labor—is highly esteemed. Wisdom knows no vocational dichotomy, no "sacred-versus-secular" or tiering of classes. Take the "proverb" itself—a "wise saying"—as an example. The proverb has been described as the "workhorse" of language,[96] and properly so, for it packs much truth into a concise form that is memorable.[97] The universality of proverbs can be seen in the subjects they carry: for example, helping the poor or needy, being diligent and not lazy, having self-control, controlling the tongue, avoiding foolish behavior, being attentive to pride, etc., etc. These topics represent a common repository of insight and awareness ("wisdom") among all peoples everywhere.

Consider, by way of illustration, the following African proverbs. Non-Africans living on other continents and in radically different cultural settings will nonetheless readily—in fact, automatically—recognize the truth that these statements contain without the need for explanation:

- "No polecat ever smelled its own stink."

- "It is patience which gets you out of the net."

96. Leeuwen, "In Praise of Proverbs," 308.

97. One is surely justified in asking: *Where is proverbial wisdom today?*

- "The strength of a crocodile is in the water."
- "No one teaches a leopard's cub how to spring."
- "When it rains, the roof always drips the same way."
- "He even milks the cows that are heavy with calf."
- "He has the kindness of a witch."
- "A woman quick to love means a woman who does not love."
- "A chief is like a dust-heap where everyone comes with his rubbish and deposits it."
- "Wealth is like dew."
- "The sons of a king do not need to be taught about power."
- "When you marry a beautiful woman, you marry problems."
- "Your mouth will turn into a knife."[98]

Without an awareness of the specific cultural setting in which they are or were employed, proverbs communicate meaning, even when it is true that there is no proverb without a setting. The proverb as a form possesses its meaning wherever human community is to be found; therefore, the wisdom it conveys is universal and not a respecter of race, culture, or creedal belief.

Proverbial wisdom, then, functions to bridge all social, cultural, and educational differences, and this based on creation. It consistently touches every sphere of life and is transmitted from generation to generation. And it constitutes a common mode of discourse for all people the world over. In a very practical sense, wisdom shows itself to be a necessary and universally accessible foundation for ethics. The manner in which proverbial wisdom bridges morality and social dealings between different cultures and eras is on display in the "wisdom literature" of the Old Testament—for example, in the fascinatingly relevant and timeless wisdom sayings of the book of Proverbs but also in the complexities that are expressed in the book of Ecclesiastes. The end product of "Qoheleth's" philosophical musings— "the conclusion to the matter" and "the whole duty of man"—is to revere the Creator. Nothing in life has meaning apart from a theistic outlook. This is the "wisdom" message of Ecclesiastes.[99]

98. These examples are taken from Finnegan, "Proverbs," 389–425, and are reproduced in Westermann, *Roots of Wisdom*, 145–46.

99. This philosophical "bottom line" is intended to express universal truth and have universal application. For that reason, Ecclesiastes remains an invaluable, though supremely neglected, part of the biblical canon. In neglecting this work, Christians

Given the speculative character of wisdom as evidenced by Job and Ecclesiastes, several comments are in order. Philosophy bears some recognizable relationship to wisdom; after all, etymologically it yields the definition of a "love of wisdom." From the beginning it consisted of reflecting on the nature of the world and the nature of human existence. At the same time, philosophy came to be "spiritualized," particularly in its Hellenistic context, whereby the material realm became less and less esteemed. However, this dualism between the soulish and material realms does not exist in the wisdom perspective, since both realms are equally a part of creation and hence given equal worth. In consequence, the philosophical enterprise, at least in Western culture to the present, increasingly has been undertaken by a relatively small segment of society, among academic elites whose language and thought are often inaccessible to the average citizen.

Neither science nor philosophy (as described above) can replace wisdom. In our day, science tends to be unhampered and unconstrained, which is not a good sign. In addition, the increasing specialization within science hampers us to the extent that we thereby miss the whole. A constant temptation is the tendency of science to overestimate human capabilities. By contrast, wisdom makes us aware of our limitations, which is *the message of Ecclesiastes*. At bottom, science is incapable of producing wisdom. Wisdom cannot be manufactured; it must *grow*.[100]

Wisdom, therefore, possesses roots that are deeper than philosophy. A pressing question for our time is whether it is again possible for wisdom and "philosophy" to converge. Can philosophy find its way back to an understanding of creation as a whole, thereby allowing itself to be understood by *all* (or even *most*) people rather than being isolated in some elitist fashion?[101]

Ecclesiastes and the "Crisis of Wisdom"

In addition to the supposed pessimism and resignation that are thought to characterize Ecclesiastes, a related line of thinking needs some comment as well, given the fact that it is almost universally presumed. Professional scholars of the Old Testament, in the main, have assumed that Ecclesiastes

---

not only rob themselves of much needed insight into the complexities of life but also deprive themselves of wisdom as they attempt to find their way among competing worldviews in a pluralistic context.

100. Worth pondering are the reflections on science, philosophy, and wisdom found in Westermann, *Roots of Wisdom*, 135–37.

101. Westermann, *Roots of Wisdom*, 136–37, thoughtfully ponders the relationship between wisdom and philosophy.

is mirroring a "crisis" of wisdom. That is, the writer is to be interpreted as *challenging* or *negating* the very tenets and principles associated with the traditional "wisdom" perspective[102] or with Israel's religion.[103] According to this argument, Ecclesiastes is located in a "late phase" of the "wisdom tradition" in which the writer must wrestle with "disappointment" over the failure or collapse of earlier "wisdom" perspectives.[104] This supposed disappointment is said to be mirrored in a "revolt" or "reaction"—i.e., "protest literature"—against "the religiously conservative and dogmatic wisdom school" of the past.[105]

Among the factors in the background of Ecclesiastes being assumed to contribute to this so-called "crisis" are (1) parallels found in ancient Near Eastern "pessimism" literature, (2) differences between the books of Proverbs, Job, and Ecclesiastes, and—perhaps most importantly—(3) the almost universally assumed post-exilic dating and social location of Ecclesiastes,

102. It is typically thought that the "traditional" wisdom perspective is best represented by the book of Proverbs. And yet many compare the book of Proverbs and Ecclesiastes in a somewhat uncritical manner, assuming that the former always affirms "sowing and reaping" (in an absolute or "guaranteed" manner) while the latter challenges it. But this is often due to a simplistic reading of the former and of so-called "proverbial wisdom." Consider, by way of example, Prov 14:13—"Even in laughter the heart may ache, and joy may end in grief"—in the light of the proverbs recorded in Eccl 7:2–4—"It is better to go to a house of mourning than to go to a house of feasting . . . Sorrow is better than laughter . . . The heart of the wise is in the house of mourning . . ." The proverbs of both texts are anchored in the same "proverbial" wisdom. Or consider as another example the self-contradictory proverbs found in Prov 26:4–5.

103. Representative of this view are Hempel, *Die althebräische Literatur*, 190–92; Lauha, "Die Krise des religiösen Glaubens bei Kohelet"; Scott, "Wisdom in Revolt"; Hengel, *Judaism and Hellenism*, 1:115–28; Williams, "What Does It Profit a Man?"; Gese, "The Crisis of Wisdom in Koheleth"; Kaiser, "Die Sinnkrise bei Kohelet"; Loader, *Ecclesiastes*, 38; Fox, "Wisdom in Qohelet"; Brown, "Character Reconstructed"; Sneed, *The Politics of Pessimism in Ecclesiastes*, 7–11, 281; and Roper and Groenewald, "Job and Ecclesiastes as (Postmodern) Wisdom in Revolt." Hengel (*Judaism and Hellenism*, 1:121–26) goes to great lengths to trace in Ecclesiastes the writer's supposed absence of belief in the principles of reward and retribution—concepts considered central to traditional wisdom teaching—as a result of the influence of Hellenistic thought and the "fates" in particular.

104. So Michel, "'Unter der Sonne,'" 93–94.

105. Scott, "Wisdom in Revolt," 165. For Scott, who is representative of a host of commentators, Ecclesiastes is thought to affirm that "man cannot attain to the knowledge of God by wisdom or through revelation" (170). In support of this view, Scott writes that the "daring originality" of the writer's views was "glossed over" by "the addition of a few orthodox annotations," the result being a "minimum declaration of religious faith" that failed to "sustain the Jewish people" (172, 187). Contra Scott, Ecclesiastes affirms the faith of Israel, just as Ruth, Esther, Nehemiah, and various psalms—in their own unique way—did, and even when in their respective literary genre they depart from the *form* of the law and the prophets.

which would mirror developments spurred on by social-cultural pluralism and Hellenistic philosophy—whether Epicurean, Stoic, or Cynic in nature.[106] According to one respected Old Testament and ancient Near Eastern historian, "skepticism intensifies [in Ecclesiastes] to become fatalism."[107] It follows, then, that "[c]onsistently ethical conduct cannot therefore be commended" in the book.[108] Incredibly, one commentator asserts that the writer "betrays his wisdom heritage,"[109] while another suggests, more incredibly, that the writer "pretends" to endorse "conventional wisdom" but in actuality intends to "challenge its veracity."[110] Still another observer writes: "Irrespective of guilt and innocence, the same fate happens to all"; and, "What happens to the fool indiscriminately befalls the righteous as well."[111] "Why aspire to be wise—or just or righteous or virtuous—if everything, wisdom included, is as pointless as chasing after the wind?"[112] Accordingly, if we are to believe this line of thinking about Ecclesiastes, all that is left for the human person, at bottom, is a "resigned" attitude, whereby "enjoyment" becomes a "flight" from "the anguish of death" and human labor becomes oppressive bondage or, at best, "a questionable intermediary solution."[113] This perspective on the writer of Ecclesiastes, rooted in fatalism and resignation, has been summarized as follows:

> Koheleth stands at the parting of the way, at the boundary of two times. Under the impact of the spiritual crisis of early Hellenism, his critical thought could no *longer make sense of traditional wisdom* and, consequently, of *traditional piety* . . . So there remained for him only the pessimistic conclusion that human existence with all its toil and its apparent success amounted to nothing.[114]

106. While virtually everything about Ecclesiastes has eluded a consensus, one element that has *not* is the matter of dating. It is thought to mirror a post-exilic social setting, with most commentators locating it in the fourth or third century BCE. Challenging that consensus is Kim, "A Study of the Linguistic and Thematic Roots of Ecclesiastes," whose thorough examination of lexical-linguistic evidence in Ecclesiastes argues against the broader consensus of presumed "Hellenistic" influence.

107. Hengel, *Judaism and Hellenism*, 1:119.

108. Hengel, *Judaism and Hellenism*, 1:121.

109. Frydrych, *Living under the Sun*, 44.

110. Crenshaw, "Ecclesiastes (Qoheleth)," 508.

111. Balantine, *Wisdom Literature*, 63. Balantine adds that "Job and Qoheleth are not persuaded" that trust in God is "safe" (64).

112. Balantine, *Wisdom Literature*, 68.

113. Hengel, *Judaism and Hellenism*, 1:121, 126, and 2:82n109.

114. Hengel, *Judaism and Hellenism*, 1:127 (emphasis added). Notice the assumption at work here: not only the essence of "traditional wisdom" but *basic faith* has been

In the end, Ecclesiastes by this assessment of professional scholarship is declared to be "the literature of protest."

Given all of the difficulties surrounding Ecclesiastes interpretation—difficulties that will be addressed in greater detail in chapter 3—we are confronted with stubborn questions that require a response. As mirrored in Ecclesiastes, we are forced to ask: is "wisdom" in a "crisis"? Has the writer lost "orthodox" faith and succumbed to a despairing and an unforgiving "realism"? Is he perhaps "a wolf in sheep's clothing"[115] and indeed in revolt against "traditional" wisdom?

The present volume, which diverges considerably from much commentary on Ecclesiastes, seeks to present an alternative viewpoint to the aforementioned.[116] It proceeds on the assumption, over against the mainstream of Old Testament scholarship, that Ecclesiastes does *not* mirror a "crisis" in *wisdom itself*, even when the sheer force of the writer's argument seems to demolish some of our theological and ethical assumptions and challenges the reader in utterly unique ways by addressing the "conventional wisdom" of the surrounding culture.[117] Ecclesiastes is not "contradictory" but *complementary*; wisdom is *critical* without being in a "crisis."[118] The resignation or disappointment mirrored in Ecclesiastes is not linked to wisdom thinking *per se* or to a God "who has withheld information" and "who has stacked the deck" against humanity.[119] Rather, disillusionment arises out of the materialist's reaction to human limitations and flawed intellectual capacity over against divine inscrutability.

The present volume interprets Ecclesiastes from the standpoint that, in any era, wisdom—i.e., authentic wisdom as compared with *the world's*

---

jettisoned.

115. Hinkle, *Pedagogical Theory of Wisdom Literature*, 98–113, helpfully uses this imagery to raise important questions for the reader.

116. One can, nevertheless, agree that the writer of Ecclesiastes is a man of his time and that he is seeking to counter the spirit of the age of which he is a part. And, in the end, my principal disagreement with conventional scholarship does not concern the matter of dating or social context (which is widely assumed to be post-exilic and Hellenistic). Rather, it concerns what appears to be a relatively widespread inability of conventional scholarship to *allow the text of Ecclesiastes to speak for itself*, and I take up this matter in chapters 3, 4, and 5.

117. Two Old Testament scholars who counter the widespread view that Ecclesiastes mirrors a "crisis of wisdom" are Schultz, "Unity or Diversity in Wisdom Theology?" and Schwienhorst-Schönberger, "Via Media," esp. 197–98. Schultz argues that the claim of a "crisis" by Old Testament scholarship undermines the authority of Old Testament wisdom literature. It is difficult to disagree.

118. So Sternberg, "The Inner Coherence of the Four Wisdom Books," 156.

119. So Duncan, *Ecclesiastes*, xxv.

wisdom, or, "Wisdom" versus "wisdom"[120]—is non-fluid and dependable, based on the fact that it is woven into the very fabric of creation.[121] The creation order holds true even when it appears *not* to be true in the human experience. Because of creation, moreover, wisdom is accessible to the genuine seeker universally and makes a profound difference in the life of the God-fearer. The "crisis" needing exposure, then, is the crisis that besets a culture or society in which *false notions* of "wisdom" are believed and promoted. To that social-cultural environment, a work such as Ecclesiastes can speak—and in fact *did* speak in its original historical context. The writer sought to present a theocentric outlook on ultimate reality, but in order to do so he had to demolish contemporary understandings of meaning and happiness and destroy any illusions among his readers.[122] It is this contrast of conflicting outlooks—a juxtaposing of two diametrically opposed perspectives in life—that beckons the reader to rethink how we have typically understood the book of Ecclesiastes.

Ecclesiastes does not belong to "wisdom literature" because it "challenges" or "refutes" a so-called "traditional" wisdom, contrary to a host of commentators.[123] Rather, it belongs to the wisdom genre *precisely because* it advances a timeless wisdom—divine wisdom—even when the literary form being used to advance this wisdom tends to be philosophical and disputational in nature. Authentic wisdom stands over against the world's "wisdom." In fact, the character of authentic wisdom and the difference that it makes in a person's life, whether ancient or modern, is bountifully on display throughout the treatise:

- 2:14—wisdom facilitates discernment

- 3:1, 17b—it recognizes that there is a proper time and season
  for everything

- 3:14—it recognizes that what God does will endure

120. Thus Hill, *Wisdom's Many Faces*, 3.

121. Whether we humans discern authentic wisdom is another matter.

122. In this regard, Ecclesiastes shares much in common with the Hebrew prophets, who expose mankind's hubris, and in utterly devastating ways.

123. See n. 103 above. For example, Brown, "Character Reconstructed," 123, 126, asserts that the Teacher is seeking to "undermine" traditional wisdom. Contra Williams, *Those Who Ponder Proverbs*, 52–53, the fact that in Ecclesiastes the writer is utilizing personal "observation" does *not* mean that "Kohelet and Jesus both depart from the authority of [wisdom's] tradition" or that the writer "calls into question the traditional doctrine of self-control." Much to the contrary. Not "traditional wisdom" but "conventional wisdom" is depicted as *hebel* or *"meaningless"* (more on which, see chapter 3). It is true that Ecclesiastes and Jesus "disorient" their audiences; however, they are demolishing "conventional wisdom," not "traditional wisdom."

- 4:9-12—it recognizes the value of friendship
- 5:2-3, 6—it recognizes the importance of listening over speaking (cf. 9:17; 10:12)
- 5:12—it recognizes the value of contentment (cf. 4:6)
- 6:7—it recognizes that human appetites are never satisfied (cf. 5:10)
- 7:2a—it recognizes the importance of moral character (cf. 10:1)
- 7:2a—it exercises self-discipline over self-indulgence
- 7:4a—it empathizes with others' loss
- 7:5a—it rebukes what is foolish
- 7:8-9—it is patient and not easily provoked (cf. 10:4)
- 7:11—it is an inheritance that brings benefits
- 7:12a—it is a shelter that guards and protects
- 7:14—it recognizes God's sovereignty over all things and human limitations
- 7:19—it is better than power and strength (cf. 9:11, 16; 10:10, 17)
- 8:1b—it brightens one's countenance
- 8:6a—it discerns proper timing and proper means
- 8:12-13—it recognizes that ultimate justice does exist
- 9:18a—it is better than weapons of war
- 10:8—it affirms the reality of "sowing" and "reaping"
- 10:17—it values industry
- 11:1-2, 6—it recognizes opportunities to do good and makes the most of them, without any guarantee of reward

The above insights facilitated by wisdom as mirrored in Ecclesiastes agree not only with "traditional" wisdom but with the spirit of the New Testament, finding abundant confirmation in various writings of the New Testament. Consider alone Jesus' use of wisdom as a teaching technique. His dependence on parable, riddle, hyperbole, and the rhetorical question are on constant display throughout the Gospel narratives. Not unlike Ecclesiastes, Jesus reminds his hearers that God has hidden wisdom from some and revealed it to others (Matt 11:25 and Luke 10:21). Just as significantly, he challenges his listeners with the very rhetorical question posed at the outset of Ecclesiastes—"What does it profit . . .?"—when he asks, "For what does it profit a man to gain the whole world and forfeit his soul?"

(Matt 16:26, Mark 8:36, and Luke 9:25).[124] The Apostle Paul, similar to the writer of Ecclesiastes, juxtaposes the wisdom of this world with divine wisdom (1 Cor 1 and 2). At the same time, the apostle's prayer for believers is that God would give them wisdom and understanding, in order that they might be pleasing to God and know God better (Eph 1:18 and Col 1:9). Moreover, the epistle of James, in line with Ecclesiastes, distinguishes between two types of wisdom—an earthly wisdom and a heavenly wisdom (Jas 3:13–18). One flows from selfish ambition, while the other is the fruit of humility and the fear of the Lord.[125]

Not only does the present volume take the position that Ecclesiastes, however unique and jarring, stands in continuity with "traditional" wisdom—even as the book of Job does[126]—but it also argues that a *second theme* in the book is to be recognized—a theme that stands in contrast to "Meaningless, meaningless! Everything is meaningless!" This alternative interpretation, rather than viewing Ecclesiastes as promoting pessimism or resignation and mirroring a "crisis" of wisdom, understands Ecclesiastes to be teaching through its "indirect theology" that the God-fearer will experience distinct levels of satisfaction and contentment. Notably, this occurs in the context of the "ordinary" and one's work. Moreover, this experience, not despair and resignation, is to be *normative*, based on divine purpose and human design.[127] This thesis, of course, will need fleshing out in the chapters that follow.

---

124. ESV.

125. Note as well the use of the rhetorical question in James—for example, in 2:4, 2:6 (twice), 2:7, 2:14 (twice), 2:16, 2:20, 2:21, 2:25, 3:11, 3:12, 3:13, 4:1 (twice), 4:4, 4:5, 4:12, and 4:14. The three questions found in 4:13–14, however, are not rhetorical; they are hortatory.

126. The widespread view among Old Testament scholars that Ecclesiastes and Job mirror a "crisis in wisdom" is predicated largely on assumptions about dating and social context that tend to be read back into the text of the book rather than through exegesis of the text and writer's literary-rhetorical strategy.

127. To argue that satisfaction and contentment in our work is "normative" is not to deny hardship and suffering; it is only to underscore our design as human creatures—we are *designed* for work and for flourishing, based on our creation in God's image—and to distinguish between a theistic and non-theistic outlook on ultimate reality.

— 3 —

Interpretive Strategy in Ecclesiastes

On Reading Ecclesiastes

TWO GENERATIONS AGO ONE Old Testament commentator offered this rather banal and wildly understated observation: "The book of Ecclesiastes is not as well known as it should be."[1] That state of affairs, vastly underestimated, has not changed. In fact, it is far worse today than it was in our grandparents' generation. Rarely will one hear teaching or preaching from Old Testament wisdom texts—and this among churches that are purported to have a *high regard* for Scripture.

Then or now, part of the problem is the character of this "strange and disquieting" book.[2] The major interpretive problem, alluded to in chapter 1, is this: how to understand and explain its apparent internal contradictions, and thus, how to make sense of its intended message. For example, one contemporary scholar who summarizes commentary to the present day observes that "one is tempted to despair when one realizes the extent to which scholars still disagree about it."[3] A survey of the literature will reveal that even professional scholars who have devoted their entire lives to the study of the biblical text seem to despair over Ecclesiastes. The reason for this vexation is that the book presents "enigmas of every kind,"[4] thereby rendering any sort of consensus on interpretive matters well nigh impossible. This state of affairs leads one commentator to assert: "In fact, it [Ecclesiastes] denies some of the things on which the other [biblical]

1. Paterson, *The Book That Is Alive*, 129.

2. Fox, *Ecclesiastes*, ix. For a helpful overview of modern interpretation of Ecclesiastes as well as relatively recent proposals for reading the book up until about 2000, see Bartholomew, "Qoheleth in the Canon?"

3. Bartholomew, "Qoheleth in the Canon?," 13.

4. Whybray, *The Intellectual Tradition in the Old Testament*, 67.

writers lay the greatest stress—notably that God has revealed himself and his will to man."[5] Another commentator is equally frank in his rejection of the book's authority: "His [the writer's] God is not the God of Israelite faith."[6] And yet another laments:

> Life is profitless . . . totally absurd. This oppressive message lies at the heart of the Bible's strangest book. Enjoy life if you can . . . for old age will soon overtake you. And even as you enjoy, know that the world is meaningless. Virtue does not bring reward. The deity stands distant, abandoning humanity to chance and death.[7]

The complaints, however, are not confined to a few. One well-respected Old Testament scholar protests, "It is truly difficult to give an overall picture of the work. Qoheleth's thought is tortuous . . . The book provides no basis for relativizing the fundamental perception of 'vanity.'"[8] Yet another commentator discounts the presence in Ecclesiastes of any "epistemological, ethical, or metaphysical" guidelines, being resigned to the book's message of life's "ultimate worthlessness"[9]—a state of affairs leaving one more commentator to object that the teaching of Ecclesiastes is frankly "incompatible" with the orthodoxy of the Hebrew Bible[10] and causing another to opine, "his [the writer's] claims for universal truth become, in fact, almost ludicrous."[11] Still another commentator summarizes the "value" of reading Ecclesiastes in the following manner: "Its shallow philosophy ignores all that is best and noblest in human character and experience, and thus robs youth of its dreams, manhood of its rewards, and old age of its consolations."[12] And if all this were not *bad enough*, the authors of the best-selling *How to Read the Bible for All Its Worth* offer the following unflattering view, which deserves to be cited at length:

---

5. Scott, *Proverbs-Ecclesiastes*, 191. Moreover, Scott writes, "In Ecclesiastes God is not only unknown to man through revelation; he is unknowable through reason, the only means by which the author believes knowledge is attainable"; the book constitutes "a philosophy of resignation."

6. Lauha, *Kohelet*, 17. The German original reads: "Sein Gott ist nicht der Gott des israelitischen Glaubens."

7. Crenshaw, *Ecclesiastes*, 23.

8. Murphy, *Ecclesiastes*, lviii–lix.

9. Gericke, "Axiological Assumptions in Qohelet," 6.

10. Shields, *The End of Wisdom*, 1, 6, and 135.

11. Sharp, *Irony and Meaning in the Hebrew Bible*, 205.

12. Mitchell, "'Work' in Ecclesiastes," 138.

[I]ts [the book's] consistent message (until the very last verses)
is that the reality and finality of death mean that life has no
ultimate value. After all, if we are all going to die anyway, and
pass and be forgotten like all the rest, what difference does it
make if we lived a generous, productive, godly life, or a selfish,
wicked, miserable life? . . . Enjoy life as much as you can while
you are alive (8:15; 11:8–10; et al.) because *that is all* that God
has provided for you—there is *nothing else*. Live as well as you
can *now*. After this, there is no meaning . . . But this advice has
no eternal value. It is given mainly to help make one's meaningless life somewhat more pleasant and comfortable while one is
still young. *Ecclesiastes seems to deny an afterlife . . . , criticize key*
aspects of the Old Testament faith . . . , and generally encourage
attitudes very different from the rest of Scripture . . . Why, then,
you ask is it in the Bible at all? The answer is that it is there as
a *foil*, i.e., as *a contrast to what the rest of the Bible teaches* . . . It
is the *secular, fatalistic wisdom* that a *practical* (not theoretical)
atheism produces . . . The book thus serves as a reverse apologetic for *cynical wisdom*; it drives its readers to look further because the answers that the "Teacher" of Ecclesiastes gives are so
discouraging. The advice of 12:13 (keep God's commandments)
points away from Ecclesiastes to the rest of Scripture . . . where
those commandments are found.[13]

The preceding litany of indictments—and these truly are indictments
(not least of which comes from "experts" on "how to read the Bible for all its
worth")—is truly remarkable and should give us pause. When professional
interpreters of the Bible hold Ecclesiastes to be a distortion that teaches "practical atheism" and to be *counter* to Scriptural teaching, one is left to ask, in
all seriousness: *With so-called "friends" like these, who needs "enemies" when*
it comes to interpreting Scripture?! By rendering the book of Ecclesiastes so
problematic, so "heterodox," and so dubious, Old Testament scholarship
tragically has rendered it virtually *inaccessible* to the average reader.[14] Little

13. Fee and Stuart, *How to Read the Bible for All Its Worth*, 192–93 (emphasis
added).

14. While this is my own view, I find support for it elsewhere. Literary critic Leland
Ryken is one of the few who would seem to concur; see his essay "Ecclesiastes," which
is chapter 19 of *A Complete Literary Guide to the Bible*, 268–80. And the observation
of Ellul, in *Reason for Being*, 12, seems accurate: what strikes the student of Ecclesiastes is commentators' extraordinary knowledge of Hebrew or Hellenistic history or
ancient Near Eastern culture yet their relatively shallow reading and understanding of
the text. Worst of all, Ellul notes, their theology is empty. Strangely, in contrast to this
rather unfortunate state of affairs, the amount of literature on Ecclesiastes published
particularly in the last three decades is extensive, most of which is devoted to matters

wonder that Ecclesiastes is viewed as the "black sheep" and "problem child" of the Bible. If we are to believe mainstream biblical scholarship, one truly questions why this book is even in the Bible in the first place.

Complicating matters is the fact that many "interpreters" of this most "questionable" of biblical books will not resist the temptation to read and interpret it ideologically and in twenty-first-century terms. One commentator wishes to inform us that Ecclesiastes represents "an optimal arena" for "postmodern" interpretation, given its "shifting and unstable constellation of freighted signifiers, structuring devices, and rhetorical tools."[15] Another commentator describes the book's "virtually unintelligible" and "tauntingly seductive" nature as "an arena of fruitful thought," inasmuch as its "breakdown of coherence" can surely "delight us."[16]

Perhaps the more ideologically minded among us will approach the text of Ecclesiastes with an "ecological" reading or a "feminist" reading or a "liberationist" reading or a "post-colonial" reading or even an "animal theology" reading. And in fact, one commentator does us the service of collecting and summarizing these very hermeneutical perspectives of the present day as they are applied to Ecclesiastes.[17] Thus, we should not be surprised at the appearance of one recent title—*Ecclesiastes: A Peculiarly Postmodern Piece.*[18] And it should not be all that surprising that contemporary "postmodern" readings of the book are inclined to praise the writer's "heterodoxy," as if his purported "doubt, disbelief, and despair" are some *necessary corrective* to a dogmatic Christian theology.[19] While indeed Ecclesiastes may well serve as

---

of form rather than content. Whatever we make of this, treatment of Ecclesiastes in the literature is clearly disproportionate to its understanding and place in the life of the church. Sadly, much of the literature does not serve the church well in terms of its teaching and preaching ministry.

15. Sharp, *Irony and Meaning in the Hebrew Bible,* 196.

16. Berger, "Qohelet and the Exigenices of the Absurd," 141–42.

17. See Dell, *Interpreting Ecclesiastes,* 59–94. Gericke, "Qohelet's Concept of Deity," is one of the few to challenge many of the more contemporary readings of Ecclesiastes. Gericke specifically takes to task representative Old Testament commentators for their "romanticizing" of the writer's supposed "deconstruction of religious dogma." Gericke's counsel to such commentators is straightforward: theologically, Ecclesiastes contains "too much that just does not enter into the consumer culture of postmodern God-talk" (2), and this content needs an accounting. Whatever one thinks of the broadly "reader-response" approach to reading texts that has been dominant in our generation, it needs emphasizing that the newer interpretations are *no more authoritative or superior* than the "pre-critical" readings against which they are reacting. Simply said, texts cannot mean whatever we, the readers, wish them to say.

18. Ingram, *Ecclesiastes.*

19. Or, as in the case of Tamez, *When the Horizons Close,* 1, 16, the interpreter of Ecclesiastes rails at the free market system of democratic societies and the "ideology of

a corrective to shallow belief, the sort of "postmodern" readings that have
become fashionable, particularly in academic circles, tend to be flawed at
several levels. In addition to importing meaning and inferences that are for-
eign to the text, they tend to be evasive, failing to wrestle with (and discern)
the author's intent as expressed through the language of the text as we have
it, through recognizable literary-rhetorical strategies at work, and through
the structure of argumentation.[20]

Because of the widespread assumption that Ecclesiastes is theologically "heterodox," as the above negative comments by Old Testament
scholars make clear, a measured response is in order. For one, modern
scholarship has generally overlooked the interpretation of Ecclesiastes
found in rabbinic traditions and hence the precise nature of rabbinic questioning of the book.[21] Even when it is true that the contents of the book
created difficulties for both the synagogue and the church, the rabbis of old
never cite "orthodoxy" as a problem with the book. Their concerns, as they
evaluated the book's authority as well as its canonicity,[22] were generally—
with the exception of "internal contradictions"—not those of modern and
ultra-modern interpreters. Thus, for example, according to the lines of
rabbinic thinking, so-called "interpolations" or "pious additions" would
have automatically excluded Ecclesiastes from consideration in the Hebrew canon.[23] In the end, a rabbinic consensus regarding inclusion in the
canon emerged if it was thought that the book indeed "defiled the hands,"[24]
a rabbinic metaphor for its sacred and authoritative character.[25] In vari-

---

capitalism" and of "imperial power." Tamez's ideological biases, issuing out of her South
American perspective, permit her reading of Ecclesiastes only to find application in a
critique of North American or "first-world" cultures, without giving serious attention
to the *actual text* of Ecclesiastes itself.

20. German Old Testament scholar Norbert Lohfink, *Qoheleth*, 1, perceptively
notes that not a few commentators today find Ecclesiastes a "back door" by which to
express *their* unorthodox views and skepticism. These often are sentiments, he notes,
which normally would be "refused entry" at the portals of orthodox faith.

21. So Hirschman, "Qohelet's Reception and Interpretation in Early Rabbinic
Literature."

22. On rabbinic debates regarding the inclusion of the five "disputed" books of the
Old Testament—Ezekiel, Proverbs, Esther, Song of Songs, and Ecclesiastes—see Beckwith, *The Old Testament Canon of the New Testament Church*, 274–337.

23. For a helpful and reasonably non-technical discussion of rabbinic attitudes toward the matter of "heterodoxy," see Gutridge, "Wisdom, Anti-Wisdom, and the Ethical Function of Uncertainty," 184–96.

24. The school of Shammai ruled that Ecclesiastes did not defile the hands, while
the school of Hillel ruled that it did.

25. On the rabbinic notion of "defiling the hands," see Leiman, *The Canonization of
Hebrew Scripture*; Beckwith, *The Old Testament Canon of the New Testament Church*,

ous places in Talmudic literature, we find that this expression is applied to three Old Testament books—Esther, Song of Songs, and Ecclesiastes. What is more, evidence indicates that the Qumran community accepted Ecclesiastes as authoritative and therefore "canonical."[26]

Second, against the great majority of commentators, Ecclesiastes mirrors *notable*, and not just marginal, affinities with "traditional" biblical wisdom, which is thought to accord with the language and theological orientation of the book of Proverbs.[27] In truth, the evidence supporting the view that Ecclesiastes is "orthodox," as we attempted to argue in the previous chapter, is compelling, even when we may acknowledge that the book is utterly unique in its character and composition.

Consider, for example, not only the many sayings in the book of Proverbs but the various "wisdom" Psalms that juxtapose the righteous and the wicked or the wise and the foolish. Not a few psalms contain this sort of language. And proverbial wisdom such as is found in Prov 13:22 ("A good man leaves an inheritance for his children's children, but a sinner's wealth is stored up for the righteous"), Prov 28:8 ("Whoever increases wealth by taking interest or profit from the poor amasses it for another, who will be kind to the poor"), or Job 27:17 (". . . what he [the wicked] lays up the righteous will wear, and the innocent will divide his silver")[28] finds substantiation—and parallel expression—in Eccl 2:26. What is striking in standard commentary on 2:24–26 (see chapter 5) is the common contention that the dualism found in 2:26 is "non-moral" in nature, i.e., that a "righteous-versus-wicked"/"wise-versus-foolish" contrast is *not* being mirrored here,[29] when in fact this is *precisely* the contrast that the writer is making: "For to the one who pleases him God has given wisdom and knowledge and joy, but to the sinner he has given

---

278–91; and Broyde, "Defilement of the Hands."

26. Hereon see Muilenberg, "A Qoheleth Scroll from Qumran." On definitions of, witnesses to, and the structure of "canon," see Beckwith, *The Old Testament Canon of the New Testament Church*, 16–180.

27. The wider assumption among scholars that Ecclesiastes is "challenging"—if not negating—"traditional" wisdom is anchored in three general presuppositions or interpretive biases that are interlocking. The first is dating; the book is assumed to be post-exilic, based on evidence of its language, social setting, and philosophical arguments. The second issues out of the supposed "internal contradictions." And the third is an inability to distinguish between two kinds of "wisdom" in the book—a "worldly" and a "godly"; this inability itself proceeds from an inattention to the writer's literary-rhetorical strategy of juxtaposition or comparison, the argument for which is developed in the present chapter.

28. NIV.

29. So, for example, Murphy, *Ecclesiastes*, 26; Longman, *The Book of Ecclesiastes*, 110; Crenshaw, *Ecclesiastes*, 90; and Duncan, *Ecclesiastes*, 35.

the business of gathering and collecting, only to give to one who pleases God."[30] That "righteousness" in Ecclesiastes is indeed intended to connote a foremost moral condition—thereby standing over against wickedness or foolishness—is strengthened by statements found, for example, in 7:20 and 9:1–2,[31] as well as reminders of divine judgment.[32]

Relatedly, the strong dual emphasis in Ecclesiastes on (a) the foolishness of trusting in wealth and (b) the human's "creaturely" status at death finds confirmation in numerous "wisdom" psalms. Consider, for example, Psalm 49:

- 49:6—some trust in their wealth and boast of their great riches
- 49:10—the foolish leave their wealth to others
- 49:12, 14—man is like the beasts that perish and destined for the grave
- 49:17—no one takes anything with him into the grave
- 49:20—a person with riches yet without understanding is like the beast that perishes

In fact, the similarities are particularly striking between Ps 49:12, 20, as noted above, and Eccl 3:18–20, which reads:

> I also thought, "As for men, God tests them so that they may see that they are like the animals. Man's fate is like that of the animals; the same fate awaits them both: As one dies so dies the other. All have the same breath; man has no advantage over the animal. Everything is meaningless. All go to the same place; all come from dust, and to dust all return."[33]

In the end, to remind human beings of their creaturely status is a "wisdom" feature of the Psalms—for example, Ps 8:4: "What is man that you are mindful of him?" (cf. Heb 2:6)—wherein we find the cry of the psalmist as he contemplates the utter incomprehensibility of the cosmos from the perspective of a mere human being.

Further evidence of Ecclesiastes being commensurate with—rather than challenging—the "traditional" wisdom perspective lies in its

---

30. RSV.

31. Eccl 7:20: "There is not a righteous man on earth who does what is right and never sins"; 9:1–2: "the righteous and the wise and what they do are in God's hands . . . All share a common destiny—the righteous and the wicked, the good and the bad, the clean and the unclean . . ." (NIV).

32. Eccl 3:15b; implied in 5:6b and 9:2; 11:9d; and 12:14

33. NIV.

comparison to Job.[34] The commonalities are notable and deserving of attention, even when Job probes the matter of righteous suffering while Ecclesiastes addresses the meaning of life and human happiness.[35]

- Both share the perspective on human limitations and divine inscrutability, human beings' smallness and God's greatness.

- Both demolish false certainty, hubris, and human autonomy.

- Both teach that failure to recognize human limitations is *the* central human dilemma.

- Both underscore divine sovereignty and God's "otherness," by which God is neither predictable nor manageable.

- Both expose a false wisdom.

- Both conclude with the fear of the Lord and teach that human beings should revere God.

- Both mirror a "listening" disposition before God.

- Neither "resolves" the dilemma of divine inscrutability.

- Both feature a great "wise" man.

- Both depict alienation from God—or, more accurately, a *sense* of alienation.

- Both counter a naïve theology as well as doctrinaire self-righteousness.

- Both affirm the reality of human suffering—a suffering that is not always the result of "reward" or "punishment."

- Both view death as the great leveler and final arbiter.

- Both stress our creaturely status.

- Both affirm divine justice and judgment, even when human beings do not see it in their experience.

- Both teach that a proper response to God is listening, receptivity, and awe.

34. Regardless of attempts to date the book, I am assuming that Job belongs to the "normative" wisdom perspective, which includes not only *declarative* maxims for how to live (e.g., proverbial wisdom) but also more *speculative* reflections on the meaning of life and the meaning of human suffering.

35. In Ecclesiastes the writer is not wrestling with the problem of evil, as is the case with Job; rather, his focus is life's meaning and purpose.

At this point, it is necessary to grapple with discerning the writer's purpose for writing. *How* should we read Ecclesiastes? Is the book's message pessimism, optimism, an absurd mix of the two, or something that is simply indiscernible? After all, the book has received a mixed review throughout history, and it is surely instructive that for the better part of two millennia it was read allegorically. What might that suggest? Based on the language employed, the structure of thought unfolding,[36] and the peculiar use of literary devices such as repetition[37] and refrain, what is the writer's aim? Given the exclamation "Everything is meaningless!" that frames the work (1:2 and 12:8), does this motto represent the writer's *own* position, i.e., the position that *everything* in the cosmos—*categorically*—is "meaningless" and without purpose?

Literary-Rhetorical Strategy in Ecclesiastes

The present volume takes the position that the literary-rhetorical strategy at work in Ecclesiastes is intended to be neither narrative[38] nor sermonic; nor is the work foremost a theological tract,[39] even when it possesses a *very clear theological framework*. It is rather a mixture of observations—"I devoted myself to explore," "I sought to understand," "I saw," "I thought in my heart," "I know that," "I realized." These are not "isolated," unrelated, or seemingly "conflicting" observations, as is often thought[40]; they are, rather, philosophical (and as chapter 4 argues, theologically freighted) observations about life's meaning and human endeavor that are couched intermittently in an almost brooding skepticism. This probing by the writer is so relentless,

36. As noted in chapter 1, evidence of a structural design in Ecclesiastes indicates that there is more than what is "under the sun." See in this regard chapter 5.

37. Repetition in Ecclesiastes occurs both in terms of substance and style, even to the point of the writer employing sound-play for literary effect. Hereon see Carasik, "Qoheleth's Twists and Turns."

38. That is, Ecclesiastes does not represent events (whether real or fictive) in a time sequence, even when it is true that the book at time reads like a story. I derive this definition of narrative from Prince, *Narratology*, 1. Holding an opposing view are Fox, "Frame Narrative and Composition in the Book of Qoheleth," and Christianson, *A Time to Tell*.

39. This is not to argue that the writer does not advance theology. It is only to acknowledge that in the wisdom perspective theology is implicit in nature.

40. Much commentary views these observations as unrelated or disjointed. Representative are Staples, "'Profit' in Ecclesiastes," 96; Murphy, "The Pensées of Qoheleth"; Armstrong, "Ecclesiastes in Old Testament Theology," 20; and Brown, "Book of Ecclesiastes I," 276. Staples (above) complains that Ecclesiastes "might well have been entitled" something akin to *Guesses at the Truth*.

so unremitting, so thorough that "he can easily be taken for a sceptic or a pessimist."[41] Altogether, his observations might seem at times to contradict and at other times to support earlier observations. In fact, his voice changes so often that virtually all commentators assume two or three "voices" at play in Ecclesiastes.[42]

Consistent with a standard technique found in wisdom literature, however, the wider strategy of the writer of Ecclesiastes[43] is to contrast and compare—that is, to juxtapose—and to repeat various insights.[44] This is to

41. So Kidner, *A Time to Mourn, and a Time to Dance*, 13.

42. Remarkably, over a century ago, Siegfried, *Prediger und Hoheslied*, 2–12, posited as many as *nine* different voices in the book.

43. I will simply assume *Qoheleth*, the Hebrew form of the word translated "Preacher" or "Teacher" (1:1, 2; 7:27; 12:8, 9), to be the writer, whom I shall also call the "Teacher" (based on his reference in 12:9). Being implied here is one who "gathers" or "convenes" (*qahal*) and, thus, teaches publicly. Intriguingly, in Aramaic and Syriac, the root *qhl* connotes not only "to assemble" but also "litigious" or "quarrelsome." It is quite fitting, then, if the writer's title is "the arguer." See Ullendorff, "The Meaning of *qhlt*." This surely strengthens the case that Ecclesiastes is intended to be an "apologetic." The position taken in the present volume is that the question of whether one equates Solomon with Qoheleth or understands Qoheleth to be either speaking on behalf of Solomon, adopting a Solomonic persona, or extending Solomonic tradition is, in the end, secondary. As someone has said, the *song* is more important than the "singer." And, unfortunately, the "singer" seems to have received far more attention among professional scholars than the "song." Eaton, *Ecclesiastes*, 17, has stated the matter correctly: "we do not need a date for Ecclesiastes in order to receive its message," for the genius of the author is reflected in the fact that the book "stands on its own feet at any time and in any place." Is the writer transcribing oral lectures? Is he compiling? Did subsequent editors compile? Is the work a running dialogue with an imaginary opponent? These and related questions, fascinating as they are, must be consigned to our own speculation; we simply do not know, even when scholars have not been shy about positing theories. As indicated in chapter 1, the present volume does not examine questions of authorship, dating, social-economic setting, or canonicity, nor does it focus heavily on literary genre or language; these matters together are sufficiently addressed in standard critical commentaries. It does attempt, rather, in a very limited fashion to assess the value of wisdom as it informs an important sub-theme in the treatise—i.e., the meaningfulness or meaninglessness of human labor—which in particular requires an accounting since *all human activity* is said to be "meaningless." The significance—indeed, the greatness—of a work such as Ecclesiastes arises less from its form—over which scholars disagree greatly—than its *content*. However, I reject the view of Kreeft that "[t]he form of Ecclesiastes is simple, direct, and artless" (*Three Philosophies of Life*, 15). On all three counts Kreeft is mistaken. The writer utilizes reflective narrative, proverbs, comparative sayings, rhetorical questions, autobiographical material and more—not to mention techniques such as alliteration, repetition, satire, didactic poetry, and parallelism. In short, the writer is a literary master. Hereon see, for example, Hobbins, "The Poetry of the Book of Qohelet."

44. Wright, "The Interpretation of Ecclesiastes," discerns a pattern of refrain in Ecclesiastes but does not develop this sufficiently. Moreover, he says nothing about

recognize that the writer moves back and forth throughout the treatise seamlessly without telling the reader along the way, "Now, pay attention: this is a
contrast," or "Now a shift." Not once, not twice, but continually this technique
is employed, often to the consternation of the average reader, who is perhaps
hoping for a clearer, "straight-line" approach to interpretation.[45] And, as it
happens, juxtaposition and repetition are two trademarks of Ecclesiastes, with
the latter recurring in terms of both vocabulary and phraseology.

One means of discerning the message of Ecclesiastes—indeed, of any
literary work—is to observe whether any statements recur as a sort of refrain. Indeed, as a closer reading of the text reveals, this is in fact the case. A
key in interpreting both the form and content of Ecclesiastes is to grasp the
dialectical method underlying the entire work. Contrast is the organizing
principle. Everything between 1:2 and 12:8 ("All is meaningless!") does not
constitute "variations on a theme," as one commentator has argued;[46] rather,
it constitutes variations on *two* themes. And in this contrast of two philosophies of life—this juxtaposition—the writer's strategy is to keep despair in
the foreground, with unblinking persistence hammering away and utilizing
periodic—and strategically placed—glimpses of the alternative. For in order
for people to see clearly, they must receive shock therapy, as it were, having
their false hopes pulverized.[47] With other words, the writer "disillusions us
to bring us to reality."[48] And facilitating this juxtaposing of two clashing
perspectives, the Teacher is comfortable trafficking in both worlds—the
Jewish and the pagan—as he addresses the question of happiness and life's
meaning.[49] His concern is to probe "the boundaries of life."[50]

---

satisfaction in work, which is a key element in this refrain. A clearer sense of juxtaposition is found in the arguments presented by Eaton, *Ecclesiastes,* and Lee, *The Vitality
of Enjoyment.*

45. One plausible way in which to interpret the writer's literary-rhetorical strategy—a matter that, truth be told, bedevils both ancient and modern readers—is to
understand the writer to be utilizing "Janus" statements—that is, statements which,
thematically and structurally, look both back and forward. Hereon see Dell and Forti,
"Janus Sayings."

46. Contra Jarick, "The Hebrew Book of Changes," 80.

47. Hendry, "Ecclesiastes," and Kidner, *The Wisdom of Proverbs, Job & Ecclesiastes,*
93–94, are among the few commentators to grasp this rhetorical strategy in Ecclesiastes. Otherwise, Scott's famous remark (*Proverbs-Ecclesiastes,* 203), that "all this [Eccle-
siastes] sounds like an argument for suicide" would seem to be true, if indeed we fail to
get the message right.

48. Kidner, *A Time to Mourn,* 36.

49. To communicate truth about happiness and life's meaning, one must address
the philosophers of any age. And this is what the Teacher seems to do, which makes the
message of Ecclesiastes timeless and ever relevant.

50. Kidner, *A Time to Mourn,* 13.

Having observed contrast or dialectic in Ecclesiastes, we must sharpen this thesis a bit. Not only are two ways of thinking, two approaches to life, two views of ultimate reality being compared in the book, they are also presented in sharpest relief. That is, they stand in diametric opposition; they are antitheses. The despair that arises in Ecclesiastes emanates from the writer-teacher's oft-repeated lament that in spite of *everything*, he fails to find *anything* of meaning. If, however, the writer were a real pessimist to the bone, he would have struck a different note throughout the treatise. He would, it seems, have assumed an attitude of disgust, with death serving as *release* from this absurd and cruel world. But such represents neither the tone nor the rhetorical strategy at work. The materialist-secularist outlook being critiqued and lamented is real and "true" in the human experience. However, it is not the whole truth; a theistic outlook transcends that which is temporal and materialistic.

There are essentially three ways in which to interpret the "contradictions" in Ecclesiastes. One is to view the writer as being autobiographical and thus "evolving" in his outlook. Another is to view the writer as standing in conflict, caught in a tension between the two poles of "meaninglessness" and hope that again and again will be dashed.[51] The third possibility is to understand the writer to be contrasting two competing metaphysical outlooks on life, a position being advanced by the present volume. If we allow the tensions and ambiguities—the perceived "contradictions"—in Ecclesiastes to stand, we may discover that there is interplay between two polarities of thought, between two contradictory perspectives. Contradiction does not cancel out coherence.[52] The writer, it needs emphasizing, is not contradicting *himself*. The contradictions are placed side by side for the purpose of forcing the reader to render a verdict. After demolishing the materialist's outlook by insisting that "Nothing matters," the Teacher shifts and argues that "Everything matters." Why? Because of the Creator and Maker of all things (3:11; 7:14, 29; 11:5; 12:1) who is to be revered (3:14; 5:7; 7:18; 8:12–13) and who will judge all people and all things (3:17; 5:6;11;9; 12:14).

What in the end seem to amount to *blatant contradictions* in the human existence (at least, in our perception of human existence) are, in fact,

51. As we noted in chapter 1, this approach reads Ecclesiastes as if the writer is affirming a sort of "sweet-and-sour" view of ultimate reality.

52. Thus, for Loader, *Polar Structures in the Book of Qoheleth*, internal coherence of Ecclesiastes entails recognition of polarities or "polar structures." Miller, "What the Preacher Forgot," describes contradiction or antithesis in the book in terms of "destabilizing" and "restabilizing" the intended audience's belief system. The latter is understood by Miller to be a reconstruction of a world- or life-view as evidenced by the writer's admonitions, most of which are developed progressively.

"reconcilable" in terms of the writer's literary-rhetorical strategy.[53] Consider, for example, the reflections gathered in the didactic poem beginning at verse 3:1—reflections that seem to bear out the reconciling of what are incongruities in human experience. There is a "time"[54] and "season"—and this "under heaven"—for "everything"; hence, seeming contradictions and absurdities, which encompass virtually everything in the human experience, are put in proper perspective *if* viewed according to a proper framework of reality. The poem reconciles chaos (our perspective) with order (the divine perspective) in a remarkable literary fashion. "Seasons" of life have the effect of reminding us of—and reinforcing—our limitations. These "seasons," presented as opposites in the form of fourteen pairs[55] of poetic verse, include: (1) birth and death/planting and uprooting; (2) killing and healing/destroying and building; (3) weeping and laughing/mourning and dancing; (4) removing stones and gathering stones/embracing and withdrawing; (5) searching and giving up/retaining and throwing away; (6) tearing down and sowing/being silent and speaking; and (7) loving and hating/war and peace. Within the literary form of poetry, the writer is here employing the language of proverbs. In truth, every one of these statements, in its form, could appear in the book of Proverbs. The writer comprehends the temporality of human existence in terms of polarity, in the same way that proverbial wisdom stereotypically does.

While the verses of this didactic poem are some of the most well-known (or at least oft-cited) verses from the Bible, precisely how they inform the overall message of Ecclesiastes—i.e., that life and human existence must be Creator-centered[56]—is less well known. In fact, because the paired elements appear to be blatant contradictions, they are routinely dismissed—when, that is, they are not misunderstood.[57] Thoughtful medi-

---

53. The manner in which many commentators "reconcile" the book's "internal contradictions" is to conclude that *both* emphases—"All is meaningless" and "Life is a gift of God"—are true. But this "solution" itself is absurd and is self-contradictory.

54. The proper way in which to understand "time" here accords with "season"; thus, it should be rendered "occasion" or "appropriate time" (hereon see von Rad, *Wisdom in Israel*, 38–43). The sense of these verses, it should be noted, has to do not with a mechanistic or deterministic predestination but rather with human discernment.

55. The numeration here—two pairs times seven—can be viewed as a poetic expression of sovereignty or utter perfection.

56. The message of the book is *not* the importance of living a so-called "balanced" life (contra, for example, Curtis, *Ecclesiastes and Song of Songs,* 2) or the need to somehow reconcile the absurdities of life with its more pleasant aspects, as the vast majority of commentators maintain.

57. Contra, for example, Blenkinsopp, "Ecclesiastes 3.1–5," this poetic material is neither a "foil" to the writer's own view of human existence, nor is it a "stoicizing" of

tation and reflection on what they suggest, from a wisdom perspective, and how they illuminate life's meaning and purpose are very much needed. While our natural reaction is to view many of the elements in these pairs as absurd, wretched, and scandalous, every one of them possesses meaning and purpose if interpreted by divine providence. (Whether human beings actually discern meaning and purpose in them, of course, is another matter.) Such a conclusion accords with the statement that follows: "[God] has made everything beautiful in its time" (3:11).[58]

Hence, an important lesson of this didactic material is *discernment*—discernment of (a) the particular season that impacts our lives and (b) what action or actions would be appropriate, given that particular season. With this material the writer is navigating between divine sovereignty and human responsibility, similar to other wisdom sayings such as Prov 16:9 ("A man's mind plans his way, but the LORD directs his steps.") and Prov 21:1 ("The king's heart is a stream of water in the hand of the LORD; he turns it wherever he will.")[59]; he is not affirming any sort of fatalism or determinism.[60] The context and theological framework here are quite clear: any measure of discernment presupposes the recognition of divine omnipotence and providence.[61] The declaration that everything has a "season" or "proper time" reinforces the writer's own theological stance—everything has a *purpose*—and hence represents a response to "everything is meaningless" (1:2).[62]

As we look at Ecclesiastes as a whole, assisting the reader in the interpretive process is the writer's repeated use of catchwords (for example, "meaningless"/"meaninglessness" [*hebel*], "enjoyment" [*śimhâ*] or "rejoice" [*śāmah*], "gain" or "profit" [*yitrôn*], "portion" or "lot" [*heleq*], "good" [*tôb*], and "labor" [*'āmāl*],[63] catchphrases ("under the sun," "under heaven," "chas-

---

Hebrew wisdom, an element that would have permitted suicide in some instances.

58. In the words of Fredericks and Estes, *Ecclesiastes and the Song of Songs*, 117, these words constitute "the greatest statement of divine providence in the whole of Scripture" and parallel Rom 8:28.

59. RSV.

60. Contra Rudman, *Determinism in the Book of Ecclesiastes*, and Hubbard, *Ecclesiastes, Song of Solomon*, 100–101.

61. Omnipotence and providence are conveyed not only in 3:11 but also in 3:14–15 as well. Past and present are open to God the Sovereign, who stands outside of time.

62. Contra Fox, *Qohelet and His Contradictions*, 102, "everything has a season" does not mean "everything will reoccur." Purpose, not circularity, is the intended meaning. Much commentary focuses on the limits placed upon human beings by divine sovereignty—i.e., purported negative implications—rather than the fact that divine sovereignty grounds human *meaning and contentedness*.

63. Of the three terms translated "labor" or "work" in Ecclesiastes, *'āmāl* appears most frequently.

ing after the wind," "what God does/has done," "the gift of God," "what God has given," "nothing better than"), and recurring themes ("This, too, is meaningless," "so that men will revere God," "this is a gift of God"). Moreover, all aspects of human activity—that is, *everything* in human existence and human experience, whether accumulating knowledge, pursuing pleasures, seeking justice, or toiling in one's work—are said to be "meaningless"; hence, the purpose of the bookends in 1:2 and 12:8 with the declaration "Meaningless, meaningless . . . everything is meaningless!"

Interpreting the "All Is Meaningless" Thesis

Precisely here it needs emphasizing that no consensus exists among students of the Old Testament as to the precise translation of the Hebrew term *hebel* (lit., "vapor," "smoke," or "breath"), which appears thirty-eight times in Ecclesiastes. In fact, translations differ wildly in terms of rendering this keyword, as was noted in chapter 1. Variations range from "vanity," "meaninglessness," "futility," "absurdity," "deception," "pointlessness," or "profitlessness" to "transience" or "fleeting" to "enigmatic," "mysterious," "incomprehensible," even "ironic," with a few commentators choosing to render it literally as "vapor" or "breath." Most commentators—though by no means all—are willing to acknowledge the remarkable flexibility and ambiguity of the term, depending on the context in which it appears. However, this variance in connotation is *not,* I would argue (against most commentary), the only reason—or even the *chief* reason—for Ecclesiastes generating such divergent interpretations, even when it is doubtless a contributing factor. Notwithstanding the fact that the term does allow a wide range of inflections, these lexical possibilities bear *some association to one another* and are not *worlds* apart in terms of their connotation. More telling as it concerns the book's interpretation, it would seem, are (1) the structure of the argument developed in Ecclesiastes,[64] (2) the use of various catchwords and catchphrases that highlight particular themes, (3) the use of literary-rhetorical devices such as rhetorical questions[65] and repeti-

---

64. At the outset in chapter 1, I noted that virtually everything about Ecclesiastes—inclusive of the work's basic structure—is contested and has eluded consensus. In speaking of "structure," I am not referring to the basic organization of (1) superscription (1:1), (2) body (1:2–12:8), and epilogue (12:9–14); that much "structure" is very obvious to all. Rather, a consensus has eluded scholarship regarding the "structure" of the main *body* of the work.

65. Remarkably, thirty-five rhetorical questions in the book are identified by Carasik, "Qoheleth's Twists and Turns."

tion, and (4) recurring shifts or "refrains" in the writer's argumentation, which can easily go unnoticed.

Against the grain of much biblical scholarship, the present volume proposes that the motto "All is *hebel*" (1:2 and 12:8) is to be taken as an exaggeration or as a metaphor rather than literally (i.e., as a "vapor" or "breath, and by extension, "fleeting" or "transient").[66] That is to say, everything *within the writer's purview and investigation* is *hebel*; everything is *hebel* existentially, but not metaphysically or cosmologically. In addition, if we translate *hebel* as "transient" or "vaporous" in the superlative, as it appears in 1:2 and 12:8 (i.e., "Transient of transience" or "Vapor of vapors"), the statement simply does not make sense; if, however, we render it "futile," "meaningless," or "absurd," it does acquire meaning. Moreover, and most importantly, how the term is used in Ecclesiastes varies and is thus dependent on context; parallel expressions in the book serve to guide us—for example, "chasing after the wind" and "a sore affliction." While the position being taken in the present volume is that *hebel* is multivalent, with differing inflections in Ecclesiastes, at the same time it makes very little sense to declare that "everything is a vapor" (and hence "fleeting"), particularly in passages of the treatise that appear to have a clear moral implication. Thus, for example,

- the context of *hebel* in 2:15 is foolishness over against wisdom;

- in 2:19 it is lack of control of the future;

- in 2:23 it is pain and grief and sleeplessness;

- in 4:4 it is envy of the neighbor;

- in 4:8 it is lack of friendship;

- in 4:13–16 it is the foolishness of morally flawed leadership;

- in 5:7 it is promiscuous imagination and talk;

- in 5:10 it is the love of money;

- in 6:9 it is the unquenchable appetite of the human being;

- in 7:6 it is the laughter of fools;

- in 7:15 it is injustice;

- in 8:9–10 it is the end of the wicked; and

- in 8:14 it is injustice.

66. The position being assumed here is that the use of *hebel* in Ecclesiastes by the writer is both metaphorical and multivalent, a position also represented by Holmstedt et al., *Qoheleth*, 50. Taking an opposing position *inter alios* are Whitley, *Koheleth*; Ogden, *Qoheleth*, 14; Fredericks, *Coping with Transience*; Caneday, "'Everything is Vapor'"; and Duncan, *Ecclesiastes*, 2–9.

Virtually all of the above are *moral* matters and, from the standpoint of accurate translation, have *little or nothing* to do with life's "brevity," "transience," or the "fleetingness" of the moment. In Ecclesiastes the writer is not coping with the brevities of life, for "brevity" does not connote failure or futility. Rather, he is coping with despair and meaninglessness;[67] he is making *value-judgments*,[68] as his frequent use of the metaphor "chasing the wind" indicates. After all, to "chase the wind" does not bespeak brevity or the fleeting nature of life; it connotes futility, pointlessness, meaninglessness, and vanity. Hence, the standard translation of *hebel* as "meaninglessness," "vanity," "futility," or even "profitlessness"[69] seems preferable and best suited to the writer's argument in most instances. In fact, the sense in which *hebel* is used in Ecclesiastes has echoes and finds confirmation in the New Testament as well:

- Acts 14:15—turning from "worthless" things to the living God

- Rom 1:21—humankind's understanding becoming "futile" with human hearts being darkened

- Rom 8:20–21—creation having been subjected to "futility"

- 1 Cor 3:20—the wisdom of the world being "futile"

- 1 Cor 15:17—without the resurrection our faith being "futile"

- Eph 4:17—the "futility" of the unbeliever's thinking

- Titus 3:9—avoiding controversies that are unprofitable and "useless"

Furthermore, *hebel* is used elsewhere in the Old Testament to depict what is idolatrous;[70] rarely does the term connote the sense of "vapor." One example of this usage is Ps 78:33—"So he [God] ended their days in futility . . ."—wherein *hebel* carries the strict sense of "futility," not "transience." Thus, rendering the term in Ecclesiastes according to its literal sense—"vapor" or "transience"—simply does not adequately capture those contexts in which it is used to depict what is evil, repugnant, or worthless.

---

67. Contra *inter alios* Fredericks, *Coping with Transience*, 96.

68. As noted by DeRouchie, "Shepherding Wind and One Wise Shepherd," 20n27, of the thirty-eight occurrences of *hebel* in Ecclesiastes, only six of these have no association with moral judgment.

69. Few commentators render *hebel* as "profitless," but this rendering captures the predominant sense in which the writer uses *hebel* throughout. A further reason for preferring this translation is that it answers the "What profit is there?" rhetorical question posed at the outset (1:3) and raised thereafter.

70. For example, Deut 32:21; 1 Kgs 16:13, 20; Ps 31:6; 78:33; Isa 57:13; Jer 2:5; 8:10; 10:8, 15; 14:22; 51:18; and Jonah 2:8.

Hebel must be understood—and translated—in the light of sin's curse, not mere "transience" or the "fleeting" nature of life. Even in the opening section of the book (1:3–2:23), the writer is not lamenting life's "brevity," "mystery," or "enigma"; he laments that *any and all* attempts to "create" meaning utterly *fail*; they offer no *gain* (cf. 1:3). This failure is *qualitative* and not merely *quantitative*.

Yet another factor strengthens the interpretation for which we are arguing. Divine judgment, which is an important sub-theme in Ecclesiastes, does not exist for that which is "vaporous" or "fleeting"; it exists to condemn—and then ultimately eliminate—what is evil or idolatrous. If everything "under the sun" is *hebel*, then various human myths—for example, human "progress," wealth and possessions, fame and reputation, accumulating knowledge, and conventional approaches to pleasure—must be exposed for *what* they are and *why* they fail.[71] Alas, the argument being presented in the present volume is that the *hebel* being decried in Ecclesiastes, because it is *freely chosen* by human beings, is not some brute, unchangeable fact without cause; it is, rather, a symptom.[72] It is, indeed, a symptom of the fall and part of the "curse." *Hebel* "infects" all of life, as the lament in 1:3–2:23 graphically portrays; however, life in its essence is not *hebel*. Rather, *hebel* can drive human beings to their Creator.[73] And yet because it is, in truth, a symptom, it does not release human beings, who are fashioned in the "likeness" of God, from being moral agents and choosing rightly. For this very reason, as noted above, divine judgment awaits all. Divine judgment would be meaningless—indeed, less than "meaningless"—if human actions and motives were not the essence of authentic meaning and happiness in life. Judgment only has meaning in a moral universe.

Beyond linguistic considerations, a further interpretive clue is the initial rhetorical question, "What do people gain from all their labors at which they toil under the sun?" (1:3), which follows on the heels of the opening lament that "All is meaningless" (1:2). This rhetorical question can be interpreted more broadly—i.e., "What do people gain through any of their efforts in any sphere of human existence?"—or more narrowly—i.e., "What

71. Here Ecclesiastes shows itself ever relevant to our own cultural context—a context which is heavily materialist in orientation and which assumes that human beings are evolving to a higher plane. Contra the "new biologists" and social engineers of our age, human beings do not evolve beyond the brute fact of their limitations in the created order. Man and beast go to their appointed end; death awaits, and beyond it we cannot see.

72. Webb, *Christian Reflections*, 104, is one of the few commentators to press this salient point.

73. In fact, this appears to be the point of the argument culminating in 3:14–15: God does this in order that human beings will revere him—the very point on which the book ends (12:13–14).

do people gain through their work, occupations, and specific endeavors in this life?" Given the broader aim of the writer to probe the meaning and purpose of human existence, the implied answer is that *nothing* is "gained" or "earned" or "accomplished" by means of human striving and effort.[74] Compelling evidence for that utter failure is laid out in excruciating detail in the material that follows (1:4–2:23)—evidence that is attested to by history and all of nature (1:4–11), philosophy (1:12–18), pursuit of pleasure (2:1–3), accomplishments, reputation, and wealth (2:4–11), intellectual pursuit (2:12–16), as well as human labor and endeavor (2:17–23).

Contrasting Two Competing Outlooks

At the same time, periodic shifts occur in the writer's thinking—shifts that begin in 2:24–26 as a response to the lament of 1:3–2:23. Significantly, these "shifts" in perspective invariably contain references to God or the Creator.[75] Thus, at play in Ecclesiastes is a contrasting of two perspectives on life: one issues from what we might call "under-the-sun secularism," while the other might be termed "under-heaven theism." Two approaches to interpreting reality, two understandings as to what is meaningless or meaningful, two competing teleologies or ultimate ways of viewing human existence. "All is meaningless" is existentially true "under the sun," but it is not the *whole* truth,[76] as the writer's literary-rhetorical strategy and the structure of the book suggest. Those things that appear meaningless when viewed "under the sun" take on a different cast and possess meaning *if* they are viewed in the light of the Creator whose providential ways are impenetrable.

In our interpretation, then, the musings of Qoheleth the teacher might be viewed as an invitation to "listen in," as it were, on a "dialogue" or "dispute" between two contrasting positions that stand diametrically opposed. This exegesis, alas, goes against the interpretation of much standard commentary on Ecclesiastes, which assumes either that the writer is "debating with himself," that he is conflicted, or that he is on some sort of evolving philosophical "journey."[77] And, indeed, without the "shifts" that are exam-

74. Cf. Matt 16:26, Mark 8:36, and Luke 9:25; Jesus poses essentially the same question to his listeners.

75. Of the roughly eight "shifts" or recurring "enjoyment refrains" (see chapter 5), only one—3:22—lacks an explicit reference to God, although the material immediately preceding—a defense of divine sovereignty and inscrutability (3:14–21)—contains the densest allusions to God in the entire book.

76. So Eaton, *Ecclesiastes*, 57, correctly in my view.

77. Kidner, *The Wisdom of Proverbs*, 93–94, observes that there are essentially two ways of interpreting the book's tensions: either we see Ecclesiastes as (1) an inner

ined in chapter 5, there is no reasonable interpretation of the book other than resignation and despair. Militating against the "philosophical journey" interpretation of Ecclesiastes, moreover, is the fact of innumerable citations throughout the treatise. The generous use of citations in the book mirrors several likely intentions on the part of the writer: facilitating dialogue or debate, expressing a counter-viewpoint, presenting a foil, offering a hypothetical position, or buttressing an argument.[78] One might argue that all of these, in some fashion, are being employed by the Teacher.

To fail to discern this comparative strategy—a strategy in which the writer is juxtaposing *two diametrically opposed* outlooks—is to lapse into an interpretation typical of a great many commentators that was identified in the previous chapter. It is to presume that Ecclesiastes is mirroring a "crisis" of wisdom. That is, the writer is thought to be challenging—or negating— the tenets and principles associated with the traditional wisdom perspective and Israel's religion.[79] Stated more drastically, it is to adopt one of the following interpretations: (1) that Ecclesiastes reflects "a loss of trust in the goodness of God" who, in the end, is "unknowable,"[80] with the result that the message of Ecclesiastes is "rigorously hopeless" and hence mirroring a forced resignation;[81] (2) that the faith as depicted in Ecclesiastes *cannot be squared* with "the faith of the other biblical writers";[82] and/or (3) that the book mirrors a "total abandonment of the traditional religious concepts of the Jewish people" and an "unvarnished declaration that religious actions, worship, and morality are ultimately irrelevant."[83] Each of these positions is

---

"debate" on the part of the writer, wherein he is torn and his thinking progresses and whereby he learns to live with a basic tension between "meaninglessness" and divine determinism, or (2) a thorough critique and demolition of materialistic, non-theistic thinking. One observes yet a third reading strategy among commentators: (3) attempting to situate the Teacher *between* the two poles of meaninglessness and joy and thus caught in an existential tension that allows little interpretive coherence, though leaning toward pessimistic resignation. This option does little or no justice to the positive refrains throughout Ecclesiastes.

78. See Gordis, "Quotations as a Literary Usage."

79. For representatives of this view, see chapter 2, n. 103. Virtually all commentators follow this line of thinking to some degree, under the assumption that the writer is questioning or countering the traditional "wisdom" principles undergirding reward and punishment, cause and consequence. However, this line of thought ignores the fact that the writer clearly believes in justice and judgment (so, for example, 3:17; implied in 5:1–7; 11:9; and 12:13–14), even when he does not necessarily see it in the human experience or understand its timing (again, cf. 3:1–8).

80. So Crenshaw, *Old Testament Wisdom,* 116–17.

81. So Watson, *Text, Church and World,* 283.

82. So Murphy, *The Tree of Life,* 58.

83. So Loader, *Ecclesiastes,* 14.

underpinned by certain presuppositions that have already been suggested thus far—among them: a presumed late date and assumed socio-economic setting, a multiauthored or multiedited literary construction, an epilogue that "adjusts" the book's argument, seeming contradictions throughout, the lack of an identifiable structure, and supposed glosses by redactors to correct "unorthodox" theological statements.

In the end, a failure to discern literary-rhetorical strategy at work in Ecclesiastes forces upon the interpreter a sort of literary and interpretive schizophrenia, inasmuch as statements that stand in *blatant*, diametric opposition are forced to stand side by side.[84] An interpretive "resolution," then, is typically found in a multiauthored (i.e., multiedited), patchwork (or "tossed salad") explanation that is incoherent and has the effect of undermining the book's authority.[85] Thus, the authors of one standard Old Testament introduction can write: "the message of the book is not the message of Qoheleth's speech; it is rather the simple instruction in the last few verses . . . What he [Qoheleth] did not have was hope."[86] Similarly, another professional scholar of wisdom literature writes: "Ecclesiastes shows signs of later adjustments to soften its pessimism."[87] The reason for such "later adjustments"? "The summary is alien to anything . . . [the writer] has said thus far."[88] Yet another insists that the "optimistic wisdom" perspective found, say, in the book of Proverbs is being "challenged" by the writer in Ecclesiastes: "His bold challenge to orthodox Judaism was regarded as dangerously close to heresy." Consequently, "the book was touched up here and there to make it more palatable to orthodox taste."[89] In the end, one is left, unhelpfully, to posit two theologies in Ecclesiastes: that of the writer, "Qoheleth," and that of the concluding

---

84. Those holding to this position of split thinking typically refer to it, somewhat euphemistically, as a "synthesis."

85. Alas, based on this sort of misguided thinking, there exists *no compelling reason* why Ecclesiastes belongs to the canon of Scripture.

86. Dillard and Longman, *An Introduction to the Old Testament*, 255. Dillard and Longman are merely representative.

87. Crenshaw, "Unresolved Issues in Wisdom Literature," 222. Similarly, Hengel, *Judaism and Hellenism*, 1:128, asserts that the writer of the second epilogue applies a "corrective hand."

88. Crenshaw, *Ecclesiastes*, 192. In a similar vein, Alter, *The Wisdom Books*, 343, considers the epilogue "a not more than hopeful rhetorical gesture" and "an effort to conclude the book with a seal of official approval unlikely to fool anyone about its actual contents."

89. Anderson, *Understanding the Old Testament*, 501.

epilogue.[90] Or, in a similar vein, one must conclude that the book's epilogue is "an oversimplification of the book's message."[91]

At bottom, the standard reasoning behind the multiauthor/multieditor supposition offered by most commentators is not persuasive.[92] It seems very odd to imagine an editor—or several editors—introducing so-called "pious insertions" or an epilogue to a treatise which is deemed dangerous or heterodox. No "wisdom" literature exists in which two opposing theologies—orthodox and heterodox—are affirmed side by side in a sort of philosophical tossed-salad approach to living.[93] And why would an orthodox writer produce a work of pessimism or skepticism?[94] If, for example, several editorial hands were needed to make Ecclesiastes palatable, then Qoheleth the teacher (1:1, 2; 7:27; 12:8; cf. 12:9, 10) was not wise enough in the first place—a conclusion that makes a mockery both of the doctrine of scriptural inspiration and of canonicity.[95] In fact, if several editorial hands *were* needed to make the book palatable, then the statements in 12:9–10—attesting to the Teacher's wisdom and knowledge, ability to discern, appropriateness of language and thought, uprightness, and truth—may be judged to be *outright falsehoods*.

A more reasonable explanation is that the book was written by a wise person, as stated by the editor in 12:9–10. This person was able to reflect seriously on—and adjudicate between—life's seeming "contradictions." The work was preserved and handed on, then commended by another teacher-editor who reiterates that there is a *true* wisdom and a *false* wisdom, the arbitrator of which is supreme Judge (12:13–14).[96] In truth, the epilogue serves to *support* rather than "correct" or dismiss the observations being made by the Teacher throughout the book.[97] As we have at-

90. So Longman, *The Book of Ecclesiastes*, 30–32.

91. So Murphy, *Ecclesiastes*, lxv.

92. A minority voice among interpreters in this regard is Fox, "Frame-Narrative and Composition in the Book of Qohelet," 91, who views the entire book to be "by the same hand."

93. Eaton, *Ecclesiastes*, 40, is one of the few commentators to raise this point.

94. The writer is a "skeptic" only insofar as he rejects the "wisdom of this world" and its pretensions.

95. Crenshaw, *Ecclesiastes*, 189–90, is representative of those who see a second epilogist in the book's conclusion as adjusting the first.

96. Not insignificantly, Seow, "'Beyond Them, My Son, Be Warned,'" 141, notes that the epilogue in Ecclesiastes has notable parallels in Egyptian wisdom text, which (a) are written in the third person, (b) contain a final warning, and (c) praise the author as a sage.

97. Eccl 12:9–14 bears some similarity to Deut 34:5–8, which describes Moses's death. Indeed, most books of the Old Testament, in their final state, have been edited

tempted to argue, the writer is juxtaposing conflicting outlooks—i.e., flat contradictions—in order to create a contrast that requires observation and decision on the part of the reader. This juxtaposing, as it is, permits us to discern an internal organizing logic at work in Ecclesiastes. At bottom, the essence of much contemporary literary analysis is to *explain away* literary and theological dissonance; after all, dissonance creates embarrassment for the reader, and Ecclesiastes is the most "embarrassing" of literary texts.[98] In the final analysis, the present volume rejects the basic assumption that the writer of the book and its editor(s) stand at cross-purposes, in which case it is impossible to (a) identify the book's purpose and message and (b) assign to it any measure of authority.

Discerning the Message of Ecclesiastes

Again, we are forced to ask, *What is the purpose of the book of Ecclesiastes?* And what on earth—"under the sun," so to speak—is this book doing in the Bible? In the words of one commentator whose view is *not* representative of most Old Testament scholarship, Ecclesiastes is a work of "apologetics"—that is, a work that defends divine providence by underscoring "the grimness of the alternative."[99] The writer's tactic is to put the reader "in the shoes of the humanist or secularist"[100] and to confront us with the brute facts of human experience as we perceive them, apart from divine revelation. The work serves as a reminder to human beings of their mortality and finitude. Against the backdrop of the lament "All is meaningless!," the writer's response—his apologetic *counter*-argument—is that "Life is a gift, not gain,"[101] and only in this realization are true happiness and contentment to be found.

The writer's argument or "defense," however, is directed not so much against other religions or against "religious pluralism" as it is against a wider outlook on life that, to be sure, is religious, theological, and philosophical in its assumptions about ultimate reality. This argument, when we as readers truly listen to it, mirrors the writer's awareness and penetrating

---

and are anonymous.

98. "Embarrassment" is precisely the word used by Armstrong, "Ecclesiastes in Old Testament Theology," 21, to describe the argument advanced in Ecclesiastes. One very simple literary prerequisite remains on the "endangered list," as one astute observer has noted, and that is "the naïve and linear or sequential reading of the text itself"; so Perry, *Dialogues with Kohelet*, xii.

99. Eaton, *Ecclesiastes*, 44.

100. Kidner, *A Time to Mourn*, 14.

101. Provan, *Ecclesiastes, Song of Songs*, 56, has correctly distilled the essence of the book's message.

critique of the mind-set of his own cultural surroundings (and ours, for that matter). The writer-teacher proceeds on the basis of what might be called "concealed premises,"[102] so that, in a certain sense, Ecclesiastes might be viewed as a work of "apologetic theology."[103] Moreover, as chapter 5 will hope to demonstrate, this apologetic argument, in which two diametrically opposed outlooks are pitted against one another, finds confirmation in the recurring "enjoyment" refrains, wherein divine language—for example, the "hand of God," a "gift of God," "what God has done," and divine "portion" or "lot"—is conspicuously present.

The Teacher is writing to those in his cultural surroundings whose view of human existence "is bounded by the horizons of this world; he meets them on their own ground, and proceeds to convict them of its inherent vanity."[104] The world, perceived in their terms, borders the absurd. The alternative outlook, with its focus on human limitations and divine sovereignty, understands the world not as a theater of the absurd but rather the arena of God's inscrutable glory. If we let Ecclesiastes speak for itself and we assume a literary unity (regardless of how difficult that unity may be to ascertain), we discover that three recurring and interconnecting theological elements comprise the writer's wider literary strategy: (1) a thorough, rational, and despairing examination of the meaninglessness of all attempts to find meaning and purpose through human accomplishment; (2) God the creator and his providential work behind life's mysteries; and (3) human beings' inability to discern God's doings.[105] In spite of the writer's depressing observations, which are inclined without further context to induce despair, he is not arguing that events in the cosmos are random and without purpose. There is a "time" and "season" for *everything*, he insists, even when this remains veiled in the human experience.

102. Hendry, "Ecclesiastes," 570.

103. Hendry, "Ecclesiastes," 570. That Ecclesiastes constitutes an *apologetic* work is the most reasonable explanation of its purpose, based on the linguistic, structural, and literary-rhetorical evidence found within, notwithstanding the mild objection of Garrett, *Proverbs, Ecclesiastes, Song of Songs*, 275, that an "apologetic" interpretation renders it "surely unlike any other defense of the faith we know." Indeed, St. Paul's "apologetic" in Athens before the Areopagus Council (Acts 17:16–34), as well, is unique in all of the New Testament insofar as the apostle does not cite the Hebrew Scriptures but rather utilizes cultural artifacts and cites poet-philosophers who are meaningful to the city's own history. This appeal, based on "general revelation," serves as a parallel to Ecclesiastes, in which *Elohim*, the God of creation, and not *Yahweh*, the covenant God of Israel, is employed by the writer. It is the *God of creation* who makes demands of *every living creature*, a moral reality that has not been nullified by the New Covenant.

104. Hendry, "Ecclesiastes," 570.

105. Von Rad, *Wisdom in Israel*, 227–37, is one of the few to recognize the interplay of these three themes.

We have thus far argued that recurring "shifts" in the writer's thinking are to be detected throughout Ecclesiastes. A common complaint in the literature is the lack of a clear, linear structure to Ecclesiastes. And upon perusing various commentaries the reader indeed will find a bewildering array of suggestions as to the book's overall structure. One is here reminded of the lament of a celebrated Old Testament scholar expressed over a century ago concerning Ecclesiastes: "All attempts both up to now and in the future not only to establish a unifying principle in the book but to identify its genre, its overall purpose, and its organizing structure are *destined to fail*."[106] Indeed, the frustration expressed in this lament is felt by the average reader, who more than likely struggles with each of these elements, and more.

In broader terms, any sort of consensus regarding the structure of Ecclesiastes has eluded Old Testament scholarship. Over the last 150 years, scholarly opinion on the matter has generally fallen into three major camps, with a few exceptions. One view holds Ecclesiastes to be only a loose collection of sayings with no discernible structural pattern.[107] According to an opposing view, the book has a brilliantly ordered and curiously detailed structure and design.[108] A third perspective divides the book roughly into two halves or four quarters, on the basis of supposed progression in the writer's thought.[109] The present volume represents yet a fourth position insofar as it would seem to best fit the internal evidence based on the logic of the writer's argument. This position assumes a greater sense of design than is normally recognized, even when structural markers are not always clear. It gives particular attention to (a) strategic use of catchwords and catchphrases, (b) continual use of rhetorical questions, (c) and repetitions and refrains, which are accompanied by (d) increased references to God. All of these together aid the reader in marking recurring shifts in the Teacher's argument. These "shifts" designate contrast or juxtaposition, and they mirror a structure of thought that is intentional.[110]

106. Delitzsch, *Hoheslied und Koheleth*, 195 (my translation, emphasis added). The original German citation reads: "*Alle Versuche, in dem Ganzen nicht nur die Einheit des Geistes, sondern auch genetischen Fortgang, alles beherrschenden Plan und organische Gliederung nachzuweisen, mussten bisher und werden ins künftige gescheitern*." Similarly, closer to our day, Murphy, *Ecclesiastes*, xxxi, has opined, "There is no satisfactory solution to the literary form of the book."

107. So, for example, Delitzsch, *Hoheslied und Koheleth*, and Bickell, *Der Prediger über den Wert des Daseins*, 1–45.

108. So, for example, Wright, "The Riddle of the Sphinx Revisited," 38–51; Wright, "Additional Numerical Patterns in Qoheleth," 32–43; and Loader, *Polar Structures in the Book of Qohelet*.

109. So, for example, Seow, *Ecclesiastes*, 43–47.

110. In the words of Steele, "Enjoying the Righteousness of Faith in Ecclesiastes,"

The fact that very little agreement among Old Testament scholars exists as to the structure of the overall argument of Ecclesiastes quite naturally is linked to the difficulty they have in discerning the book's message. Illustrating commentators' general reticence to acknowledge a literary-rhetorical strategy of juxtaposition or contrast at work in Ecclesiastes, one commentator offers this rationale:

> Because Qohelet experiences life as finally incoherent, it is appropriate that the reader too should struggle with the question of form and meaning. If indeed Qohelet's failed quest . . . is taken seriously, it suggests that in Qohelet's attempts to make sense of the universe, things don't add up. It is appropriate that Qohelet's expression of human experience is communicated in a book in which the overall structure is at least enigmatic and perhaps incomprehensible.[111]

This sort of appraisal of Ecclesiastes by a "professional" student of the Old Testament should give us pause. If we may summarize her conclusion, because the Teacher is thought to find life *incoherent*, it is appropriate that *our* reading of Ecclesiastes be incoherent as well, and *incomprehensible*.

Interpreting the Enjoyment Thesis

The above-cited interpretive conclusion (confusion?) well illustrates that if we get the nature and structure of the Teacher's overall argument wrong, we get the message wrong. The "shifts" described in the present chapter that inform the book's overall message and structure—and hence illuminate the book's teaching on the relative value of human labor—are evidence of a literary-rhetorical strategy at work. This strategy has the writer moving back and forth between two philosophies of life, two metaphysical outlooks, which yield either "meaninglessness" (*hebel*) or "enjoyment"/"contentment" (*śimhâ*).[112] In Ecclesiastes, *śimhâ* intention-

---

229, structurally "Ecclesiastes is not a mess, but a masterwork." This is true even when no structural concept is air-tight.

111. Huwiler, "Ecclesiastes," 169.

112. Over against much scholarly commentary, two resources that capture a proper sense of the structure of the argument developed in Ecclesiastes are Ellul, *Reason for Being*, 36, and Ogden and Zogbe, *A Handbook on Ecclesiastes*, 9–10. Ellul describes the structure of the book in terms of a tapestry, with its interlocking threads that appear again and again. One might even draw parallels between Ecclesiastes and Job, whereby the reader encounters successive "cycles" of discourse before the conclusion is reached.

ally stands in contrast to *hebel*.[113] What is more, the shift to the former, significantly, is always accompanied by references to the Creator God, in bald contrast to the material that either precedes or follows.

The "enjoyment" thesis in Ecclesiastes, which is not lacking in grammatical-lexical and literary-textual evidence, has not been taken seriously by the majority of Old Testament scholars, having found only a few minority voices.[114] Strangely, it has been all but discounted by many, on the assumption that the message of Ecclesiastes is pessimism and resignation based on the above-noted "incoherence" of life.[115] Consequently, it is thought, any admonitions toward enjoyment that are found in the book are to be attributed to a quasi-Epicurean mind-set: "Enjoy yourself, the little that you can, because everything in life is vanity and incoherence, with death awaiting anyway."[116] Thus viewed, joy is not thoroughgoing and God's "answer" to the *hebel* of life "under the sun"; it is merely for the moment, a temporary respite from the pain and agony of normal living.

In order to appreciate the magnitude and sheer persistence of this prevailing negative consensus, consider the following appraisal of the "enjoyment" thesis by a professor of Hebrew Scripture at a well-known divinity school:

> "Qoheleth's" exhortation to delight in the moment, to embrace joy, cannot serve . . . to undermine the relentless cynicism and despair of the rest of his discourse, *pace* those interpreters who want to privilege the motif of joy in the book. "Qoheleth's" rhetorical grasping for joy is a desperate, unconvincing paraenesis [exhortation or counsel] . . . His claim that the savoring of joy is paramount rings hollow . . . He is an unreliable sage, and he is not joyful. We believe what "Qoheleth" says only at our peril.[117]

113. Gianto, "The Theme of Enjoyment in Qohelet," 52, presses the argument that the Teacher's use of *śimhâ* is just as "artful" as his use of *hebel*.

114. Exceptions to mainstream scholarship are Whybray, "Qoheleth, Preacher of Joy"; Ogden, "Qoheleth's Use of the 'Nothing Better'-Form"; Ogden, "'Vanity' It Is Certainly Not"; Ogden, *Qoheleth*; Lohfink, "Qohelet 5:17–19—Revelation by Joy"; Lee, *The Vitality of Enjoyment*; and to a lesser extent, Eaton, *Ecclesiastes*, 40–49, and Kidner, *A Time to Mourn*, 71.

115. This is the modern interpretation of Ecclesiastes. In fairness, it needs to be acknowledged that the book's calls to enjoyment were not well received by medieval Jewish commentators either. However, the reason for their discomfort was the *literal* application; hence, medieval Jewish as well as Christian interpretations of Ecclesiastes were in the main metaphorical-spiritual in nature. Hereon see Neriya-Cohen, "Rashbam's Understanding of the Carpe Diem Passages in Qohelet."

116. In truth, however, no book was ever less "Epicurean" than Ecclesiastes.

117. Sharp, *Irony and Meaning in the Hebrew Bible*, 211.

We believe the writer of Ecclesiastes only at our peril . . . Clearly, if we accept the above assessment, we must conclude that teaching and preaching Ecclesiastes in the church *imperils* our faith. And yet the above citation, it needs emphasizing, is by no means an isolated case. Consider other representative assessments by Old Testament commentators of an "enjoyment" thesis in Ecclesiastes:

- Enjoyment in Ecclesiastes is expressed as "Eat, drink, and be merry for tomorrow you die."[118]

- Enjoyment in Ecclesiastes amounts to a "flight" from "the anguish of death."[119]

- In the end, "there is no goodness in life."[120]

- In the book it is impossible to discern "any meaning or purpose" in life.[121]

- The book teaches that "God does not care" how humans behave, and that because of God's "capriciousness," the writer "recommends enjoyment."[122]

- Any "good" in Ecclesiastes is a "relative" good.[123]

- The enjoyment directive is a "Spartan philosophy of resignation to the limits and boundaries of life which are imposed."[124]

- Enjoyment in Ecclesiastes serves as a "distraction" and a "palliative," in order to forget "the pain of life."[125]

- Enjoyment in Ecclesiastes is an expression of "resignation," "strident desperation," a "momentary respite" to "dull the pain" of life, and an "anesthesia" which mirrors the writer's "lack of enthusiasm," even "reluctance."[126]

---

118. Paterson, *The Book That Is Alive*, 146, and McKane, *Tracts for the Times*, 78.

119. Hengel, *Judaism and Hellenism*, 1:126.

120. Walsh, "Despair as a Theological Virtue in the Spirituality of Ecclesiastes," 46.

121. Alter, *The Wisdom Books*, 345.

122. Spangenberg, "Irony in the Book of Qohelet," 67–68.

123. Horne, *Proverbs-Ecclesiastes*, 461, 474.

124. Fuerst, *The Books of Ruth, Esther, Ecclesiastes, the Song of Songs, Lamentations*, 125.

125. Fox, *Ecclesiastes*, 38.

126. Longman, *The Book of Ecclesiastes*, 107, 122, 123, 168, 221, and 231.

- Joy in Ecclesiastes becomes a "tease," insofar as life is a "bad business" (1:13 and 4:8).[127]
- The book's counsels of joy are expressions of the writer's "psychological disturbance and conflict."[128]
- Emphasizing the so-called "joy" passages in Ecclesiastes is like telling a chronically depressed person just to "cheer up," for the writer "certainly has little joy."[129]
- The book's counsels of joy are "self-serving" and "almost certainly less affirmative than they appear."[130]
- The joy passages are only "wishful thinking" and "invalidated" by the book's pervasive emphasis on meaninglessness.[131]
- Enjoyment in Ecclesiastes is "paradoxical at best."[132]
- "Arbitrary pleasure" is "the only antidote" to an "impenetrably absurd existence."[133]

The above comments, the reader needs reminding, come from *professional scholars* who have devoted their careers to the study of the Old Testament text. In the end, the enjoyment refrains in Ecclesiastes have generally suffered three unfortunate interpretative fates: (1) they have been ignored, (2) they have been dismissed as peripheral, or (3) they have been viewed as counter to the Teacher's argument, only distracting us from the book's true message. Is it, then, any wonder that the average lay person is intimidated by this "wisdom" book and that Christian leaders and teachers conspicuously avoid it in standard teaching and preaching? At bottom, what benefits can possibly accrue from its reading when Old Testament scholars themselves have difficulty offering a *compelling* reason for its inclusion in the canon of Scripture?

This depressing state of affairs notwithstanding, an intriguing clue in our attempts to interpret accurately the book's message, which has received little (if any) attention by Old Testament commentators, invites the attention of the serious reader. It is the fact that, in the Jewish calendar, Ecclesiastes has been used in association with Sukkot, the Feast of

127. Balantine, *Wisdom Literature*, 73.
128. Zimmerman, *The Inner World of Qohelet*, 8.
129. Fox, "The Inner-Structure of Qohelet's Thought," 227–28.
130. Shields, *The End of Wisdom*, 204, 236.
131. Anderson, *Qoheleth and His Pessimistic Theology*, 73.
132. Brown, *Wisdom's Wonder*, 173.
133. Horne, *Proverbs-Ecclesiastes*, 493.

Booths (or Feast of Tabernacles).[134] This feast, of course, was an annual event, celebrated for seven days, and commemorated God's provision in the wilderness. With the season of harvest at end, Israelites of old would have journeyed to Jerusalem and the Temple to worship and give thanks for divine sustenance and faithfulness. The obvious question needing to be answered—the "elephant in the (interpretive) room," as it were—is *why or how the book of Ecclesiastes would play a role in Jewish celebration.* The most natural answer is that Israel learned that it is God alone who protects and provides for her.[135] In consequence, *Israel's gratitude for God's sovereign provision and gifts* expressed itself, on an annual basis, in *joy and celebration.* That joy and celebration, most assuredly, were *not* because "everything is meaningless (*hebel*)" and life is "incoherent."

This historical reality, alas, calls into question the predominant view of skepticism and quasi-hedonism surrounding most commentary on Ecclesiastes. Despite the flurry of literature published in the 1990s and 2000s on the book, its interpretation, to the present day, remains steeped in a *negative* appraisal.[136] And among the most recent interpreters, the assumption exists that Ecclesiastes is "an early embodiment of the deconstructive spirit and therefore eminently relevant for the postmodern age" in which we live.[137] As suggested already in this chapter, much contemporary, "postmodern" interpretation of Ecclesiastes fails to do the hard hermeneutical work—the "heavy lifting"—of seriously reading the canonical text in the light of overall biblical revelation. Moreover, many of these contemporary readings, in addition to spurning serious interaction with biblical theology in favor of "socially relevant" appraisals, are bankrupt in terms of their approach to "Christian ethics." And when "mainstream" biblical scholarship remains doubtful that Ecclesiastes constitutes a "viable theological [or ethical] resource,"[138] such is an accurate (and infinitely tragic) mirror of where biblical scholarship stands.

134. Lev 23:33–44, Num 29:12–40, and Deut 16:13–17; cf. John 7:2–13.

135. Lee, *The Vitality of Enjoyment*, 125, believes that an important reason for the scholarly neglect of enjoyment as a recurring theme in Ecclesiastes is that joy and the fear of God—two significant themes running throughout the treatise—are pitted against one another rather than viewed as organically connected. This observation, it would seem, is entirely correct.

136. Thus, for example, Sneed, *The Politics of Pessimism in Ecclesiastes.* Wishing to instruct us, Sneed writes that skepticism and pessimism in Ecclesiastes function to "lower expectations of the audience about . . . wisdom, God, and . . . morality"—what Sneed calls a "necessary strategy" in "resolving the theodicy problem" (279).

137. So, Lee, *The Vitality of Enjoyment*, 123.

138. So, for example, the venerable wisdom scholar Roland Murphy, in "Qoheleth and Theology?," 30–33.

In the end, the church has not been served well. If we are to imbibe and believe standard commentary, we are hereby left with a contradiction in our own thinking. The point needs reiterating that Israel celebrated the Feast of Booths *not* because "everything is meaningless." Rather, Israelites celebrated because they had *received* from God—a theological feature of Ecclesiastes that has been all but ignored by much commentary, even when it is a recurring theme throughout the treatise (as chapters 4 and 5 will attempt to demonstrate).[139]

One conspicuous and recurring shift in the book concerns the value of human toil and work. So, for example, 1:2–2:23 catalogues the "meaninglessness" of varied expressions of human activity, including human labor. This lament, however, is followed by a shift in perspective in 2:24–3:22. Whereas human toil and work were "meaningless" in the lament ending in 2:23, they are presented in a vastly different light in 2:24 and following, wherein the reader is told that the Creator "has made everything beautiful in its time" and "has set eternity in their [humans'] heart" (3:11).[140] The consequence of this is that "every man who eats and drinks sees good in all his labor—it is the gift of God" (3:13).[141] This conclusion is strengthened by the following observation: "So I saw that there is nothing better than that all should enjoy their work, for that is their lot (3:22).[142] Much standard commentary, as we have lamented above, fails to reconcile these two contrasting outlooks on the subject of work. Human labor cannot be both "meaningless"—and excruciatingly so—as well as a source of satisfaction and "the gift of God." Such an interpretation is nonsensical, both philosophically and exegetically. Neither does it square with biblical theology.

Similar shifts regarding human activity and work occur again later in Ecclesiastes. One of these is the following rather remarkable observation: "When God gives any man wealth and possessions, and enables him to enjoy them, to accept his lot and be happy in his work—this is a gift of God . . . because God keeps him occupied with gladness of heart" (5:19–20).[143]

139. Ellul, *Reason for Being*, 42–46, is one of the few to note this connection in Ecclesiastes.

140. NASB. The sense of the "eternal" that God has placed within the human heart may be understood in two fundamental, corresponding ways: first, as basic knowledge of the creator, of self, and of moral accountability—that is, that which accords with the natural law, the law "written on their hearts" (Rom 2:14–15); and, second, as a certain awareness of or yearning after meaning and purpose. Both aspects are anchored in our having been created in the image of God.

141. NASB.

142. NRSV. The Hebrew term *heleq* can be translated "lot," "portion," or "reward." In Eccl 3:22 it suggests a "down-payment" or "in-breaking" of the *ʿōlām* of 3:11.

143. NIV.

Notice the reasoning behind this statement: satisfaction in one's work is "a gift of God" (a repetition, and thus underscoring, of an earlier statement). And if this is not enough, later on the writer reinforces this fact: "joy will accompany him [the God-fearer] in his work all the days of the life God has given him under the sun" (8:15[144])—this despite humans' inability to comprehend what God does.

Discerning Life's Meaning

What might we make of these statements and the context in which they are made? Again, as noted in chapter 1, the entire argument suspended between 1:2 and 12:8 builds on the linchpin observation made in 1:13: "What a heavy burden God has laid on men!" We observed that this "heavy burden" is the "burden" to discern ultimate meaning, happiness, and fulfillment in life. This discernment, moreover, is tethered to the sense of "eternity" implanted in the human heart (3:11)—a discernment that is anchored in a *theistic* view of ultimate reality.

In addition, we have argued that the reader must keep the writer's literary-rhetorical strategy—namely, juxtaposition—in view, and this strategy extends throughout the entire treatise. Either one finds statements scattered throughout Ecclesiastes that are blatantly self-contradictory in nature, rendering any rational attempt at interpretation meaningless, or two points of view that are in conflict with one another are being compared on a back-and-forth basis. An example of this seeming "contradiction" concerns the portrayal of "wisdom" in Ecclesiastes. On the one hand, Ecclesiastes insists that wisdom is meaningless, like chasing the wind, and on the other hand extols wisdom in a number of places. Both of these viewpoints, at face value, cannot be correct—unless, that is, they are part of a literary strategy at work that distinguishes between two types of "wisdom." In Ecclesiastes, "conventional" wisdom and wisdom as a "gift of God" are being juxtaposed, and this contrast—this rhetorically effective juxtaposition—is part of the Teacher's genius, helping to explain the book's utterly remarkable appeal through the ages. Herewith the Teacher is seeking to shake the foundations of conventional thinking.[145]

In his portrayal of work within a theistic framework, the Teacher is not seeking to *idolize* work—or *any* human activity, for that matter. Neither is

144. NIV.

145. Contra Brown, *Wisdom's Wonder*, 158, wisdom does not remain "forever beyond the sage's reach." True wisdom, rather, remains beyond the materialist/secularist's reach.

he writing in the manner that popular "self-help" gurus of our day utilize—promising personal happiness, "realization," and "self-fulfillment." The universe is *theo*-centric, not ego-centric. Work is being described in Ecclesiastes in two very different ways: (a) it is "meaningless" or "futile" when and where it is performed out of self-striving and for the purposes of self-exaltation; (b) it is part of a joy-filled, contented lifestyle that humbly accepts human limitations and embraces divine sovereignty and divine inscrutability.

Two outlooks on life and all of reality are on display and being contra-distinguished.[146] If life is viewed apart from the Creator, without reference to God and transcendent reality, humans will indeed experience meaningless-ness and despair. Recall a central element of the initial "enjoyment refrain": "apart from God, who can find enjoyment?" (2:25). One commentator has helpfully summarized the burden of Ecclesiastes: "The Preacher will have his readers see the grimness of the pessimist viewpoint before he points to a life that derives from God himself."[147] The theistic perspective does not deny the experiential reality of the other perspective; rather, it transforms it.

146. Hence, to be rejected are several related conclusions. One is that of Walsh, "Despair as a Theological Virtue," 46–49, who fails to discern juxtaposition at work and ignores the progressively building admonitions in the book toward enjoyment. According to Walsh, the writer's "world-weary cynicism" and "near agnosticism" mir-ror an "acceptance" of despair's "permanence." Another is that of Brown, "Character Reconstructed," 149, who writes: "The book of Ecclesiastes is at root a confession of disillusionment about life in general and the frustration of work in particular."

147. Eaton, *Ecclesiastes*, 55.

— 4 —

Wisdom and the Work of God
in Ecclesiastes

The Witness of Wisdom

GIVEN THE WELL-KNOWN INTERPRETIVE problems outlined in the previous chapter and given the fact that theology in wisdom literature is not explicit, it is not at all surprising that little attention in the relevant literature has been devoted to the concept of God in Ecclesiastes. A fascinating and little-examined element in the book is the sheer number of references to God that occur throughout the work. It is possible to identify as many as forty texts that speak of God—this in a total of 222 verses.[1] (In stark contrast, in another of the "disputed" books of the Old Testament, Esther, God is not mentioned once.) What is more, this frequency is even greater than the number of occurrences of the keyword *hebel* ("meaningless"). Surely the fact of so many divine references in this relatively brief treatise is significant. In the words of one astute observer, "Clearly if you remove everything about God in this book, thinking to produce a text on secular wisdom, you utterly dismember it."[2] And indeed this is the case.

Significant for most commentators is the fact that in Ecclesiastes the writer always uses the term *Elohim*, which designates "God" in general and is used in the Genesis creation narrative. The Teacher does not refer at all to *Yahweh*, the God who reveals himself to his covenant people. But creation, if viewed ontologically, is not a "neutral" object, without meaning or reference. It is, rather, an object of supreme significance, both physically and morally: everything that was created was declared to be "good" (Gen 1:10, 12, 18, 21, 25, and 31). The God of all creation gives life, and that life is intrinsically

---

1. Lys, *L'Ecclésiaste ou Que vaut la vie?*, 78, and Murphy, *The Tree of Life*, 57.
2. Ellul, *Reason for Being*, 214.

"good"—which is to say, it mirrors the *very likeness* of the Creator himself. Given the depiction in Ecclesiastes of God as Creator of all life, it is thus very plausible that the writer uses *Elohim* to speak in universal terms and to eliminate any sense of Hebrew particularity, not unlike the Apostle Paul in his discourse before the Council of the Areopagus (Acts 17:16–34) while working in the "university" city of Athens during the mid-first century.

Paul's method and message in addressing the Areopagus Council are unique in several respects, in large part because of his apologetic thrust. The apostle seeks to communicate in language and categories that are familiar to his audience. He builds on pagan concepts and utilizes pagan illustrations. For example, he exploits an "altar" to an "unknown God," of which there were many in the city, and draws from two particular philosopher-poets who were highly esteemed by Athenians based on the city's history. In this regard, it is significant that Paul does not cite from the Hebrew Scriptures as he addresses his audience, which is comprised mostly of Epicureans and Stoics. After building bridges to his audience by means of appropriating "general revelation," he then adjusts the assumptions of his audience about the Creator and creation, before introducing "special revelation."[3] The point needing emphasis is that in both Ecclesiastes and Paul's work in Athens, creation is the basis on which the appropriate apologetic is built and on which moral reality rests.[4]

Divine Inscrutability

The argument being set forth in Ecclesiastes, in accordance with the "wisdom" perspective and which the previous chapters have attempted to show, is of a universal character. It is valid for Egyptians, Persians, Greeks, and Jews. In sum, it is true for all. And given its "apologetic" character, it has as its basis (a) life's limitations, mystery, and impenetrability, and (b) the resultant seeming absurdities applicable to all that lead to despair apart from the mystery of divine providence. The elements of human limitation and suffering, such as one finds in both Job and Ecclesiastes, are part of the wisdom perspective, even when they are not the *whole* of it. Mystery and divine inscrutability remain at the end of both books. And while the Judeo-Christian tradition

3. For a more detailed examination of Paul's method in Athens, see Charles, "Engaging the (Neo)Pagan Mind," and Charles, "Biblical Resources for Ethics," which is chapter 6 of *The Unformed Conscience of Evangelicalism*, 144–57.

4. While this comparison with the Apostle Paul in Athens is my own view, I discover that Eaton, *Ecclesiastes*, 47, and Rylaarsdam, *Revelation in Jewish Wisdom Literature*, 18–46, stand in fundamental agreement.

confesses that this God is in fact knowable, Ecclesiastes constitutes a necessary reminder that God cannot be calculated, manipulated, localized, or humanly understood.[5] "What God does"—a catchphrase in Ecclesiastes—is unknowable and impenetrable, and hence "hidden."

But here a caveat is in order. God is "hidden," though not distant; he is inscrutable, though not arbitrary; he is transcendent, though not removed. To say that God is "hidden," however, is not to argue that God is "in hiding" or utterly unknowable.[6] Historic Christian belief affirms that God is in part knowable, even when he seems "hidden" and his works are inscrutable. Even in the Old Covenant, the psalmist's confession—"Be still and know that I am God" (Ps 46:10)—can be understood as normative and is in fact comparable to the elements found in Eccl 5:1–7: (1) guard your steps when going to worship; (2) draw near with a listening disposition; (3) don't be hasty with your speech or vows; (4) take your vows seriously; (5) stand in awe of God.

"Knowing" God, to be sure, is a mark of the New Covenant (so, for example, John 17:3, 1 John 2:3 and 3:24). Nonetheless, it is a "knowing" that is still veiled, to the extent that God is—and remains—inscrutable. No Christian can say that he or she knows the mind of God, the works of God, and the purposes of God. The New Covenant does not alter the reality of divine inscrutability.

And it is precisely this element, divine inscrutability, that is a stumbling block for many. One esteemed student of wisdom literature, in passing verdict on the theology of Ecclesiastes, is left to complain, "One never knows the way things will turn out with this God."[7] This sort of condescension, offered by a professional student of the Old Testament, well illustrates the difficulties associated with making this book relevant to the average pastor, teacher, or lay person. While from a human vantage point God's nature and God's work may strike us as arbitrary, Ecclesiastes serves as a necessary reminder that God seems "arbitrary" when we have *preconceived notions* of what he is like or what he should do. Indeed, his inscrutability

5. As noted earlier, we may assume the position that theology is *implicit* in Ecclesiastes rather than explicit. This accords with Old Testament wisdom literature in general, wherein theology in the strictest sense is not the focus. Where it does speak of God, it is not in the form of a specifically theological discourse; rather, God's depiction stereotypically stands in contrast to human beings—Creator and the creature. On theology's implicit character in wisdom literature, see Westermann's remarks on "Wisdom and Theology" in *Roots of Wisdom*, 131.

6. Contra Walsh, "Despair as a Theological Virtue," 47.

7. Murphy, *Ecclesiastes*, 27.

and mystery have the effect of exploding any human pretensions, whether
religious or secular in nature.

An example of "human pretentiousness" that has a religious cloak
might be noted. At first glance the reader may be baffled by the rather
strange admonition of 7:16: "Do not be excessively righteous and do not be
overly wise. Why should you ruin yourself?"[8] Commentators interpret this
advice in essentially two ways. Some understand it as expressing a sort of
"golden mean," a middle path "between vice and virtue." After all, in v. 18
we read that the God-fearing person will "avoid all extremes." Others understand the exhortation to be saying, "Don't overly strive to be righteous;
a little vice is permissible, and perhaps even commendable." Both of these
interpretations, however, are ethically deficient; both contradict the wider
message of Ecclesiastes and, significantly, fail to find parallels elsewhere in
Scripture. A preferred interpretation—one that comports with the theme
of meaningless striving—is that this is a warning against *self-righteousness*,
which itself should be understood as a case of *human effort and striving*.
Thus, we are better to understand 7:16 as saying, "Don't be self-righteous"
or "Don't be a self-styled righteous person."[9] This reading, moreover,
seems to agree with the general tenor of 5:1–7, which admonishes silence
and sobriety, and 5:4–6 in particular, which warns against pretension and
self-righteous tendencies.

Divine Sovereignty and Human Limitation

A second example of human pretension (over against divine inscrutability) can be measured by the admonition in 7:13–14 (more on which, see
chapter 5). Here the admonition is to "consider" the works of God. The
temptation—i.e., the human inclination and therefore the predilection
toward pretension—is to conclude, based on our experience and limited
purview, that God is the author of evil and, relatedly, that human beings
are mere puppets, without moral agency. And indeed this interpretation
can be found in assorted commentaries on Ecclesiastes.[10] The context in
which this admonition is to be understood is divine inscrutability, the

---

8. NASB.

9. So Whybray, "Qoheleth the Immoralist?," 195. Whybray is one of the few commentators who seems to perceive the proper sense of the admonition.

10. See chapter 5. To illustrate this distortion even among commentators, Murphy,
Ecclesiastes, 66, suggests that evil is "God's doing"; Shields, *The End of Wisdom*, 236, argues that Qoheleth "ascribes evil to God," accusing God of making things "irrevocably
corrupt"; and Anderson, *Qoheleth and Its Pessimistic Theology*, 98–99, views God as the
cause of evil.

theology of which anchors the entire treatise. The Teacher is not saying, nor is he insinuating, that God causes evil; he is, however, saying that because God is sovereign he *uses* both "blessing" and adversity in our lives; nothing is outside of his sovereign purpose, even the evil that humans can manufacture. In this regard it is important to recognize that suffering and evil are not the main thrust of lament in Ecclesiastes, as is widely thought to animate Job; rather, the focus is God's incommensurability and the meaninglessness of all things apart from providence. Verses 13–14 are intended to address not suffering but inscrutability.

The relationship between divine sovereignty and human freedom in Ecclesiastes is further illustrated by the Teacher's explanation of the didactic poem (3:1–8) which follows (3:9–22). Because of the poem's teaching that various "seasons" are "set" by God and being used for his purposes, some commentators gravitate toward a more fatalistic or deterministic interpretation of the book.[11] The poem's explanation, however, indicates the writer's belief in human freedom and moral agency. That agency is clearly based on two pieces of evidence: the writer's observation that wickedness and injustice are to be decried (vv. 16–17) and the exhortation to "revere" God (v. 14).[12]

In this light, then, the book of Ecclesiastes cannot be claimed to be a "determinist" or "fatalist" treatise which undermines "free will." Such is not the case, despite assertions by commentators to the contrary:

- "Man is not a free agent."[13]
- "In the last resort, for Koheleth man no longer has free will."[14]
- God "predestines *everything*—every action, every event—for both the pious and the oppressor," rendering "wisdom and human talents," in the end, "of no value."[15]

But divine sovereignty and human responsibility are not at odds in Ecclesiastes; neither do they cancel one another out. Although the question of the relationship between the two is both a theological and a philosophical issue, its "resolution" in the historic Judeo-Christian tradition—and its attestation in the wisdom perspective (in addition to Ecclesiastes, consider Prov 16:1;

---

11. Thus, for example, Staples, "'Profit' in Ecclesiastes," 96; Hengel, *Judaism and Hellenism*, 1:119–20; Crenshaw, *Ecclesiastes*, 92–100; and Rudman, *Determinism in the Book of Ecclesiastes*.

12. Samet, "How Deterministic Is Qohelet?," captures the proper balance of divine sovereignty and human freedom in these verses.

13. Rankin, "The Book of Ecclesiastes," 44.

14. Hengel, *Judaism and Hellenism*, 1:120.

15. Ginsberg, "The Structure and Contents of the Book of Koheleth," 145–46.

19:21; and 20:24)[16]—is one that allows both elements to co-exist based on humans' creation as whole persons in the image of God.

Historic Christian belief affirms neither a fatalism or determinism nor an "unbridled" human freedom so as to render one side of the theological conundrum null and void and indiscernible. While it is true that Ecclesiastes offers what may seem to be a withering commentary on humankind's limitations in light of divine inscrutability, it does *not* teach—indeed, it *cannot accurately* be interpreted to teach—that the writer is denying the moral responsibility or moral freedom of the individual. Alone the *carpe diem* found in 9:10—"Whatever your hand finds to do, do it with all your might!"—as well as the many vibrant exhortations in 11:1-10—"sow–give–sow," "rejoice" (twice), "remember," "follows the ways of your heart," "banish anxiety," and recall divine judgment—militate against such an understanding.

In the end, divine sovereignty and inscrutability in no way negate the glorious realm of human freedom.[17] Rather, they establish theological boundaries: human beings simply cannot claim to be God's equal. Fallibility and depravity firmly establish humans' distance from their Maker,[18] with the Teacher emphasizing the fact of human limitations for "apologetic" reasons, as was argued in the previous chapter. In fact, the divine portrait in Ecclesiastes bears some similarity to that of St. Paul in his letter to the Romans, who is citing Isaiah the prophet:

> But who are you, O man, to talk back to God?
> Shall what is formed say to him who formed it,
> "Why did you make me like this?"
>
> Shall what is formed say to him who formed it,
> "He did not make me"?
> Can the pot say of the potter,
> "He knows nothing"?

16. Prov 16:1, 3: "The plans of the heart belong to man, but the answer of the tongue is from the LORD . . . Commit your works to the LORD, and your plans will be established"; Prov 19:21: "Many plans are in a man's heart, but the counsel of the LORD will stand"; Prov 20:24: "Man's steps are ordained by the LORD. How then can man understand his way?" (NASB).

17. In this regard, the present volume assumes a theological position that not only rejects fatalism and determinism but also its opposite, i.e., a denial of divine sovereignty that is motivated to "protect" free will and moral agency. This error is prone to denying that God's purpose and plan as well as his knowledge are exhaustive—that is to say, encompassing past, present, and future—and perfect.

18. On this basis, we can reject the position of Davidson, *The Courage to Doubt*, 201, who asserts that Ecclesiastes "rejects much that lies close to the beating heart of Israel's faith."

Woe to him who quarrels with his Maker,
to him who is nothing but a potsherd
among the potsherds on the ground.

Does the clay say to the potter,
"What are you making?"
Does your work say,
"He has no hands"?[19]

The question of divine "distance" as mirrored in Ecclesiastes, which is widely assumed in much commentary, needs a measured and firm response. God's inscrutability and "hiddenness" do *not* equate to divine "distance" or "arbitrariness."[20] Nor does the emphasis on human limitations and creatureliness. As was noted in chapter 2, in Ecclesiastes the writer's argument, from beginning to end, unfolds against the theological backdrop of divine sovereignty and inscrutability. Humans can only plumb "wisdom" in a superficial way; they cannot understand "what God does"—in *any* manner. Much remains hidden behind a veil, which is precisely St. Paul's argument in 1 Cor 13:9–12: "For we [now] know in part . . . , but when perfection comes, the imperfect disappears . . . Now we see but a poor reflection as in a mirror, then we shall see face to face. Now I know in part; then I shall know fully, even as I am fully known."[21] In the end, wisdom beckons human beings, in reverence and awe-struck silence, to adore an all-wise Creator; hence, the admonition to "draw near and listen" (5:1–7). Where faith is found, this "hiddenness" itself breeds neither cynical resignation nor despair nor the conclusion that God is "arbitrary"; where it is *not* found, the result is the view of one commentator: the "pessimism and disillusionment" in Ecclesiastes arises from a God "who has withheld information" and "who has stacked the deck" against humanity.[22] A related mistaken view is to conclude that, in emphasizing divine transcendence, the writer has excluded God's immanence from his search for meaning.[23] But Ecclesiastes teaches us that true piety, anchored in the fear of God, consists of humble receptivity over against vanity, self-righteousness, and presumption.[24]

19. Rom 9:20; Isa 29:16; and 45:9 (NIV).

20. Contra, for example, Scott, *Proverbs-Ecclesiastes*, 198, 203; Ginsberg, "The Structure and Contents of the Book of Koheleth," 147; Crenshaw, *Ecclesiastes*, 72–73, 90, 101, 125, and 159; Murphy, "The Sage in Ecclesiastes and Qohelet the Sage," 263–71; Longman, *The Book of Ecclesiastes*, 122–23; and Huwiler, "Ecclesiastes," 173–74.

21. NIV.

22. Duncan, *Ecclesiastes*, xxv.

23. So, for example, Longman, *The Book of Ecclesiastes*, 66.

24. The same lesson emerges from the book of Job as well. It is significant that the

God's "hiddenness," however, has another feature—one that is consistently on display through the Old Testament. It concerns the matter of unjust suffering on the part of the righteous. Consider alone the experience of the prophets. Elijah is crushed, not understanding, rather wanting suicide than to live. Jeremiah is crushed, persecuted for declaring what is unpopular and not understanding. Habakkuk is crushed, wondering how long his cry for help will be ignored and not understanding. Job feels crushed, suffering unjustly and not understanding. And the Psalmist feels crushed, crying out "How long, O LORD?" and not understanding.

This tension, it goes without saying, invites confusion and even opposition from the human vantage-point, since no one understands the *why* of suffering and injustice. One commentator on Ecclesiastes asserts that the writer "accuses God of moral evil."[25] Can this claim hold up to scrutiny? And can we distinguish between suffering that results from "adversity" and suffering that is the result of moral evil? One renowned Christian theologian has stated what certainly is a truism: most believers, when they suffer for seemingly unknown reasons, see "no outward sign of a rational, moral God ordering them [in their lives] at all."[26] How true this is, and not even religious faith in a transcendent God shields us from thinking in this way. Even when St. Paul writes to the Christians in Rome that "all things work together for good" to those who love God, this does not mean that Christian believers have "privileged insight" into their suffering;[27] invariably, they do not.[28] Alas, fathoming God, his ways, and his works, in the language of Ecclesiastes, is like chasing the wind or taming the sea. Yet to acknowledge that God is inscrutable is *not* to attribute evil to him, since "goodness" is the essence of his moral character.[29]

---

largest amount of discourse in the book is devoted to Job's three "friends," whose presumptuous speech will require repentance and atonement (42:7–9).

25. Longman, *Ecclesiastes*, 100.

26. Packer, *Knowing God*, 104.

27. So, properly, Caneday, "'Everything is Vapor,'" 27. Caneday's reflections on moral evil, suffering, and divine sovereignty (26–40) are well worth pondering.

28. Hence, we must take issue with Chang, "Suffering and Enjoyment/Hope in the Progress of Revelation," who argues that Romans 8 "completes" or "answers" Ecclesiastes in terms of suffering and hope (5). Packer, *Knowing God*, 104, and Caneday, "'Everything is Vapor,'" 27, are correct: even Christians do not have "privileged insight" into why they suffer, despite the assurance of Paul's statement recorded in Rom 8:28. Moreover, Ecclesiastes does not intend to address the matter of suffering and hope, as does Job; rather, its focus is the reality of human limitations against the backdrop of providence and divine inscrutability.

   Significantly, the Heb. *tôb* ("good") is a keyword in Ecclesiastes, appearing an fifty-two times—the most of any term in the entire book. This alone would

One of the "joy refrains" noted above and considered in the following chapter reads as follows: "In the day of prosperity be joyful, and in the day of adversity consider: God has made the one as well as the other, so that man may not find out anything that will be after him" (7:14).[30] This declaration is preceded by the following statement: "Consider what God has done: Who can straighten what he has made crooked?" (7:13). In our attempts to understand the language here, our guide is "what God has done." *What God does* is consistent with his moral character, and as we argued above, he cannot cause evil because of his moral perfection. Hence, what is "crooked" is not meant to convey that God causes or wills what is evil; such is heresy—pure and simple. Rather, it is meant to convey divine inscrutability and human limitations.[31] No one can know the divine purpose, and no one can alter that purpose.

The Work of God

What, however, the Teacher *does* tell his readers throughout the treatise about this Creator God—i.e., what is *not* "hidden"—is significant and worthy of consideration, aiding us in discerning an interpretive strategy by which to understand the book and, ultimately, helping us to discern the book's message. Throughout Ecclesiastes God is depicted in essentially three roles: as creator, as inscrutable and impenetrable sovereign, and as judge.[32] Consider some of what we know about God from the writer's argument in Ecclesiastes and how these specific elements, in some form or fashion, express creation, inscrutability, and judging:

- 1:13—God places a burden on humans to comprehend meaning in life (cf. 3:10)

---

seem to undermine any claims by commentators that God as depicted in Ecclesiastes is harsh or cruel and arbitrary. Hereon see Anton Schoors, "Words Typical of Qohelet," 37.

30. ESV.

31. It is fascinating that although this text is intended to highlight human limitations, a "straight" path occurs in the book of Proverbs seventy-five times, which suggests that the Teacher is employing the stock vocabulary of "wisdom literature." In addition, "straightness" is part of the epilogue (12:10).

32. Kidner, *A Time to Mourn*, 15–17, is one of the few who understands Ecclesiastes to depict God in essentially three ways. I diverge in collapsing Kidner's second and third divine features—sovereignty and inscrutability—into one (my second) while adding judgment as a third.

- 2:24–26—God grants enjoyment, satisfaction in our work, wisdom, and happiness
- 2:26—God gives to those who please him
- 3:10—God places a burden on humans to comprehend meaning in life (cf. 1:13)
- 3:11a—God has made everything beautiful in its time
- 3:11b—God has placed a sense of the eternal in human hearts
- 3:12–13—God gives gifts of contentment, one of which is satisfaction in human labor
- 3:14—what God does endures, and nothing can be added or subtracted from this reality
- 3:15–17—God will judge all, the wicked and the righteous, and that judgment will be according to our deeds
- 3:18—God tests human beings
- 3:22—God assigns a "portion"
- 5:1–7—God is to be approached, worshipped, and served
- 5:1—God has a presence (the temple)
- 5:2—God hears
- 5:2—God is "in heaven" and thus incommensurate and "other"
- 5:6—God is angered
- 5:7—God is to be revered
- 5:18—God gives life
- 5:19–20—God gives gifts such as wealth, satisfaction in work, and gladness of heart
- 5:20—God "occupies" the human heart with joy
- 6:2—God gives wealth, possessions, and honor
- 7:13–14—God orders things; what God has done is to be pondered
- 7:13–14—God has a purpose in adversity
- 7:18—God is to be feared
- 7:29—God created the human person upright
- 8:12–13—God is to be feared and revered
- 8:15—God gives life and joy in human labor

- 8:16–17—What God has done is unsearchable

- 9:1—God holds the righteous and wise in his hands

- 9:7—God is pleased by what we do in the moment

- 9:9—God grants life

- 11:5—God has made everything, which is to say, he guides things— even human evil—toward an ultimate purpose that he alone knows

- 11:9—God will call human beings to account and judge

- 12:1—God the Creator is to be remembered in our youth

- 12:6–7—God is to be remembered before we grow old and near death

- 12:7—God gave the spirit of life

- 12:13—God is to be feared and his commandments to be kept

- 12:14—God will bring every deed—good and evil, hidden and open— into judgment

What is the prominent verb describing God's action in the treatise? It is that God "gives."[33] He gives life, he gives or assigns us a portion, he gives gifts that are spiritual, psychological, and material, he gives meaning and purpose, and he gives satisfaction in our labors. But despite the accent on God's gifts in Ecclesiastes, many commentators take a negative view of the writer's theology. "Qoheleth's God is a hard ruler," laments one commentator, a ruler who "must be feared, not cherished . . . This is an uncomfortable theology, and one need not accept it as valid—the other Biblical authors *wouldn't have*—but this is Qoheleth's teaching."[34] With this pronouncement we are witnesses to the interpreter confusing divine inscrutability for harshness and hence missing the mark theologically. And, of course, we're left to wonder, *what on earth is Ecclesiastes doing in the Bible?* Another commentator similarly misses the mark by speaking of "Qoheleth's harsh criticisms of God" and asserting that the writer "blames" God.[35] In truth, however, nowhere in Ecclesiastes are there found "harsh criticisms" of God. Another commentator describes divine activity in

33. Müller, "Wie Sprach Qohälät von Gott?," examines God's work and God's action in Ecclesiastes, observing that "to give" is the most frequently occurring verb in the treatise. This is compelling evidence for Müller that the writer is *not* "challenging" the "traditional" wisdom perspective, as is widely assumed, but rather is critiquing the surrounding cultural climate.

34. Fox, *A Time to Tear Down*, 136–38, emphasis added.

35. Enns, *Ecclesiastes*, 116, 210.

Ecclesiastes as "desperate trickery."[36] Still another claims this God to be a "sovereign despot,"[37] while yet another asserts that the cosmos is governed with "rigidity" and "tyranny" by the God of Ecclesiastes.[38]

The Fear of God

As mirrored in the above very unflattering comments (all of which come from "professional" students of the Old Testament), not only is God's "hidden-ness" a stumbling block to many but God's seeming "harshness"/"tyranny" as well. The perceived "harshness," as viewed from a human perspective, issues from the fact that God's ways and works are *impenetrable*. But this is *as it should be*; otherwise, we construct God *in man's image*. In the words of one eminent theologian, "the inscrutable God of providence is the wise and gracious God of creation and redemption."[39] The sort of aforementioned commentary that assumes divine harshness and distance in Ecclesiastes—and representative examples from Old Testament scholarship could be multiplied—errs at several basic levels. For one, it fails to recognize that Ecclesiastes concerns itself, in a detached manner, with life's totality from the standpoint of human anthropology and not *theology proper*. God as depicted in the book is not absent, only as a God who is deserving of rever-ence; hence, "fearing God" is a fitting last word.

In addition, it fails to discern the literary-rhetorical strategy of con-trast at work in the treatise. This strategy, as we have sought to argue, issues out of the writer's burden to *dethrone human autonomy*. And correlatively, it misses or ignores *inter alia* recurring admonitions in the book concern-ing life's "enjoyment" and God's "gifts"—admonitions that actually consti-tute robust "theological statements of faith in a just and loving God."[40] In fact, we must insist, along with one perceptive interpreter, that fear of God and joy co-exist in Ecclesiastes.[41] In the end we must insist, against most of the literature, that Ecclesiastes does *not* mirror a theological or theocentric deficiency. In truth, its theology squares with that of the New Testament:

36. Murphy, *Ecclesiastes*, 39.

37. Frydrych, *Living under the Sun*, 189.

38. Perdue, *Wisdom and Creation*, 239.

39. Packer, *Knowing God*, 107.

40. Ogden, *Qoheleth*, 26.

41. Lee, *Vitality of Enjoyment*, 83–122, is one of the few to devote considerable attention to this linkage. Joy as the *fruit* of the fear of God forms the basis for Lee's argument.

"Consider therefore the *kindness and severity* of God" (Rom 11:22).[42] Human response to the divine, as mirrored in Ecclesiastes more broadly and in 5:1–7 more specifically, calls for reverence, silence, acceptance, and awe. Indeed, these responses are what we often find in the Psalms. Such response, alas, is not "deficient"; rather, it is what is properly *due*.

Thus far in the present volume we have noted the prominent view of the Creator represented in Ecclesiastes as mirrored by most modern commentators (and as distinct from ancient and pre-modern commentators). Based on the literature, their interpretation of this Creator God can be summed up in the following words: distant, harsh (even cruel), despotic, restrictive, frustrating, and unknowable. In chapter 2's discussion of the character and qualities that underpin wisdom literature, we observed the centrality of the fear of God in Israel's wisdom perspective—a component that is found in numerous "wisdom" texts of the Old Testament. This foundation, predicated on God's holiness, otherness, and unapproachable nature, accords with the teaching of the entire biblical canon. As a guiding motivation of the believer, the "fear of God" suggests that discernment and wisdom are at odds with—and oppose—the hubris, autonomy, and false confidence that are characteristic of human nature. However, not a few biblical commentators, in their reading of Ecclesiastes, wrongly assume that this "fear" amounts to dread and terror. One commentator well summarizes this distortion: to "fear God" means "to be on guard against God."[43] Another asserts that the God depicted in Ecclesiastes is "a despot before whom we must cringe in fear and abject submission."[44] Yet another holds that the Teacher's theological convictions are rooted in not "awe and wonder" but "shock and terror," not "awed joy" but "terrorized compliance."[45]

Alas, this sort of false caricature proceeds from a theological deficiency in commentators themselves, which is then imported into the text itself. But inhering in the fear of God, properly understood, is an element of confidence, trust, self-surrender, and—indeed—wonder as well.[46] And, in Ecclesiastes, as we shall observe, it also expresses itself in joy and gratitude—precisely what we find in recurring refrains (see chapter 5) that climax in *carpe diem* admonitions of 9:7–10 and 11:7–10. One theologian is justified in identifying the "wedge" of Ecclesiastes' message: the writer seeks

---

42. Emphasis added.

43. Bickermann, *Four Strange Books of the Bible*, 149.

44. Paterson, *The Book That Is Alive*, 145.

45. Balantine, *Wisdom Literature*, 72.

46. See, for example, Job 1:8; Prov 3:7; 8:13; 14:2; and 16:6.

the "dethroning of all autonomous wisdom."[47] Because this "dethroning" requires an exposure that is utterly bleak in character, the Teacher's message strikes the average reader as "pessimistic," "despairing," or "cynical," and in the end "resigned." Failure to distinguish between an autonomous, *anthropocentric* wisdom and *divine* wisdom—the latter being anchored in the fear of God—may be one reason why, in wider Ecclesiastes scholarship, "the positive elements are on the whole too little regarded."[48] Consequently, that failure leads to the tendency among scholars to interpret the fear of God in the book in such utterly negative ways.

The fear of God is *the* mark of "wisdom literature." But it is more. It is the most important motivation that underpins faith in the Creator God, with *both* the Old and New Testaments serving as authoritative witness. Herein Judeo-Christian faith distinguishes itself from other metaphysical outlooks, whether ancient, modern, or "postmodern." It alone explains— and informs—the ethic by which the religious believer lives. At bottom, the believer who fears God has confidence as he or she lives in a world that is hostile toward a theistic outlook, because that person is aware that divine judgment[49]—both in the present and in the future—ultimately reveals what a person's true motives for living are. In stock "wisdom literature" vocabulary, people are depicted as "wise" or "foolish," "righteous"/"God-pleaser" or "wicked"/"sinner" (Eccl 2:26).

Human beings cannot fear or "revere" God (Eccl 3:14; 5:7; 8:13; 12:13) without the *'ôlām*, the sense of eternity, implanted in the human heart based on their created nature (3:11). It is the opposite of—indeed, the answer to—*hebel*. If in fact there is a season and purpose for everything "under heaven," then all is not "meaningless"; otherwise, the writer is teaching absurdity. "There can be no doubt," asserts one of the most highly esteemed Old Testament theologians of the past several generations, "that in the Old Testament statements about the fear of God the inward agitation produced by the *mysterium tremendum* [awe-inspiring mystery] emerges with extraordinary emphasis."[50] This can be seen from the creation narrative and the Garden of Eden through Moses and the patriarchs down through the entirety of Israel's history until its exile. The Law, the Prophets, and the Writings witness to the fear of God as *that which sets apart* both the believing community and the individual believer. God's holiness—his

47. Eichrodt, *Theology of the Old Testament*, 2:88.

48. Eichrodt, *Theology of the Old Testament*, 2:89n2.

49. The emphasis on divine judgment in Ecclesiastes clearly shows that the writer affirms moral retribution, cause and consequence, reward and punishment, contrary to the view held by many commentators.

50. Eichrodt, *Theology of the Old Testament*, 2:269.

transcending and impenetrable "otherness"—creates a "distance" between him and all of creation, to the extent that nothing and no one can approach him—apart, that is, from his own condescending miraculous works. Even among the covenant people of old, Israel's representatives, the priests, entered the "holy of holies" with fear and dread and only under tightly prescribed conditions, without which death was automatic.

And yet this aspect of "terror," dreadful as it is, did not (and does not) have the character of *panic* or servile *anxiety*, as one might expect. Rather, it contains "a mysterious power of attraction which is converted into wonder, obedience, self-surrender, and enthusiasm."[51] We see this in the canonical part of the Old Testament designated the "Writings," which are often exuberant in their tone. Hymns of praise are expressed to the God of creation and redemption, whose mighty acts and in-breaking are repeatedly demonstrated in human history and celebrated in the course of Israel's own history. Not anxiety, horror, or consternation, which stereotypically depict the response of adherents of other religions surrounding Israel to their deities, but joy—*exuberant joy*—characterizes the psalmist in these many and varied hymns of praise and adoration. Reverence, then, over against an irrational fear or paranoia, expresses Israel's attitude toward the Creator. In fact, this godly "fear" has a decidedly *rational* component, insofar as it motivates one's behavior and guides one in the ways of wisdom; hence, the importance of the Law and the keeping of God's commandments (Eccl 12:13). Wonder and self-surrender, it needs emphasizing, cannot be forced; they are drawn out of us by that which transcends us. At the same time, wisdom—properly understood—is more than knowledge and even more than "wonder," for it entails sound judgment and ethical discernment.[52]

The admonitions associated with worship found in Ecclesiastes 5 are fitting in the light of the "wisdom" accent on divine reverence. Consider the focus of 5:1–7, which is how to approach God. Four warnings (vv. 1a, 2a, 4a, and 6a) in these seven verses caution against being casual, even flippant. The particular focus is speech.[53] The worshipper is admonished toward listening rather than brash utterance; the nature of worship is to be relational, not

---

51. Eichrodt, *Theology of the Old Testament*, 2:270.

52. Zuck, "God and Man in Ecclesiastes," 54–56, summarizes man's responsibilities, according to the Teacher, as (1) being wise, (2) worshipping and pleasing God, (3) remembering the Creator, (4) fearing God, (5) being diligent, and (6) enjoying life.

53. The matter of paying vows is a prominent theme in the Psalms—so, for example, Pss 22:25; 50:14; 61:5, 8; 65:1; 66:13; 76:112; 116:14; and 132:2. What's more, the warning against rashly making of vows found in Ecclesiastes 5 is precisely the warning found in Prov 20:25. Cf. as well Prov 7:14 and 31:2.

mechanical. The unit ends with the very same exhortation that concludes the book: to "revere" (i.e., "stand in awe of"—NIV) God (v. 7).[54]

The Unchanging Character of God

As already noted, of the words describing God's work in Ecclesiastes, the one that occurs most frequently is the verb to "give." God *gives* life, wisdom, joy, wealth and possessions, a sense of the eternal, satisfaction in our labors, as well as an awareness of human limitations. In addition, he "assigns" human beings their "lot," "portion," or "reward." Significantly, joy or life is the divine "gift" in numerous statements in Ecclesiastes that depict God's works.[55] The wisdom perspective on God's action—he *gives* and he *judges*—alone constitutes evidence that the writer of Ecclesiastes is not "challenging" or negating the "traditional wisdom" perspective, contrary to what is widely assumed among commentators.

An important interpretive question confronts the reader: *Can "meaninglessness," "absurdity," or resignation be reconciled with joy in Ecclesiastes?* If so, how? Standard responses by biblical commentators tend to be variations on a "no, but . . ." answer. That is to say, Ecclesiastes seems to many a reader (and not a few commentators!) both "sub-Christian" and out of character with the rest of the Old Testament, but "because it was accepted in the biblical canon we must be reconciled to its presence." This sort of less-than-enthusiastic rationale can take several forms. One is to argue that Ecclesiastes is a "dramatic foil to the really 'new thing' that has happened in Jesus Christ."[56] Another is to say, however well-intended, that "we follow Jesus anyway, no matter what."[57] Yet another is to assert, "Jesus Christ is the one who redeems us from the vanity, the meaninglessness under which Qohelet suffered," and "[a]s a result, Christians can experience deep significance precisely in those areas where Qohelet felt most oppressed."[58] Still

54. Demonstrating a good grasp of 5:1–7 in terms of its function in Ecclesiastes is Fletcher, "Ecclesiastes 5:1–7."

55. Gordis, *Koheleth—The Man and His World*, 129, even describes joy in Ecclesiastes as "God's categorical imperative for man." The God of Qoheleth and the Allah of Mohammed are *not at all* closely related, contra Paterson, *The Book That Is Alive*, 145.

56. So Dempster, "Ecclesiastes and the Canon," 399.

57. So Enns, "Ecclesiastes according to the Gospel," 38.

58. So Dillard and Longman, *An Introduction to the Old Testament*, 255. Elsewhere, Longman writes: "It is noteworthy that the New Testament never directly quotes Ecclesiastes" (*The Book of Ecclesiastes*, 30), giving the impression that the book's authority and place in the canon are to be questioned. However, the same can be said for Esther, Nehemiah, Ezra, and several of the prophets; hence, such is no argument against its

another asserts that Ecclesiastes "cries out for the revelation of the future" as witnessed to "in the Gospels."[59] All of these attempts to make sense of Ecclesiastes, in a form of Christianized resignation, miss the book's message and fail to discern the writer's literary-rhetorical strategy, which is to contrast two philosophies of life, two metaphysical outlooks.

But if we view the writer's argument from the standpoint of the wisdom technique of contrast or juxtaposition, even contradiction, and if we observe the "back and forth" nature of that argument as the juxtaposing of a despairing "under-the-sun secularism" (by which the world and human existence are not *self*-explanatory)[60] and an acknowledging of the Creator whose ways are unfathomable, we are permitted to see a pattern or general "movement" of thought throughout the book. This movement, furthermore, is broadly "apologetic" in nature, as we have attempted to argue thus far, and not "sub-Christian," as is often argued (or intimated) in various commentaries. That is to say, the function of Ecclesiastes is not to "point us to a Christian perspective on life,"[61] just as the aim of "wisdom literature" is not to "point us toward Christ" but rather to inform human beings everywhere at all times—*including Christians*—on how to live wisely, and this based on the realities of the *created order*.[62] After all, as chapter 6 of the present volume will attempt to illustrate, until the decisive break with standard interpretation of Ecclesiastes that occurred in the form of Lutheran reformation during the early sixteenth century, Ecclesiastes had been interpreted spiritually/allegorically and *christologically* for most of Christian history. And based on this allegorical-christological reading of Ecclesiastes, Luther was adamant that the church had gotten it wrong.

At the same time, even when it is true that the function of wisdom literature is not eschatological or prophetic or pointing toward salvation-history *per se*, it needs emphasizing that the Christian agrees with Ecclesiastes on *significant* elements. These elements, more often than not, are glossed over by standard commentary and hence need our recognition and our affirmation. Consider the following teachings which emanate from the book:

- The doctrine of the fear of God, anchored in divine reverence and awe

---

authority. What's more, contra Longman, Ecclesiastes *is* cited in the New Testament; 7:20 is utilized by the Apostle Paul (see Rom 3:10).

59. So Ellis, *The Men and the Message of the Old Testament*, 489.

60. Recall that the wisdom perspective is intended to bring us *beyond* the world and human experience and awaken basic moral intuitions.

61. Contra Gibson, *Living Life Backward*, 27.

62. Christians need reminding of the fact that the doctrine of redemption is the doctrine of creation *restored*.

- The doctrine of providence and divine sovereignty
- The doctrine of divine inscrutability
- The doctrine of creation
- The hiddenness of God in human experience
- The contrast between divine wisdom and worldly wisdom
- The effects of sin's curse on humankind due to the fall
- Life as a gracious gift of God; "receiving" rather than "earning" meaning and purpose; grace and not merit
- Joy, wisdom, and contentment as gifts of God
- Work as a gift of God and hence the importance of vocational calling

At bottom, the teachings that emerge from Ecclesiastes end up informing the very cardinal "doctrines" that lie at the heart of Christian faith. Hence, any commentary that depicts the book as "sub-Christian" misses the mark and is itself theologically deficient—and indeed "sub-Christian."

As the previous chapter attempted to argue, and as the present chapter reiterates, the juxtaposing of two diametrically opposed outlooks on life underpins the structure of the book of Ecclesiastes. This literary-rhetorical strategy of shifting back and forth from despair to divine mystery, from self-sufficiency to receiving from the Creator's hand, entails even moments of celebration and human gratitude, based on the alternative theistic outlook. In this light, considering several key passages or "refrains" throughout Ecclesiastes that serve as a counterpoint to the book's purported pessimism and resignation is an illuminating next step. It is to these passages that we now turn.

— 5 —

Wisdom and Human Labor in Ecclesiastes

A Closer Look

Joy in Ecclesiastes

ALTHOUGH "MEANINGLESSNESS" IS APPLIED to all human activity "under the sun"—that is, to wealth and possessions, health, sensual pleasures, honor and prestige, pursuing justice, acquiring earthly wisdom and knowledge,[1] and human labor—and although this state of affairs, as manifest in all spheres of human existence, is reiterated throughout the treatise, "meaninglessness" is *not* applied to human work *categorically* or *metaphysically*. It applies existentially to anything that stands outside of or apart from a theocentric outlook on life. As we have attempted to argue in chapter 3, the ongoing contrast in Ecclesiastes—a "dialogue" of sorts—is between an "under-the-sun" secular materialism and what might be called an "under-heaven" theism. And in the latter portrayal, work is depicted as an aspect of satisfaction and enjoyment that constitutes a "gift" from God.

Several misperceptions already noted concerning the role of enjoyment in Ecclesiastes require measured commentary. One concerns the prevailing consensus among commentators regarding the writer's supposed gloomy and at times despairing tone. In response, we would argue that this "negative" voice, where it does occur, is intended to meet the audience "where they live," so to speak, and thereby gain a hearing for the alterative and positive response that follows in the way of a recurring refrain. The

---

1. Ecclesiastes distinguishes between a wisdom that emanates from the fear of God (3:14; 5:7; 7:12, 18; 8:1, 12; and 12:13) and an autonomous or self-sufficient wisdom "under the sun" that, in the end, is futile (1:12–18 and 2:12–16). This comparison finds parallels in the New Testament. In his first epistle to the Corinthians, the Apostle Paul distinguishes between the wisdom of the world and godly wisdom (1 Cor 1:18–2:16), a comparison also made in the epistle of James (Jas 3:13–18).

grim tone is intended to dispel a "false consciousness about the world" and undermine "false dreams and hopes."[2]

A second common misperception about the book is that "enjoyment" only seriously appears late in the book (9:7–10 and 11:7–10), or that when and where it does appear in the text it is a "lowest-common-denominator" approach to enjoyment ("Get what you can, the little that you can"), given the reality of surrounding disappointment and despair.[3] On closer inspection, quite the opposite is, in fact, the case. Admonitions toward "enjoyment" of life are laced throughout the book, although they do seem to reach a crescendo in 9:7–10 and 11:7–10, as is often noted. These occurrences are not random; rather, they are strategically located, representing what one commentator even describes as "climactic moments" in the book.[4] In fact, one literary critic identifies fifteen negative sections of material in the book and thirteen positive sections, even when greater length is devoted to the former.[5] Given this quantitative measurement, we are therefore justified in calling "enjoyment" a prominent theme in terms of literary-rhetorical emphasis.

Moreover, while the frequency of the term "meaningless"/"vanity" (Heb., *hebel*)—appearing thirty-eight times—would lend the impression that the writer believed nothing in the temporal life could be called "good," in fact the Hebrew *tôb* ("good") occurs even more frequently than *hebel* in the book—roughly fifty times.[6] In addition, and central to the basic argument of this volume, the writer also employs both the verb *śāmah* ("to enjoy") and the noun form *simhâ* ("enjoyment," "joy"), which are prominently featured in the passages that are treated below (2:24–26; 3:12–13; 3:22; 5:18–19; 7:14; 8:15; 9:7–10; and 11:8–9), a remarkable seventeen times.[7] At the same time,

---

2. So, correctly, Provan, "Fresh Perspectives in Ecclesiastes," 403.

3. Representative of this widespread and mistaken view is Longman, *The Fear of the Lord Is Wisdom*, 35, who writes: "it is hard to disagree with the majority of scholars who detect resignation, sadness and frustration in these [enjoyment] passages. In other words, the gist of Qohelet's thinking is that since life is difficult and then comes death, we should eke out of life whatever we can."

4. Ogden, "'Vanity' It Certainly Is Not," 301–6.

5. Ryken, "Ecclesiastes," 269–70.

6. Whybray, *The Good Life in the Old Testament*, 186, and Ogden and Zogbo, *A Handbook on Ecclesiastes*, 4, identify "good" as a catchword in Ecclesiastes.

7. The verb *śāmah* (to "rejoice," to "enjoy," to "find enjoyment/satisfaction/contentment") occurs nine times—2:10; 3:12, 22; 4:16; 5:18; 8:15; 10:19; and 11:8, 9—while the noun form, *simhâ* ("joy," "enjoyment," "mirth," "contentment," "satisfaction") occurs eight times—in 2:1, 2, 10, 26; 5:19; 7:4; 8:15; and 9:7. For an examination of the Teacher's use of words deriving from the root *śmh*, see Gianto, "The Theme of Enjoyment in Qohelet."

he makes a clear distinction between authentic joy as a "gift" of God and the mindless frivolity of the fool. Together these verbal indicators suggest a picture that departs radically from conventional thinking about Ecclesiastes: there *is indeed* meaning, purpose, and satisfaction in life, *if* life—from a metaphysical standpoint—is viewed properly.

The Enjoyment Refrains

Because much commentary is broadly unified in the assumption that the writer has a fatalistic, at times despairing, and ultimately "resigned" view of life, interpretive and theological honesty requires that we acknowledge the presence of a cluster of statements spread throughout Ecclesiastes in which a full-throated recognition of enjoyment and satisfaction in this temporal life is acknowledged.[8] The presence of this material presents the interpreter with a serious obstacle—if, that is, the message of Ecclesiastes, relatively speaking, is futility and the God depicted therein is "harsh" and "distant," as is broadly assumed. Taken together, these "refrains"—eight in number—blatantly contradict the "meaninglessness" thesis that is expressed throughout. Moreover, they are clearly more than mere "marginal notes" or "escape clauses" on the part of the writer. Rather, by the manner in which they punctuate the entire treatise they constitute something of a *Leitmotif* or recurring theme and, therefore, must be taken seriously as part of the writer's interpretive strategy.[9]

What is more, the next-to-last of these passages noted below, 9:7–10, is the most forceful of the writer's admonitions toward enjoyment—emphatic advice to *make the most* out of life while one can—and may properly be viewed as part of a bridge leading into the book's concluding section. Finding enjoyment, as it turns out, is an important counterpoint and subtheme,[10] even when it is not to be confused with "pleasure-seeking" (cf. 2:1–11 and 7:1–6). Additionally, and significantly for our present purposes, in five of these passages or refrains an explicit connection is made between *work*[11] and

8. Contra *inter alios* Walsh, "Despair as a Theological Virtue," 46, who insists that the writer "perceives no correlation between moral goodness and prosperity" and that "there is no goodness in life."

9. This fundamental assumption has been argued by Whybray, "Qoheleth, Preacher of Joy"; Ogden, "Qoheleth's Use of the 'Nothing is Better'-Form"; Ogden, "'Vanity' It Certainly Is Not"; and Lee, *The Vitality of Enjoyment*. Nonetheless, it is rejected by the majority of Old Testament scholars doing commentary on Ecclesiastes.

10. As a theological theme, joy in Ecclesiastes has received relatively little attention in the literature. Exceptions to this are Whybray, Ogden, and Lee (see n. 9).

11. Three words in Ecclesiastes are used to depict "work"—'āmāl, 'asâ, and 'anah.

enjoyment—a state of affairs that does *not* exist in a materialist-secularist account of human life. (In Ecclesiastes as a whole, the noun form of *'āmāl* occurs twenty times and the verb form fourteen times; altogether, the fact of thirty-four occurrences is significant.)[12] And because of the trademark of repetition in wisdom literature, the reader may be assured that the recurring accent being placed on *contentment through human labor* is not a minor point. Moreover, eight times in Ecclesiastes the writer speaks of a human being's "lot" or "portion" (*heleq*) that has been "assigned" by heaven (2:10, 21; 3:22; 4:9; 5:18; 9:6, 9; and 11:2); several of these appear in a positive context of one's delight or contentment through work (see below).

The eight passages that speak of enjoyment or contentment—and we may call them "refrains"—may be understood as corresponding to eight intervals in the writer's argument.[13] At each interval, joy and contentment[14] are reaffirmed in contradistinction to the absurdities that characterize "secular" existence. Ecclesiastes may be said to represent the Jewish understanding of the "good life," in contradistinction to various pagan conceptions of the same.[15] Relatedly, the implication in each of these "interval" statements is that temporal enjoyment should not be dissociated from the *source* of contentment, since it is a "gift" of God. And far from being a "distant" God, as much commentary mistakenly assumes or asserts, "God keeps them [i.e., those who fear him] occupied with gladness of heart" (5:20 NIV). Simply said, one cannot have it both ways in one's interpretation of Ecclesiastes; either God "teases, taunts, and tortures" humans as a "distant" and "harsh" God, or he gives the "gifts" of life, wisdom, and contentment. Theologically,

---

These are variously rendered "toil," "work," "deed," "labor," or "business." It is unfortunate that the English word *toil* has an almost universally negative connotation. In Ecclesiastes, on occasion the context calls for a negative translation, while on other occasions it does not. Sometimes a particular translation will use the word *toil* when the context is in fact positive.

12. On the significance of this keyword, see Castellino, "Qohehelt and His Wisdom."

13. Whereas Whybray, "Qoheleth, Preacher of Joy," and *Ecclesiastes*, 64, points to seven allusions to enjoyment in Ecclesiastes, Lee, *The Vitality of Enjoyment*, identifies eight. I follow Lee for reasons of structure.

14. Perry, *Dialogues with Kohelet*, 31, makes the case that the Hebrew noun *śimhâ* is perhaps best rendered "contentment" in the rabbinic sense of being "happy with one's lot" (cf. 5:19).

15. Whether the precise nature of pagan conceptualizing of the "good life" as mirrored in Ecclesiastes is ancient Near Eastern, Hellenistic, or other is a matter of speculation and impossible to identify with precision, even when the majority of commentators assume a Hellenistic backdrop. In any case, the writer affirms a Jewish belief system, although he is "comfortable" trafficking in the two worlds of belief and unbelief. He addresses the question of meaning and happiness, doing so from the standpoint of a theism that is anchored in the fear of God.

any attempt to reconcile these contradictions by arguing that *both* are a part of the writer's cosmic outlook is absurd.[16]

2:24–26

[24] There is nothing better for a man than to eat and drink, and *find enjoyment in his labor.* This also, I saw, is from the hand of God. [25] For who can even eat or have enjoyment more so than I? [26] For to a man who is pleasing before Him, God gives wisdom, knowledge, and joy; but to the sinner He gives the work of gathering and collecting to give him who is pleasing before God. Also this is vanity and chasing the wind. (2:24–26, MEV, emphasis added)

These statements represent an initial—and in some ways, unexpected—turning point and introduce a theological grounding to an alternative outlook—an outlook stemming from divine sovereignty and providence. A veil is lifted. This alternative outlook, described by Martin Luther in his pathbreaking "Notes on Ecclesiastes" (see chapter 6) as the book's "principal conclusion,"[17] will be developed in more theological detail in 3:1–22 and will be recurring throughout Ecclesiastes. Several features of this alternative outlook are worth noting: (1) allusions to God are introduced (aside from 1:13, God is not mentioned up to this point); (2) joy and contentment in the ordinary are presented as normative; (3) life is said to be a "gift"; (4) wisdom is suddenly viewed differently—as a "gift" of God; (5) work is presented as satisfying, which comes from the "hand of God"; and (6) pleasing God is a condition. All of these elements stand in marked contrast to the despairing tone of the previous lament (1:2–2:23). The observation that both recreation (eating and drinking[18]) and labor, which together encompass all of life, are a "gift of God" serves as a counterpoint to the preceding material, namely, the futility, pain, grief of toil, and endless effort poured into labor done "under the sun" (2:17–23). Eating and drinking and finding satisfaction in our labors represent a picture of contentment and are reminiscent of a similar depiction of God's provision in the Psalms:

> He makes grass grow for the cattle,
>
> And plants for man to cultivate,

---

16. The point being made is not that adversity and hardship are not a part of life; it is, rather, that one cannot have *two over-arching metaphysical outlooks* (one issuing out of a despairing resignation and one out of meaning, purpose, and joy).

17. Luther, *Notes on Ecclesiastes*, 46.

18. Seow, *Ecclesiastes*, 157, properly notes that eating and drinking refer to "a general attitude toward life" and not merely those two activities in the narrowest sense.

> Bringing forth food from the earth,
>
>   Wine that gladdens the heart of man,
>
> Oil to make his face shine,
>
>   And bread that sustains his heart . . .
>
> When you give it to them,
>
>   They gather it up;
>
> When you open your hand,
>
>   They are satisfied with good things. (Ps 104:14–15, 28, NIV)

Together, the statements recorded in 2:24–26 constitute a response to the failure of all attempts—philosophical (1:12–18), sensual (2:1–2), commercial (2:3–11), intellectual (2:12–17), and work-related (2:18–23)—to find meaning in human existence based on human striving. Life is empty and futile (*hebel*) apart from the Creator.

These statements also answer two strategic rhetorical questions posed earlier: (1) that which was posed at the very outset—"What profit [*yitrôn*] is there in human endeavor under the sun?" (1:3)—and (2) the question concerning what is "good" (2:1). Regarding the first, 2:24–26 serves as an alternative response and contrast. The implied answer to "What profit is there?"/"What does man gain?" is *nothing* (1:4–2:23).[19] If there is no "return" or "gain" in the human experience, then life truly is without meaning and purpose. Regarding the second rhetorical question, it is significant that the "good" (Heb.: *tôb*)—a supremely important term in Ecclesiastes, occurring a remarkable fifty-two times in the book—is mentioned three times in 2:24–26. For the non-theist, "good" is wholly relative—in truth, an impossibility—inasmuch as it resides in the Creator whose standards are transcendent and abiding. Apart from God, everything in this life "under the sun" is *hebel*, "meaningless"; apart from the Creator, there can be no *intrinsic* "good."[20] Furthermore, there is moral agency being expressed in these statements, contrary to much commentary;[21] the "good" and

---

19. The rhetorical question posed in 1:3 ("What does it profit . . . ?") and later on is reminiscent of a similar rhetorical question posed by Jesus: "What does it profit a man to gain the whole world and forfeit his soul?" (Mark 8:36, ESV; cf. Luke 9:25).

20. This is the implied answer to the rhetorical question in v. 25: "For apart from him who can . . . find enjoyment?" (ESV).

21. It is telling that virtually all commentary on these verses is unified in the assumption that the writer is *not* making moral statements here. Representative is Murphy, *Ecclesiastes*, 26, who asserts: "No moral connotation is to be given to the terms . . . 'good' . . . and . . . 'sinner.'" Remarkably, Longman, *The Book of Ecclesiastes*, 110, insists that the context of 2:24–26 "forbids" a moral—i.e., "good"-versus-"sinner"—interpretation,

"pleasing God" are evidence thereof, the latter of which reveals the condition for experiencing joy.[22] Two persons are depicted here—the one who pleases God and the "sinner," or, in wisdom terminology, the wise and the foolish.[23] This contrast of the "God-pleaser" and the "sinner" appears again in Ecclesiastes—in 7:26 and in 9:2.[24] Verse 26, then, expresses a "crowning irony" in the light of the announced "meaningless" thesis; for the righteous it expresses a "crowning vindication."[25] Divine sovereignty, which is further developed in the material to follow (3:1–22), demonstrates itself in how God even uses those who reject him.

Wisdom, knowledge, and joy—a joy that includes satisfaction in one's work—are gifts from "the hand of God" (cf. as well 9:1) given to those who "please" him.[26] Joy is not pursued and earned based on human merit (1:3 and 2:11); it is *received*, in contradistinction to the outlook being critiqued in the previous material. Meaning in life is found not through our own efforts but through receiving God's gifts with thanksgiving.[27] Moreover, all three of the "gifts" given by God (v. 26)—"wisdom, knowledge, and

---

when in fact this is *the very language*—language that is typical of wisdom literature—being employed by the writer. And Crenshaw, *Ecclesiastes*, 90, prefers to understand the two persons depicted in v. 26 as "lucky" and "unlucky." Against these interpretations, Coralie Ann Gutridge, "Wisdom, Anti-Wisdom, and the Ethical Function of Uncertainty," 359–88, points out that the majority of scholars are misguided here, failing to account for why the LXX translates the Hebrew as *poein agathon* rather than *eu prattein*. In classical Greek, *poein agathon* connotes doing honorable ethical acts.

22. Cf. Heb 11:6. Standard commentary tends to deny this condition, assuming that 2:26 mirrors a God who is "arbitrary." So, for example, Scott, *Proverbs-Ecclesiastes*, 219, who is merely representative: "*Why* God favors one and regards the other as a sinner is to Qoheleth another of the baffling phenomena of life . . ." (emphasis present). On the matter of causality, we may state the wisdom perspective as follows: on occasion (when not *always*), the "wise" person *is* better off than the "fool"/"sinner," as the book of Proverbs suggests.

23. Against the flow of much commentary, in 2:26 the writer is affirming an "orthodox" view of reward and punishment, as Whybray, *Ecclesiastes* , 64, points out.

24. Eccl 7:26: "The man who pleases God will escape her [the woman who is a snare], but the sinner she will ensnare"; 9:2: "All share a common destiny—the righteous and the wicked, the good and the bad, the clean and the unclean, those offer sacrifices and those who do not" (NIV).

25. So Kidner, *A Time to Mourn*, 36.

26. The question of the justice of God in taking from the "sinner"/"fool" and giving to those who please him presents problems for not a few commentators. Yet it has parallels in other "wisdom" texts—for example, in Job 27:16–17, 19; Prov 13:22; and Prov 28:8.

27. This teaching in Ecclesiastes agrees with Paul's admonition to Timothy: "For everything God has created is good, and nothing is to be rejected if it is received with thanksgiving, because it is consecrated by the word of God and prayer" (1 Tim 4:4–5, NIV).

joy"—were previously described as *hebel* and fleeting in the opening lament (1:13–18). That these come "from the hand of God" disqualifies any quasi-hedonistic interpretation on the reader's part. What is more, work, which according to the Teacher's "response" in these statements yields a satisfaction that comes from "the hand of God" (v. 24), had been previously lamented as "painful" and "grievous" (1:17 and 2:23). In Ecclesiastes, work is depicted either as vexing and oppressive or as a source of joy and contentment, but in terms of its *intrinsic* nature, *it cannot be simultaneously viewed as both.*[28] That is to say, the two views stand diametrically opposed to one another. In the Teacher's argument, the very toil that tyrannizes becomes a joy-filled, satisfying gift, when and where life is received from "the hand" of the Creator. The statements in vv. 24–26, then, represent the very *antithesis* of striving, despair, and *hebel.*

Verse 24 contains the first of four "there is nothing better" rhetorical devices applied to work in the book. It is a rhetorical device for emphasizing a final conclusion,[29] with the "nothing better" statements answering the initial rhetorical question "What profit is there?" (1:13)—one that is repeated (3:9 and 5:16). The answer is that there *is* an advantage, a gain, a profit, but only in the context of pleasing and revering God: joy and simple pleasures in life, inclusive of work, are "gifts" and the fruit of wisdom.[30] Contrary to the vast majority of commentators, the "nothing better" rhetorical construction is *not* a statement of resignation, to the effect that "All that's left in this vexing life is pleasure, if you can find it."[31] Rather, it expresses the sentiment "There is nothing more rewarding than . . ."[32] The "nothing better" rhetorical device occurs frequently in wisdom literature, employed for the purpose of making

28. This well illustrates the writer's literary-rhetorical strategy, which is one of *juxtaposition*. To argue, as many commentators do, that the Teacher is caught in a tension between the two poles of meaninglessness and joy, is schizophrenic and incoherent; such is *not* the message of Ecclesiastes.

29. See Ogden, "The 'Better'-Proverb (*Tôb-Spruch*)," and "Qoheleth's Use of the 'Nothing is Better'-Form."

30. Not insignificantly, both "profit" and "work" in association with each other are part of "wisdom" vocabulary, not only in Ecclesiastes (1:3; 2:11; 3:9; 5:16) but elsewhere; consider, for example, Prov 14:23 and Jas 2:14.

31. Crenshaw, *Ecclesiastes*, 88–90, Longman, *The Book of Ecclesiastes*, 107, and Weeks, *Ecclesiastes and Scepticism*, 67–68, are representative of those commentators who misperceive the "nothing better" statements as mirroring pessimistic, quasi-hedonistic resignation. Crenshaw notes with a touch of cynicism that "Qohelet's positive counsel rests under a cloud," since "to enjoy life is not in anyone's power" (90). And Weeks interprets the "nothing better" rhetorical device to mean the precise *opposite* of what is intended: "There is *no good* in the person who eats and drinks . . . ," since no "inherent virtues" exist (emphasis added).

32. Thus Ogden, *Qoheleth*, 62–63.

a comparison and encouraging a verdict.[33] This initial "there is nothing better" construction in Ecclesiastes is an "animated affirmation" appearing in the first of eight refrains that are "climactic moments" and part of the *alternative* outlook in the message of Ecclesiastes.[34] In their effect, the "nothing better" exclamations in the book, four of which relate to enjoyment and satisfaction in one's work, are comparable to the confession of the Psalmist in Ps 128:1–2, wherein gifts from God are a sign of his blessing:

> Bless are all who fear the Lord,
>> Who walk in his ways.
> You will eat the fruit of your labor;
>> Blessings and prosperity will be yours.

Not pessimism and resignation but the gift of joy and contentment are to be normative. This gift, moreover, though profound, is expressed in ordinary things. This profundity and simplicity stand in marked contrast to the lifestyle of the "sinner"/fool, for whom food, wine, and work become a pursuit, an obsession, or an idol.

Finally, the intended object of the concluding sentence in v. 26— "Also this is vanity and chasing the wind"—is the "sinner," not the "one who pleases God." The *hebel* of v. 26 is the "sinner's" storing up of wealth. Chasing after the wind is another way of saying that, for the "sinner," there is no "gain" or "profit" (1:3); the "heavy burden" (1:13) goes unrelieved because of one's unbelief.

Eccl 2:24–26, then, presents the opposite of—the response and remedy to—the lament recorded in 1:2–2:23. Being juxtaposed are two contrasting outlooks on ultimate reality: human striving versus receiving from the hand of God, human limitation versus divine provision. The theological rationale for this follows in 3:1–22 in the form of a defense of divine sovereignty which stands alongside the reality of human frailty.

3:12–13

> [12] I know that there's nothing better for them but to enjoy themselves and do what's good while they live. [13] Moreover, this is the gift of God: that all people should eat, drink, and *enjoy the results of their hard work.* (3:12–13, CEB, emphasis added)

33. Other examples in wisdom literature of the "nothing better" rhetorical device are Prov 17:1; 21:9, 19; 27:5, 10; and Ps 37:16. On the function of the "nothing better" construction in wisdom literature, see Klein, *Kohelet und die Weisheit Israels*, 95–105. Klein is one of the few to go against the scholarly consensus by arguing that the Teacher, through his "better than" sayings, *is* making moral claims.

34. Ogden and Zogbo, *A Handbook on Ecclesiastes*, 79.

These statements follow on the heels of the poem on "seasons"—everything, including enjoyment, has its place, its purpose, its season, and its appropriate time (3:1–8), reminding humans of their limitations—and on the heels of the rhetorical question concerning "profit" initialed raised in 1:3 and being repeated in 3:9. The obvious answer to the question is negative, as evidenced by the multifaceted lament of 1:4–2:23. However, the statements in 3:10–11 mark a shift in perspective, from an anthropocentric to a theocentric outlook on life. Verses 12 and 13, thus, serve as a counterpoint to human inability to fathom what God has done and will do "from the beginning to the end" (3:10–15). In fact, 3:10–15 furnishes the theological grounding for the writer's argument and may legitimately be viewed as the summary of the entire book. Whereas other parts of the Old Testament exalt God for his salvific acts of power and work, Eccl 3 exalts him for his seeming "hiddenness" and inscrutability. This perspective, which highlights human beings' inability to fathom the divine nature, represents the "other side of the coin" of divine sovereignty.[35]

It is significant that God is mentioned multiple times in these statements, suggesting that joy—inclusive of human labor—has theological meaning.[36] Properly viewed, God's works and actions are the focus in this material; God acts so that human beings will revere him (v. 14), which is humankind's proper place before God. And, in fact, humans are created with a sense of the transcendent—the eternal ('ôlām)—in their hearts (3:11). This statement, that God has placed "eternity" in the hearts of human beings, constitutes an interpretive key to the whole book. In its implications, the statement is utterly profound, suggesting that human person's deepest

---

35. Most commentators chafe under this teaching of Ecclesiastes—namely, that human beings cannot fathom the divine nature—and in the end impose their own skepticism on the writer. A representative sampling suffices to well illustrate. For example, Barr, *Biblical Words for Time*, 99, sees in Eccl 3 a "clear" sign of how "frustrating" it is for human beings not to be able to know divine seasons and times. Huwiler, "Ecclesiastes," 187, writes: "It is not coincidental that the letdown occurs when the role of God is made explicit"; and, "In this segment, God is explicitly and ominously present." And Crenshaw, *Ecclesiastes*, 92, opines: "An arbitrary deity shapes human lives, allowing some persons to participate in pleasure and preventing others from doing so. It does no good to fight against this external control . . . In the end he [the writer] discovers no comfort in the knowledge that God has made everything appropriate for its particular moment" (97); and, "Divine arbitrariness would vex us less if God were kindly disposed toward human beings. But Qohelet finds no evidence for this conclusion. In truth, he discovers facts that contradict such an optimistic attitude" (101). With "professional" commentary like this, it is no wonder that preachers and teachers are not expositing Ecclesiastes from the pulpit; clearly, it would destroy a person's faith.

36. To describe the joy being observed in 3:12–13 as "constrained hedonism," as do Holmstedt et al., *Qoheleth*, 130, misses the mark, both theologically and ethically.

longings cannot be filled by that which is temporal. It suggests that in the experience of true joy, something of the transcendent—something of the eternal—manifests itself. It is the antidote to the *hebel* of life "under the sun." In fact, human beings would be incapable of revering God without the *ʿōlām* dwelling within. By virtue of creation, a consciousness of the transcendent has been implanted within the human heart; it is part of our design—the *imago Dei*—and distinguishes us from animals, even when it is the case that humans suppress that awareness.[37] And that part of our design that distinguishes us from the rest of creation is the fact that we are moral agents, equipped with the capacity to sense, reason, discern, and act based on baseline moral reality.[38] (This, then, is the "natural moral law," based on the image of God. It is implanted within and corresponds to what the Apostle Paul calls "the law written on the heart" [Rom 2:14–15; cf. Rom 1:19–20]).

Hence, joy and contentment, which are the very "seeds of eternity,"[39] represent the opposite of—and the answer to—"meaninglessness" (*hebel*); a sense of the transcendent allows us to escape the "vanity of vanities."[40] Conversely, to be ruled by impersonal fate is absurd—a state of futility which, at bottom, is intolerable.[41] But if there is indeed a proper time and

37. Rom 1:18–21 and 2:14–15. Contra Murphy, "On Translating Ecclesiastes," 573, translating *ʿōlām* as "eternity" is not "too strong." Inasmuch as rabbinic literature uses the word to designate the present age and the future world, and because it captures the proper sense of 3:11, there are *good reasons* for arguing that it is the best translation.

38. Contra John Barton, *Reading the Old Testament*, 63, whose view represents not a few commentators on Ecclesiastes, the didactic poem of 3:1–8 and its explanation in the material that follows do not constitute some sort of "gloomy determinism" on the part of the writer. Nor do they stand in contradiction of the book's conclusion (12:14). Rather, they confirm that human beings are moral agents and thus exercise "free will," which alone explains the presence of recurring warnings regarding judgment (3:17; 8:6; 11:9) as well as the "conclusion to the matter" (12:14). If there is no moral agency and "free will" assumed by the writer in Ecclesiastes, then the aforementioned pronouncements in the book are meaningless, indeed an utter falsehood.

39. Perry, *Dialogues with Kohelet*, 31.

40. Some readers are sure to object to my assertion here—namely, that we "escape" the "vanity of vanities." Lest I be misunderstood, my argument is *not* that through faith we avoid pain, hardship, oppression, and despair. Such is neither the argument of Ecclesiastes nor the argument being presented in the present volume. Rather, I am arguing that the Teacher is presenting two competing ultimate outlooks on meaning and happiness in life. The one that he knows intimately and wishes to demolish is that philosophy of life that seeks, through temporal values, to earn meaning and happiness "under the sun." Faith in the Creator "allows"—indeed, it will require— that we suffer and endure hardship and injustice without understanding *why*; that, of course, is the message of Job. Ecclesiastes, by contrast, simply builds a case for the "why" behind Job's dilemma: human limitations and divine inscrutability. In a very real sense, then, Job and Ecclesiastes *complement* one another in terms of the "wisdom" perspective.

41. Contra Ginsberg, "The Structure and Contents of the Book of Koheleth,"

season for everything (vv. 1–8),[42] then not everything is *hebel*.[43] In fact, there is a beauty in the *timeliness* of something, which is the apparent sense of 3:11a. Seasons have an appropriateness; without seasons, events lack context and, therefore, meaning and purpose. Divine inscrutability is not vexing for the believer, only the unbeliever—i.e., the materialist/secularist who refuses to acknowledge the "hand of God" and the "work of God" in creation and human circumstances. Divine sovereignty and inscrutability are a scandal only to the person who is pursuing a legacy, insofar as these divine realities clip "the wings of our self-sufficiency."[44] The *imago Dei* alone survives the final reality of death.

Because God is sovereign over all earthly activity, because he has placed a sense of the transcendent within us, because all of this should cause us to revere him, and because he will judge all things, humility and wisdom will cause us to accept the reality of human limitations, and to do so joyfully. The divine purpose behind all things (3:1–15 and 7:14), resulting in our recognition of different "seasons" ("He has made everything beautiful in its time"—v. 11) prompts us, with the psalmist, to confess, "I trust in you, O LORD; I say, 'You are my God.' My times are in your hands . . ." (Ps 31:14–15).[45] Eating and drinking and working—i.e., those basics of which ordinary life is composed—symbolize the joy of being human and thus have theological significance.[46] What is more, the writer is explicit here in affirming that human beings enjoy *the fruit of their labor*. Verse 13 reads literally that all might "see the good in their labor." The term *good* appears three times in these two statements, which itself suggests purpose and intention. Verse 12, which involves a word-play on the "good," contains the second of four rhetorical devices applying to work in the book. In verse 13 and 14, two responses are enjoined: (1) receive from God and (2) revere God. This alone might well summarize the burden of Ecclesiastes.

3:22

> [22] So I saw that there is nothing better than that all should *enjoy their work*, for that is their lot; who can bring them to see what will be after them? (3:22, NRSV, emphasis added)

140–41, Eccl 3 is not about "predestination."

42. In v. 1 the theological truth is announced, with vv. 2–8 offering variations on this theme.

43. Otherwise, Ecclesiastes is teaching absurdity.

44. So Kidner, *A Time to Mourn*, 68.

45. NIV.

46. Thus, contra Longman, *The Book of Ecclesiastes*, 123, the "gift of God" (v. 13) is not some "anesthesia" against the problems of the world.

This statement functions in two ways. It serves as a counterpoint to the finality of death and divine judgment (3:16–22) and expresses, in condensed form, both the essence of chapter 3 and the overall message of Ecclesiastes: God is sovereign and *nothing that we pursue* possesses any permanence.[47] Those two aspects constitute two sides of the same theological "coin" and are embedded in proverbial form elsewhere in wisdom literature (thus, for example, Prov 16:9 and 21:1[48]). The tension between divine sovereignty and human freedom in Ecclesiastes is allowed to stand, as later "enjoyment" refrains will bear out (see below). The fact that judgment, of both the wicked and the righteous, encompasses "every activity" and "every deed" done in this present life (3:17) is to say that it is a judgment according to *works*. Which is to argue, with other words, that our work and our deeds, are important;[49] they have great value. And this—the intrinsic value of our work and deeds—mirrors the second function of the statement: it serves as a *carpe diem* ("seize the day"), which will be strengthened in later refrains (for example, in 5:18–20, 9:7–10, and 11:1–6).

In this statement eating and drinking are absent; thus, the accent is on work and human endeavor. Blessing arises out of our work, and the sense of "eternity" resident within the human heart (v. 11) gives proper perspective and vitality to our motivations. To "rejoice in one's work" is evocative of the Genesis creation account. Humans are creative, mirroring the *imago Dei* and hence representing a noble aspect of creation. The term *portion* or *lot* (*heleq*), occurring eight times in Ecclesiastes,[50] serves as a catchword. It conveys not only particular boundaries or limitations as determined by divine providence but also human possibilities, on occasion suggesting "reward" or "inheritance" in Old Testament usage.[51] Moreover, it communicates divine initiative—God is *giving* by nature—in such a way that it manifests itself in the human heart. Thus, it is accurate to argue that the Teacher is advancing the concept of grace. On several occasions, as in 3:22, this "portion" is explicitly associated with joy. The connotation is that enjoyment or

47. Fredericks and Estes, *Ecclesiastes and the Song of Songs*, 117, rightly observe: that God has "made everything beautiful in its own time" is "the greatest statement of divine providence in the whole of Scripture."

48. Prov 16:9: "In his heart a man plans his course, but the LORD determines his steps"; Prov 21:1: "The king's heart is in the hand of the LORD; he directs it like a watercourse wherever he pleases" (NIV).

49. This, of course, is the "wisdom" teaching of Jesus, as illustrated by the "parable of the talents" (Matt 25:14–30). And it is St. Paul's teaching as well (Rom 2:6; 3:13–15; 1 Cor 3:12–13; 15:58; and 2 Cor 5:10). Our work and our works are infinitely valuable, if viewed in the proper perspective.

50. It occurs in 2:10, 21; 3:22; 5:17, 18; 9:6, 9; and 11:2.

51. For example, Deut 32:9; Pss 16:5; 73:26; 119:57; 142:5; Lam 3:24; and Zech 2:12.

satisfaction is something of a "down-payment" or "in-breaking" of the *ʿôlām* mentioned previously (3:11) that penetrates the human experience. Verse 22 contains the third of four "there is nothing better" rhetorical devices applied to work. Not resignation or pessimism but *joy* is declared to be our "portion" or "lot."[52] That assigned joy, moreover, is encountered *in our work*. That is, we experience joy both in the energy expended and in the finished product. We accept and enjoy what has been allotted to us. The doctrines of divine transcendence and human mortality allow us to accept with joy, rather than with chafing, our finitude.

Finally, the rhetorical question concluding v. 22 on not knowing the future is reminiscent of another wisdom saying—one found in the New Testament in the epistle of James: "Why, you do not even know what will happen tomorrow. What is your life? You are a mist that appears for a little while and then vanishes" (Jas 4:14).[53] The argument in Eccl 3 is not that we know nothing of God, against much commentary, only that we cannot know his purpose and the ends of his works.[54]

5:18–20

> Behold, what I have seen to be good and fitting is to eat and drink and *find enjoyment in all the toil with which one toils* under the sun the few days of his life that God has given him, for this is his lot. Everyone also to whom God has given wealth and possessions and power to enjoy them, and to accept his lot and *rejoice in his toil*—this is the gift of God. For he will not much remember the days of his life because God keeps him occupied with joy in his heart. (5:18–20, ESV, emphasis added)

These statements once more signal a conspicuous shift, which occurs both in tone—the shifts seem to build in an increasingly intentional manner[55]—and in their reference to God. The frequency of allusion to God in these statements indicates an alternative metaphysical outlook: life's secret lies in an openness to—and the ability to receive from—God. This particular refrain serves as a counterpoint—indeed, the very antithesis—to greed and discontentment as observed in the surrounding material (5:8–17 and 6:1–11), which describes that which is tantalizing yet unfulfilling. According

52. Contra Duncan, *Ecclesiastes*, 55, 3:22 is not the expression of an "agnosticism" which issues out of "not knowing the parameters of life." Quite the opposite is the case: "agnosticism" only takes root where there is an inability to accept human limitations in the light of providence and divine sovereignty.

53. NIV.

54. On not "adding" or "taking away" in 3:14, cf. Deut 4:2 and Prov 30:6.

55. Whybray, "Qoheleth, Preacher of Joy," 87, and *Ecclesiastes*, 138.

to the materialist outlook on life, people are *never* satisfied, even when they attempt to acquire more and more. By contrast, the God-fearer experiences satisfaction and contentment, which has been assigned as a "portion" (*heleq*) and divine "gift."[56] It needs pointing out here that it is not wealth *per se* but *our view* of wealth that needs chastening. Wealth and possessions can be wonderful when enjoyed and used properly. An improper view of them, by contrast, is heavily critiqued in vv. 8–14. Materialists, misers, and gluttons cannot truly "enjoy"; grateful theists, however, can.

The statements also underscore not merely the "relatively good" but the genuine "good"—something that has been emphasized in earlier refrains (2:24; 3:12; and 3:22). That the "good" is mentioned twice in these verses is significant; most assuredly, this is *not* the language of *hebel*. Moreover, this is said to be both one's "portion" or "lot" as well as a "gift of God," a reiterating of what was claimed earlier (3:13 and 22) and an underscoring of the redemptive quality of the "good." Three times in these verses we read that God "gives," and a fourth time God "occupies" with joy. Truth, goodness, and a sense of beauty are conveyed through this refrain; it is a picture of well-being and contentment.

The verb "enjoy" occurs five times in 5:11–19; by contrast, 5:17 portrayed a person "eating" in "darkness," "frustration," "affliction," and "anger," while 6:1–6 similarly portrays life utterly *without* joy. Surely this contrast and emphasis are significant. In addition, what does it mean to be "occupied with joy," a remarkable description in v. 20 of God's "gift" (v. 19)? One commentator renders this declaration by the Teacher to say that God "engrosses" the human heart with joy.[57] At the very least, it indicates that God "answers" the God-fearer—that is to say, God reveals himself—with and through a sense of divine pleasure and made manifest through joy and contentment in the human heart.[58] This joy and contentment, moreover, are constant and not "erratic," "sporadic," or "enigmatic";[59] they are the fruit of a life that fears

56. There is a tendency to perceive the language of "portion" or "lot" as deterministic; however, as noted above, it should be viewed positively, as a gift, as something of value such as a reward.

57. Barton, "The Text and Interpretation of Ecclesiastes 5:19," 65.

58. To be rejected are Murphy's suggestion, in "On Translating Ecclesiastes," 579, and in *Ecclesiastes*, 53, that "God tranquilizes them" and "distracts humans" by means of pleasure, as well as that of Longman, *The Book of Ecclesiastes*, 168, who writes that these statements are intended to "dull the pain" of life. Quite remarkably, Crenshaw, *Ecclesiastes*, 125, suggests a reading of v. 20 that is the *exact opposite* of its intended (and logical) meaning: "God *afflicts* the person by the constant presence of thoughts about the good life" (emphasis added). These sorts of renderings fail to do justice to the writer's argument, not to mention to basic biblical theology.

59. Contra Murphy, *Ecclesiastes*, 27, whose view issues out of the assumption that

God and receives from his hand. Neither is this ethic of joy an "ethic of the moment," as some would suppose;[60] rather, for God to keep a person "occupied with gladness of heart" suggests a lifestyle, an abiding reality.

These verses, containing one of the densest concentrations of allusion to God in the book (along with 3:10–15), represent something of a "high point" of the entire book,[61] serving to develop further earlier statements (2:24–26 and 3:12–13) and suggesting that enjoyment is even an ethical responsibility.[62] The contentment mirrored in these statements stands in stark contrast to the declaration that human appetites are *never* satisfied (2:10–11 and 6:7). This "occupying" contentment, moreover, is contrasted with the sleepless nights (2:23 and 8:16), heavy burdens (1:13), and vexation (4:8; 8:16; cf. 11:10) that attend the unbeliever—a contrast reminiscent of Ps 127:2: "In vain you rise early and stay up late, toiling for food to eat—for he grants sleep to those he loves."[63] With contentment present, there is no room for anxiety (cf. 11:9–10). The contrast between the two states of mind—"tranquility" versus "toil"—appears in the form of a proverb in 4:6: "Better one handful with tranquility than two handfuls with toil and chasing after the wind."[64]

With these statements, then, the writer raises an opposing perspective on wealth, possessions, and human labor. And herewith he could not be more positive and affirming in his outlook; his position is the very antithesis of "meaninglessness."

7:14

In the day of prosperity be joyful, and in the day of adversity consider: God has made the one as well as the other, so that man may not find out anything that will be after him. (7:14, ESV)

This paradoxical statement serves as a counterpoint to potential disillusionment that arises from a lack of wisdom and life's disappointments (7:1–8:1). To be ruled by impersonal "fate" is simply unbearable; it is *hebel*. While the statement reiterates that joy is the heritage of the God-pleaser, with sobriety it also harkens back to the earlier argument that humans cannot fathom what God does (3:1–22). And here in the immediate context, it states for a second time the imperative to "consider": "Consider what

God's actions are "arbitrary."

60. Contra, for example, Lee, *The Vitality of Enjoyment*, 53.

61. Lohfink, "Qoheleth 5:17–19."

62. Thus Lee, *The Vitality of Enjoyment*, 53.

63. NIV.

64. NIV.

God has done" (v. 13). In both good days and bad, we are to be joyful *and* reflect—a declaration that resembles admonitions in the New Testament toward rejoicing in all things and contentment (Phil 4:4, 11; Jas 1:2; 1 Pet 1:6). The implication is that God governs, that he is sovereign, and that he is inscrutable. God's ways and God's works are simply incomprehensible, which produces in us a certain disposition, or, better said, predisposition.[65] This perspective, moreover, is part of "traditional" wisdom, finding frequent parallels in the book of Proverbs:

- There is a way that seems right to a man, but in the end it leads to death. (14:12 = 16:25)

- In his heart a man plans his course, but the LORD determines his steps. (16:9)

- Many are the plans in a man's heart, but it is the LORD's purpose that prevails. (19:21)

- A man's steps are directed by the LORD. How can anyone understand his own ways? (20:24)

- There is no wisdom, no insight, no plan that can succeed against the LORD. (21:30)

- Do not boast about tomorrow, for you do not know what a day may bring forth. (27:1)

That God's ways and works are inscrutable, however, is not to argue that God is the author of evil—a point missed by much commentary,[66] although it is a perennial human concern. In fact, vv. 13–14 are reminiscent of statements made by Job: "Does God pervert justice? Does the Almighty pervert what is right?" (Job 8:3); "It is unthinkable that God would do wrong, that the Almighty would pervert justice" (Job 34:12). What's more, the "crookedness" alluded to in v. 13 is not a "crookedness" that is perverse or fallen or representing the "absurdities" of life;[67] it refers, rather, to the divine will and the divine purpose.

65. Lee, *The Vitality of Enjoyment*, 52.

66. So, for example, Murphy, *Ecclesiastes*, 66, who suggests that evil is "God's doing," and this "as if God were keeping human beings off balance by an erratic performance." In addition, Shields, *The End of Wisdom*, 236, argues that Qoheleth indeed "ascribes evil to God," "accuses God of making things irrevocably corrupt," "and "questions God's justice." And Anderson, *Qoheleth and Its Pessimistic Theology*, 98–99, suggests God to be the cause of all evil and affliction. While Murphy, Shields, and Anderson's interpretation may well strike the average reader as extreme, it is not unrepresentative of much Ecclesiastes commentary.

67. Against, for example, Crenshaw, *Ecclesiastes*, 139n105, who complains: "The

These words are reminiscent of another wisdom utterance—"Shall we indeed accept good from God and not accept adversity?" (Job 2:10b[68])—and are important in light of the human tendency to doubt God's omnipotence, his providence, and his goodness.[69] Wisdom views adversity quite differently than does the world. Wisdom and the fear of God allow us to accept what we cannot control, moderating the human tendency toward fear and anxiety and permitting us to endure suffering, even when its causes remain to us a mystery. Divine sovereignty encourages us rather than stifling us, and mystery should produce reverence. This statement contains echoes of the didactic poem of 3:1–8: various seasons each have moral significance and purpose. And earlier in his argument, through the didactic poem, the Teacher suggests that it is not possible to know real joy without knowing sorrow; various "seasons" comprise the faith-life for the believer. In the words of one commentator, faith creates within us "a profound openness to the future," whatever that future holds.[70] According to the wisdom perspective, prosperity and adversity are not explained only in terms of reward and punishment, but rather, in terms of the rhythms of life or "seasons" in which we find ourselves and over which we have no control. Godly fear allows us to accept whatever comes our way; in the words of Martin Luther, we endure adversity differently when our contentment is in God.[71] In this statement, then, we find a linkage that is central to the writer's message: namely, a connection between joy and the fear of God. It is a linkage that is implicit in the cry of the psalmist: "Make us glad for as many days as you have afflicted us . . ." (Ps 90:15).[72]

Finally, that the God-fearer can expect not only to encounter suffering but to *willingly endure* it—itself an absurdity to the materialist-secularist outlook—helps to explain the proverb found in Eccl 7:4: "The heart of the wise is in the house of mourning." The wise person chooses to identify with those who are suffering, and the reason for this is lodged in our basic understanding of suffering itself. In suffering, whether our own or that of another, we realize—and we affirm—that God is never removed from us and that everything has a purpose (3:1–8), even when our experience seems to suggest otherwise.

twisted character of things also contradicts Qohelet's view in 7:29 that God made humankind straight . . . , but they sought out devious means."

68. NASB.

69. To describe these words as a "backhanded compliment" of divine power, as Holmstedt et al., *Qoheleth*, 207, do, seems to miss the mark theologically.

70. Lee, *The Vitality of Enjoyment*, 57.

71. Luther, *Notes on Ecclesiastes,* 120.

72. NIV.

8:15

[15] So I commend enjoyment because there's nothing better for people to do under the sun but to eat, drink, and be glad. *This is what will accompany them in their hard work*, during the lifetime that God gives under the sun. (8:15, CEB, emphasis added)

These statements, which constitute a strengthened commendation—even *extolling*—of joy, serve as a counterpoint to life's "unfairness" and "injustice" (8:11–15), based on divine inscrutability. Human wickedness notwithstanding, moral accountability *is* affirmed in 8:12–13 ("it will go better with God-fearing men"); that is to say, because the wicked do not fear God, it will not go well with them. This is a truism even when it cannot be absolutized and frequently does not seem to be true in our perception or experience. Various elements of enjoyment in previous refrains are recapitulated here—eating and drinking and the experience of joy in our work, God's "gift" of life, as well as the observation that joy accompanies the God-fearer continually. That joy can actually "accompany" us in our labors is an intriguing and profound reality, for when work is allied with joy, it becomes not merely bearable but *meaningful*. Furthermore, joy and contentment are said to accompany us "during the lifetime that God gives"; most translations here read "all the days of the life God gives" us. This is a remarkable fact, which suggests that joy accompanies the God-fearer as a *lifestyle*; it has an *enduring* quality and is neither erratic, nor sporadic, nor enigmatic.[73]

Such a state of affairs, moreover, stands in bald contrast to that which follows in v. 16: there is *no sleep or satisfaction in labor*. Moreover, it confirms that "it will go better" with those who fear God (vv. 12–13). This refrain also contains the fourth of four "there is nothing better" rhetorical devices applied to human work. It suggests that in finding satisfaction in our work, we recognize work's purpose and source. In the end, one can rest assured that "the righteous and the wise, along with their works, are in God's hands" (9:1).

9:7–10

[7] Go then, eat your bread in happiness and drink your wine with a cheerful heart; for God has already approved your works. [8] Let your clothes be white all the time, and let not oil be lacking on your head. [9] Enjoy life with the woman whom you love all the days of your fleeting life which He has given to you under the

73. Strangely, Horne, *Proverbs-Ecclesiastes*, 493, interprets 8:15 to mean the precise *opposite* of what it communicates: "Arbitrary pleasure is the only antidote to the paradoxes of an impenetrably absurd existence." And similarly, contra Fox, *Ecclesiastes*, 60, enjoyment here does not merely serve to "only palliate the distress" we experience.

sun; for *this is your reward in life and in your toil in which you
have labored* under the sun. [10] *Whatever your hand finds to do,
do it with all your might*; for there is no activity or planning or
knowledge or wisdom in Sheol where you are going. (9:7–10,
NASB, emphasis added)

At this point a shift occurs from what was previously a descriptive
mood to an imperative mood. These statements, which as a refrain reach a
crescendo by employing multiple imperatives couched in festive imagery,[74]
serve as a remarkably enthusiastic counterpoint both to humans' vain attempts at understanding God's actions (8:16–17) and to death as the universal destiny of all human beings (9:2–6).[75] Since "the righteous and the
wise and what they do are in God's hands" (9:1),[76] great confidence belongs
to those who fear God, and here there is an appropriate response. With
associated imagery that conveys a picture of well-being, even celebration
(though not hedonism), these statements constitute a powerful witness to
human moral agency and responsibility with their explicit "seize the day"
imperative, which finds its expansion in the later admonitions to give, take
risks, and sow seed (11:1–6).[77] Passivity is not the fruit of bona fide faith.
Throughout Ecclesiastes the writer connects joy and labor, and that linkage
is pronounced here in this *carpe diem* imperative. When one is contented,
that person can throw himself/herself into a task with great energy and
gusto. There is reward in the *present*, not just in the future—a reality that
gives meaning and purpose to our work. This is our "portion," our calling,
our vocation. And this reality is not eliminated by the presence of sin, since
it is part of being created in the image of God. We are *created* for energetic
involvement. The admonition "Whatever your hand finds to do, do it without all your might!" finds a parallel in the New Testament. St. Paul employs
similar words when he writes the Christian community in Colossae: "Whatever you do, work at it with all your heart . . ." (Col 3:23).[78] Being implied in
v. 10 is the fact that work is satisfying at both the physical and psychological
level.[79] In fact, the implication of v. 10 is that not only our energies but our

74. The festive language and imagery here demolish the notion, surprisingly widespread in commentary, that Ecclesiastes mirrors resignation and pessimism.

75. Ogden, "Qoheleth IX 1–16," grasps the Teacher's question-response strategy in
a way that escapes most commentators.

76. NIV.

77. Eccl 9:7–10 and 11:7–10 are not the language (or evidence) of "meaninglessness" (*hebel*). They represent the alternative outlook.

78. NIV.

79. As one commentator well notes, the admonition found in 9:10—"Whatever
your hand finds to do, do it with all your might!"—is indeed a "cruel joke" if the writer

possibilities are *unbounded*.[80] The statements "Do it with all your might!" and "Everything is meaningless!" are contradictions; the Teacher does not— indeed, *cannot possibly*—affirm or "synthesize" both.

Together the statements of this refrain offer, in an implicit manner, theological grounding for satisfaction in work, insofar as they observe the presence of gladness and a cheerful heart *and* an awareness of God's favor (v. 7). Whatever the precise meaning of "God already favors what you do," its implications are stunning, producing courage, hope, and confidence in the agent. Divine *favor*, it needs emphasizing, excludes the common perception of God as "arbitrary," "distant," or "harsh," which is indicative of so much commentary. The link between pleasing God and divine approval is central to the wisdom perspective, as indicated by Prov 16:7: "When a man's ways are pleasing to the LORD, he makes even his enemies to be at peace with him."[81]

In addition, enjoyment is depicted not as fleeting or short-lived but a phenomenon that, at its base, is present "all the days" of one's life. This, then, is the alternative and "counter" to *hebel*, which in v. 9 should be translated with a different inflection than "meaningless"; the connotation here is "fleeting."[82] Joy is said in this refrain to be one's "reward" in life—a statement that parallels the writer's use of "portion" elsewhere and further answers the original "gain" rhetorical question of 1:3 (reiterated in 3:9). Additionally, these statements are a reminder that the present represents a *theater of opportunity*; there is no working, sowing, investing, and multiplying beyond this life (v. 10b). However, there is also *no limit* as to what might be "gained" by generous "sowing" in the present life (v. 10a).

In virtually all commentary on Ecclesiastes it is standard to compare verses 7–10 with the Epic of Gilgamesh, an ancient Mesopotamian tale dating two millennia earlier that chronicles the weal and woe of a Sumerian king.[83] And, indeed, the parallels between Ecclesiastes 9:7–10 and the Epic

---

believes that *everything* is "meaningless" (Fredericks and Estes, *Ecclesiastes and the Song of Songs*, 210). A person cannot strive for excellence and do something well if it amounts to nonsense.

80. Hence, any interpretation of Ecclesiastes that suggests the writer to be breeding resignation, despair, pessimism, or determinism is misguided.

81. ESV.

82. As was suggested in chapter 3, there is a multivalence that informs the Teacher's use of *hebel*, even when his usage normally conveys the sense of "meaningless" throughout the treatise.

83. For an English translation of the Gilgamesh Epic, see Pritchard, ed., *Ancient Near Eastern Texts*, 72–98. As it applies to Ecclesiastes, the notable parallels are found in Tablet 3, lines 7–8 (Eccl 1:2–4); Tablet 10, iii, lines 7–14 (Eccl 9:7-10); Tablet 10, vi, line 29 (Eccl 9:6); and Tablet 10, vi, lines 32–36 (Eccl 1:4, 11; 2:16; and 9:5).

are striking. However, what is significant for Ecclesiastes is the fact that wholly absent from various ancient Near Eastern parallels are several conspicuous items—in particular, the fear of God, a chaste understanding of joy, and the *commendation of work*. Ancient societies as well as classical Greco-Roman culture did not view work in the way that Ecclesiastes portrays it. Such a portrait of human labor is striking, and peculiarly Judeo-Christian. In addition, it needs emphasizing that the language being employed here is *not* metaphorical or allegorical. The intended meaning finds confirmation later in Ecclesiastes: "skill applied will result in success" (10:10b), whereas where "a man is lazy, the rafters sag" (10:18a).

11:7–12:1a

> [7] The light is pleasant, and it is good for the eyes to see the sun. [8] Indeed, if a man should live many years, let him rejoice in them all, and let him remember the days of darkness, for they will be many. Everything that is to come will be futility. [9] Rejoice, young man, during your childhood, and let your heart be pleasant during the days of young manhood. And follow the impulses of your heart and the desires of your eyes. Yet know that God will bring you to judgment for all these things. [10] So, remove grief and anger from your heart and put away pain from your body, because childhood and the prime of life are fleeting. Remember your Creator in the days of your youth . . . (11:7–12:1a, NASB)

These statements—statements which dispel any possibility that the writer's own position is despair, disillusionment, or resignation—represent a "dramatic culmination"[84]—one might even say, a "call to decision"[85]—of the treatise following admonitions toward wise behavior, industry, generosity, and persistence in "sowing" (11:1–16). They begin the final section of the book and a new unit of thought, following on the heels of admonitions to "sow seed," and to do so liberally (11:1–6, esp. vv. 1, 2, and 6). They also serve as a radical counterpoint to the inevitability and finality of death in old age (11:8–12:7).

The six allusions to "youth"[86] in these verses suggest that this stage of life is strategic; youth is portrayed here as a divine gift and opportunity—unbounded potential that is to be used not impulsively but creatively,

---

84. So Lee, *The Vitality of Enjoyment*, 72.

85. So Eaton, *Ecclesiastes*, 139.

86. "Youth" or "young man" is consistent with the object of wisdom literature, as indicated by chapters 1–9 of Proverbs ("my son").

energetically yet soberly.[87] They suggest a remarkable openness to both energy and desire—forces that have been granted by the Creator (12:1). Relatedly, the term *youth* here need not be restricted, for example, merely to adolescence or later adolescence. Rather, it encompasses the season of young adulthood. Just as there is a "season" for sowing (3:2 and 11:1–2, 6), there is a "season" for "youthful" passion and strength. In fact, it is possible to argue that the writer's thrust here is not necessarily youth-versus-old age. An alternative reading is "vitality-versus-despair."[88] Inactivity, which guarantees *nothing*, is worse than ignorance and thus to be avoided.[89] Because of the image of God, human beings possess a wondrous realm of moral freedom (cf. 11:9). And the freedom to "follow the ways of your heart" is in line with earlier advice: enjoyment is the gift and the design of God, to which the previous enjoyment refrains attest.

Moreover, insofar as outcomes are out of our control, without any "guarantee," the counsel being offered here—indeed, it is not mere advice but an *imperative*—is to *make the most* of those opportunities that are available. Significantly, these statements immediately follow three forceful admonitions in 11:1, 2, and 6 ("sow," "give," and "sow") to act generously, step out in faith, and be willing to take risks (presumably, to *do good*, given that "good" is a keyword in Ecclesiastes), without any guarantee of a "return" or "gain." The "sowing" of vv. 1–6 agrees with the emphasis in Ecclesiastes on doing good.[90] What is possible in the use of our time and talents that, like "seed," may bring an unexpected "return"?[91] How might

87. This material is not idolizing of youth; rather, it represents a full-throated appreciation of its gifts.

88. Thus Ogden, "Qoheleth XI.7–XII.8," 33–34.

89. So, correctly, Holmstedt et al., *Qoheleth*, 289.

90. Verses 1–6 tend to receive two interpretations in most commentary, with no strong consensus either way. Some insist that these statements—notably 11:1–2—refer to business investments and economic affairs, while others prefer a reading that stresses charity and generosity in a more general, less literal, fashion. Since Ecclesiastes is less about financial matters than fearing God, doing good, and enjoying God's simple gifts, the latter interpretation seems more fitting. And indeed it fits with the two *carpe diem* imperatives found in 9:7–10 and 11:7–10. The burden in Ecclesiastes 11 would appear to be the maximizing of our freedom in doing good in service to God. Further evidence against an economic or financial interpretation of these verses is that finance and commercial activity require calculation, which the writer has been criticizing. Favoring the view that 11:1–6 concerns charity and generosity are Seow, *Ecclesiastes*, 335, 341–44, Magarik, "Darshanut," and Brown, *Ecclesiastes*, 99–100. Preferring the alternative interpretation—i.e., that 11:1, 2, and 6 refer to financial investments or sound economic planning—are, for example, Gordis, *Koheleth*, 320, Crenshaw, *Ecclesiastes*, 178–79, and Garrett, *Proverbs, Ecclesiastes, Song of Songs*, 338.

91. Magarik, "Darshanut," observes that, in Jewish midrashic interpretation, casting

the glory and energy of youth be channeled in a way that is meaningful, even when we do not know what tomorrow holds? Surely, it is significant that the expression "you do not know" appears four times in 11:1–6.[92] The suggestion here, which is intended to be positive, is that "you never know. what unexpectedly wonderful things might happen."[93] At bottom, uncertainty serves as an *incentive*, not a *dis*incentive, to act.[94] Simply because a farmer cannot guarantee a certain yield does not mean that he won't sow seed (11:6). What we have here is a call to invest our lives and our energies in the direction of the Creator. In this light, it is helpful to observe the various admonitions in this material:

- Rejoice in all of your years
- Consider the dark days
- Be joyful
- Let your heart give you joy
- Follow your heart
- Know that God will judge you
- Banish anxiety from your heart
- Cast off your fleshly troubles
- Remember your Creator

Such is the language of great enthusiasm, confidence, and inspiration, not frustration and resignation.[95] To rejoice in "all the years a person might

---

bread on water is a metaphor for kindness, a type of "moral investment."

92. Hereon see Glasson, "'You Never Know,'" 43–48.

93. Glasson, "'You Never Know,'" 47–48, concludes his essay with a wonderfully encouraging illustration, using the example of "sowing without knowing" done by John Wesley some 250 years ago. Following his Oxford education, Wesley began riding horseback in central Ireland and sowing seed. In time he crossed Ireland on his steed twenty-one times. "After many days" (see Eccl 11:1b), groups began springing up not only in Ireland but also in England, Scotland, and Wales. Today there are millions upon millions of Methodists and Wesleyans worldwide. In fact, if one travels to Los Angeles—a half a globe away from the British Isles—and happens to visit the campus of the University of Southern California, one is likely to visit the Bovard Administration Building, perhaps the most iconic of the campus's Renaissance-style structures. Atop that building sits a 116-foot tower with a statue of John Wesley perched thereupon.

94. So Gutridge, "Wisdom, Anti-Wisdom, and the Ethical Function of Uncertainty," 396.

95. These verses well illustrate the difference between standard interpretation of Ecclesiastes, according to which the writer is "caught" in tension between meaninglessness and the fear of God, and the interpretation being argued in the present volume:

live" (v. 8) is most assuredly *not* hebel. "Rejoice" and "remember" are the two admonitions receiving emphasis and being woven together in this unit. This link of enjoying and remembering was found in 5:18–20 as well; here, however, the material is climactic and leading to the book's conclusion. Stated in a different way, these two elements express the recurring link in Ecclesiastes between joy and the fear of God, and hence a moral realism. We "remember" our Creator because, as created beings, he has a designated pattern, and that pattern is *good*. Failure to remember one's Creator—i.e., failure to remember that we are created and not autonomous[96]—leads to the inevitable result of bitterness and regret later on in one's life.[97] Surely it is the case that virtually every human being on his or her deathbed looks back over life and regrets those opportunities that were missed or squandered. All wish that they had done more with their time, their gifts, their energies, and their possessions.[98] All in all, while this material may strike the average reader as extremely elusive,[99] it is nonetheless *very* wise counsel. And as it is, this counsel finds exact parallels in the New Testament:

- 2 Cor 9:6—"Remember this: Whoever sows sparingly will also reap sparingly, and whoever sows generously will also reap generously."

- Eph 5:15–16—"Be very careful, then, how you live—not as unwise but as wise, making the most of every opportunity."

- 2 Tim 4:2—". . . be prepared in season and out of season . . ."[100]

The resounding message here, in any event, is that life, though brief, is *not* meaningless (*hebel*); it can be utterly absorbing.[101] Joy and vexation are opposites; they are worlds removed from one another, and once again we

---

namely, that *everything* has meaning and purpose, if viewed properly (and theistically). "All is meaningless!" is not the Teacher's *own* position; it is, however, the outlook that he wishes to demolish.

96. One might argue that all of the evils of the world have a common root: they issue from human pretensions to *be like* God.

97. Garrett's comments regarding these verses (*Proverbs, Ecclesiastes, Song of Songs*, 340–41) are full of insight.

98. Perry, "Planning the Twilight Years," prefers a literal rather than conventional allegorical reading of 12:1–8.

99. Not surprisingly, both Jewish as well as early Christian and medieval exegesis of 11:1–12:7 tended to be allegorical, under the assumption of a *contemptus mundi* (contempt of the world). Luther, in significant ways, will challenge this long-standing tradition (see chapter 6).

100. NIV.

101. Kidner, *A Time to Mourn*, 59, has captured the spirit of this *carpe diem* imperative quite admirably.

are witnesses to the writer's literary-rhetorical strategy, which is to contrast opposites, in order to move the reader toward a verdict.[102] These statements together call to mind the sort of disposition undergirding the Augustinian maxim "Love God, and do what you will." Once more, the connection between enjoyment and the fear of God can be observed to surface here in this cluster of imperatives. The latter serves as a necessary guide, with its properly delineated boundaries. There exists indeed a "profit" that death, though inevitable, *cannot* eliminate. Life's uncertainties, it is true, serve as a bridle on our motivations and emotions; but they also serve as an incentive to be faithful stewards of what we have been given. Even granting life's unexpected sorrows and disappointments, as seen from a metaphysical standpoint, life *is* "sweet"; it is most assuredly not "meaningless." And that sweetness is an ultimate *good*. For if light and life are indeed "sweet" (11:7), then it is wonderful to be alive.

A Summary of the Argument in Ecclesiastes

The enjoyment refrains distributed throughout Ecclesiastes play a crucial role in identifying an overall structure to the writer's argument, and hence in properly understanding the message of the book. They serve as interludes in the wider thesis between the bookends of 1:2 and 12:8: "Meaningless! Meaningless. Everything is meaningless!" In their literary-rhetorical function they stand juxtaposed to—they are the antithesis of—the *hebel* or "meaninglessness" thesis. With supreme dexterity, the writer moves back and forth between two competing outlooks on ultimate reality, exposing the grimness of life lived not as a "gift" to be received from the Creator but as a transaction or an entity to be "gained" (cf. 1:3, 2:11, 3:9, and 5:16) by means of human striving and determination. In a world of no enduring value, life is chaotic and without meaning. If all of life is without meaning and pointless (*hebel*), then one will need to admit that it is pointless to engage in work, for therein can be found no enjoyment or satisfaction, no meaning or purpose—only misery.[103]

---

102. The painful process of reflection and reaching a verdict, perhaps after a change of thinking, is captured in the epilogue: "The words of the wise are like goads, their collected sayings like firmly embedded nails . . ." (12:11). Just as goads or nails served as a cattle prod to move livestock—often oxen—in the desired direction, so the words of the wise, if they have value, cut to the heart of the listener.

103. The average reader today can scarcely appreciate enough the weight of the Teacher's emphasis on finding *satisfaction in work*. In *all of antiquity*, up until the Christian advent, every dominant culture had a deficient view of human labor. Hence, the "Judeo-Christian" perspective on human labor is a radical departure—philosophically,

But because the writer affirms a theology of creation, several important and interrelated consequences follow; three in particular need emphasizing. First, humankind can experience life and joy as divine gifts, since life—*all* of life—has meaning and purpose. Second, the divine gift of practical wisdom in life's experiences can be recognized and acquired, even with our human limitations; true wisdom and a "worldly" wisdom are being contrasted. And third, work itself can grant a measure of satisfaction where and when it is done faithfully and with the proper motivation, since work is our vocation based on (a) our being fashioned in the image of God and (b) our "assignment" (*heleq*) from God. Enjoyment—by which the writer is signifying contentment or satisfaction and which is symbolized by eating and drinking (i.e., shared fellowship around the table) and working—is a divine "gift" as depicted in Ecclesiastes. Gifts are to be received, and these particular gifts of God are *intrinsic* to the life of faith. For this reason, they are not merely "external," "antiseptic," "sedative," or "palliative" forms of "distraction" from the "pain" of normal living, contrary to the dominant line of reasoning in much commentary.[104] Nor is joy "absurdly minimal" as depicted in Ecclesiastes.[105] To the contrary, the joy being depicted in the *carpe diem* refrains from 2:24–26 through 11:7–12:1a mirrors an in-breaking of "eternity" (3:11), as it were. They are not palliative or narcotic or external in nature; rather, they are internal, constitutive, and grounding in their character.

The fact that enjoyment and "gifts" are to be received and not pursued or viewed as *ends in themselves* illustrates the two clashing world- and life-views on display in the book. In point of fact, as noted above, the writer has used the rhetorical device "nothing is better" four times throughout the treatise to emphasize the matter of life's enjoyment, work's satisfaction, and the truth that such is a "gift" of God (2:24–26; 3:12–13; 3:22; and 8:15).[106] God's gifts, moreover, are declared "good" in six of these intervals (3:12; 5:17; 7:14; 8:15; 9:7; and 11:9). Together, these markers underscore not the Creator's *harshness* but his *benevolence*, not God's *tyranny* but his *gracious governance* of all things. The result is not a *bitter resignation* but a *joyful humility* before the Creator. Joy is the "portion" or "inheritance" (*heleq*) of the one who fears God.[107] And this joy induces us to accept our role as stewards, and thus, to

---

anthropologically, and ethically—from that of the dominant culture. The doctrines of creation and the *imago Dei* have the effect of *utterly transforming* how human beings envision their identities, their labors, and their endeavors.

104. See chapter 3.

105. Contra Brown, "'Whatever Your Hand Finds to Do,'" 281.

106. See Ogden, "The 'Better'-Proverb (*Tôb-Spruch*)," "Qoheleth's Use of the 'Nothing is Better'-Form," and "Qoheleth's Summons to Enjoyment and Reflection."

107. Based on the frequency of its appearance (eight times in the book),

make the most of life and our work. We find meaning in day-to-day activity *only* if we have found meaning at a deeper level in life. And in a culture of hedonism, materialism, totalitarian consumerism, and militant secularism, the message of Ecclesiastes is *desperately* needed.

The Essence of Joy: Finding Satisfaction in One's Work

Finding satisfaction in one's work is the opposite—the very *antithesis*—of "chasing the wind" and "futility." In granting satisfaction in our labor, God sanctifies, as it were, the ordinary. In the words of one observer, "The momentous and the mundane are wedded under God's providential work."[108] Correlatively, the Judeo-Christian tradition knows no split or dichotomy between manual and mental labor, in contradistinction to the Greco-Roman cultural tradition. The reason for this is quite simply that we are created in God's likeness (Gen 1:26–27). Furthermore, the enjoyment of our labor is not merely some momentary phenomenon—here one minute and then gone the next. Rather, it has a *residual effect* in the believer's life: "This is what will *accompany* them in their hard work, *during the lifetime* that God gives under the sun" (8:15, emphasis added). Such an understanding of work, hence, negates the belief, shared by many, that "Work has meaning only through what it produces."[109] To the contrary. The satisfaction toward which Ecclesiastes points us is both *in* and *through* the task, not merely the *result* of our tedious efforts. Moreover, as argued above, this satisfaction or contentment is an intrinsic, qualitative good to be savored, not some "pain killer" or "anesthetic" that serves to "distract" us from the evil around us.[110] Neither does enjoyment "offset" the "wearisome" nature of work, serving as "solace" or "comfort"; nor is human labor a "misfortune to be endured."[111]

---

heleq—rendered "lot," "portion," or "inheritance"—would seem to be a keyword in Ecclesiastes.

108. Brown, *Wisdom's Wonder*, 169.

109. Thus, Ellul, *Reason for Being*, 93.

110. While my response to this distortion was offered in chapter 3, it is worth reiterating that this negative interpretation and misjudging of the text (and the writer's argument) are remarkably widespread in standard Ecclesiastes commentary. Representative are Fox, *A Time to Tear Down*, 239; Longman, *The Book of Ecclesiastes*, 106–10, 123, 168–69, 221, and 230–31; and Walsh, "Despair as a Theological Virtue," 46–49. Walsh ends up extracting from Ecclesiastes the *very opposite* message of what the writer intends, asserting that the spirituality being advocated in the book is "the most total type of asceticism, since it must be carried out in the absence of a meaningful relationship with God" (48).

111. Against Mitchell, "'Work' in Ecclesiastes," 134–35, 137.

Some material in Ecclesiastes—for example, material comprising statements recorded in 1:3, 2:11, and 2:17—seems to suggest that humans are not made for work, that our efforts are futile and our energies wasted. But the grim tone employed by the Teacher in the lament of 1:3–2:23, coupled with the literary-rhetorical strategy of juxtaposition utilized throughout the book, indicate that the Teacher is mirroring and reacting against *conventional* views of work. Against much Ecclesiastes commentary and as evidenced by the "enjoyment" refrains, there *is* lasting profit in our endeavors and our labor; such is a "gift" of God to those who humbly acknowledge his providence and inscrutable ways. Consistent with "wisdom literature," which values, commends, and dignifies work, the secret of work as portrayed in Ecclesiastes lies in recognizing that, given our design,[112] we humans work not for self-promotion or the acquisition of earthly honors and pleasures but for the sheer joy, as stewards of God, of investing our lives, our gifts, and our wider callings in the lives of others and in the promotion of the common good around us. We may rest assured that this willingness to *serve* pleases the heart of God our Creator, and we need only recall Jesus' reiteration of the Great Command: serve God and serve others.[113]

Ecclesiastes, as we have attempted to demonstrate, depicts work in a way that is utterly relevant to our contemporary world, just as it always has been. Not only is human labor part of Ecclesiastes's taxonomy of joy, it is (or *should* be) part of the Christian's as well. Hence, it remains an important part of Christian ethical reflection, lodged at the very center of Christian vocation, which—properly understood—transforms our understanding of work. We are *created* for work, and as vice-regents of all of creation we *co-create* with the living God.[114] From the beginning it has been God's purpose that people find joy and fulfillment in their work, as suggested by wisdom literature elsewhere:

- Prov 12:24—diligents hands will rule

- Prov 13:11—faithful persistence brings an increase

- Prov 22:29—skill in our work creates strategic opportunities

112. Work *per se* is never presented in the Old Testament as degrading or needing an escape. Even with the fall, it is not *work* that is cursed; it is the ground (Gen 3). Human beings are designed for work, created in the likeness of God. Consequently, the Hebrew view of work was radically different from that of Mesopotamians, Egyptians, Greeks, and Romans.

113. Matt 22:37–39; Mark 12:30–31; and Luke 10:27; cf. Lev 19:18, 34.

114. While the ground was cursed due to the fall (Genesis 3), *work* itself was not; it remains part of our created nature, and creation is still "good."

And based on the creation mandate (Gen 2:15), it is our calling to exercise dominion over *all* of creation.[115] This theological reality, based on creation, means that work is *intrinsically* valuable and satisfying. This endowment and propensity, it needs reiterating, are from the Creator and a part of the *imago Dei*.

Thus, Ecclesiastes has not "lost something that was characteristic of Hebrew thought and piety [or, of the "traditional" wisdom perspective] in an earlier period,"[116] as not a few commentators—past and present—presume. Neither is the enjoyment found in Ecclesiastes either the standard utilitarian "living for the moment" ("Enjoy yourself, *the little* that it is possible") or a state of mind located somewhere between zeal and resignation ("Enjoy yourself, *if* possible"), both of which express what might be called a "hedonism born from despair."[117] In this light, it needs emphasizing that no book was ever *less* "Epicurean" than the book of Ecclesiastes, given its emphasis on satisfaction in and through *human labor*. What is more, no book has ever demonstrated more the relationship between joy and godly fear.

Nor is it legitimate to view the depiction of work in particular or enjoyment more generally in Ecclesiastes as "sub-Christian," as a surprising number of commentators assume.[118] It is misguided to read Ecclesiastes in terms of Christ's fulfillment of messianic promise or the "new covenant," and therefore to interpret Ecclesiastes as "sub-Christian," inasmuch as wisdom literature, based on its *function*, is not meant to be read as salvation history. So, for example, proverbial sayings are true because they correspond to *the reality of the created order*, whether that applies to human beings before or after the Christian advent.[119] They are as true for Christians as they are for Jews, Muslims, polytheists, and agnostics, and they are no less true today than they were for Mesopotamians, Egyptians, Persians, and Greeks before the coming of Christ. While it is true that "a greater than Solomon" has come,[120] we read Job, Proverbs, Ecclesiastes, and various Psalms as "wisdom literature," which addresses perennial matters of living and is applicable at all times to all people in all socio-cultural contexts.

115. This biblical mandate *cannot* be viewed as the *cause* of ecological abuse, particularly in our day when ecological activism (whether religious or secular) would attempt to lay the blame for abuse at religious believers' feet.

116. So Paterson, *The Book That Is Alive*, 143.

117. Whybray, *Ecclesiastes*, 64.

118. Contra, for example, Loader, *Ecclesiastes*, 15; Greidanus, *Preaching Christ from Ecclesiastes*, 24–29; and O'Donnell, *The Beginning and End of Wisdom*, 72–76.

119. In this regard we are reminded by the New Testament that *Christ himself* is the Creator of all things, as is implied in the prologue of the Fourth Gospel (John 1:1–3), stated categorically by the Apostle Paul (Col 1:15–20), and briefly reiterated by the writer of the epistle to the Hebrews (Heb 1:2).

120. Luke 11:31.

To read Ecclesiastes as biblical theology, at the center of which stands human creation in the *imago Dei*, teaches us that we are *designed* for joy and satisfaction—a norm that is *not* eliminated or abolished by the presence of suffering or sin in our lives. Human beings are created to flourish. The equivalent of joy and satisfaction being mirrored in Ecclesiastes can be found in assorted Old Testament "wisdom" psalms, which underscore—and quite typically highly extol—*God's design in creation*. Psalm 104 is one such example:

> He makes grass grow for the cattle,
> And plants for man to cultivate—
> Bringing forth food from the earth;
> Wine that gladdens the heart of man,
> Oil to make his face shine,
> And bread that sustains his heart . . .
>
> Then man goes out to his work,
> To labor until evening.
> How many are your works, O LORD!
> In wisdom you made them all . . .
>
> These all look to you
> To give them their food at the proper time.
> When you give it to them,
> They gather it up;
> When you open your hand,
> They are satisfied with good things.
> When you hide your face,
> They are terrified;
> When you take away their breath,
> They die and return to the dust. (104:14–15, 23–24, 27–29, NIV)

One Old Testament theologian beautifully captures the essence of the divine norm for human beings based on their design: "When human life is thus surrounded [i.e., surrounded by children, friendship, wisdom, opportunities for charity, the experience of beauty, and freedom] and upheld by God's blessed will, man's basic mood in relation to his task and his destiny is one of joy."[121] This, then, is the response to "meaninglessness" which unfolds in the message of Ecclesiastes—a norm that is anchored in creation, guarded by providence, and conditioned by the fear of the Lord (12:13).

---

121. Eichrodt, *Man in the Old Testament*, 34. Eichrodt observes further: "Joy is the fine expression of what it meant for the Old Testament understanding that Israel's consciousness . . . was opened to the width and richness of the world of creation" (35). And, indeed, because of the creation model the same applies to the Christian as well.

— 6 —

Concluding Thoughts on the
"End of the Matter"

FOLLOWING WHAT IS BASICALLY a "call to decision"[1] (11:1–12:8), and after all has been considered in Ecclesiastes (12:9–14), the writer's argument, presented in the postscript's third-person form, concludes: the "end of the matter" is that humankind *revere God*. The secret of human existence, then, is to acknowledge human limitations and be receptive to God the Creator and his works. Transcendence and divine inscrutability should, in the end, induce the fear of God in human beings. This posture, as mirrored in Ecclesiastes, is based on rational and joyful openness to the Creator. Where, however, human openness to the divine is absent and resisted, God's ways and God's work end up alienating us, rendering us cynical and skeptical.[2] If any wisdom is to be found among human beings, it will lead a person away from the absurdity of a metaphysical materialist outlook on life ("secularism" as we modern readers understand it) and to the acknowledgment of the mystery of divine providence.

The "fear of God," in the end, is the final word (12:13–14). Transcendent reality leads human creatures, in the words of the psalmist, to "be still and know" that he is God (Ps 46:10). The theme of divine reverence, it needs emphasizing, has occurred six times—spaced intermittently—throughout Ecclesiastes—in 3:14; 5:7; 7:18; 8:12–13 (twice); and 12:13.[3] Thus, in the mes-

---

1. So Eaton, *Ecclesiastes*, 139.

2. Thus, as an example, Murphy, *Ecclesiastes*, 39, describes divine inscrutability in terms of "desperate trickery." Inscrutability, however, it needs emphasizing, is not *injustice*. To fail to grasp God's works and God's purposes does *not* mean that God is harsh or malevolent. Murphy is simply representative of a host of commentators who bring their own theological deficiencies *to* the text of Ecclesiastes (eisegesis) rather than drawing meaning *out of* the text itself (exegesis).

3. Cf. Job 28:28; Ps 111:10; Prov 1:7; 9:10; 14:26, 27; 15:33; 16:6; 19:23; 22:4; 23:17;

sage of Ecclesiastes we clearly have no "Chicken Soup for the Soul" approach to positive thinking or spirituality, by any stretch of the imagination.[4]

A Recasting of Human Labor

All told, throughout Ecclesiastes everything that constitutes normative human activity, inclusive of human labor, has been addressed. The writer does not despise or devalue work; rather, he recasts and sanctifies it.[5] Specifically within a theocentric context, work is portrayed not as "meaningless toil" but rather as (a) a source of satisfaction and (b) a gift from God (2:24; 3:13; 5:18–20; 8:15; and 9:10 [implied]). That various translations render the three Hebrew terms designating "work" in Ecclesiastes—'āmāl, 'ānāh, and 'asâ—as "toil" is, as already noted, in some ways misleading insofar as "toil" in English almost always carries a *negative* connotation. On occasion in the treatise a negative connotation *is* intended, but on other occasions it is *not* intended, as context often makes clear.[6] Context, then, must help guide the reader when and where work is being portrayed throughout the book. Where human activity is self-serving and self-promoting, the fruits of human labor are indeed "meaningless" or "profitless," whereby—at least in common English parlance—work *is* "toil," "drudgery," and a "heavy burden." Where, in stark contrast, life is received as a "gift of God," joy and contentment express themselves both *in and through* human labor.

Because human beings are fashioned in the image of God, work is *that for which we are created*. Hence, it is not some "burdensome toil" that is meaningless (or next to meaningless) in nature or a "necessary evil," as some—even professing Christians—would believe.[7] That God himself delights in his own work and that it is called "very good" (Gen 1:31) should tell us something about the intrinsic nature and value of work.[8] Human

---

and 28:14. The fear of God, in any event, as a theme is at home in the wisdom tradition.

4. O'Dowd, "Epistemology in Ecclesiastes," 216, captures this sentiment precisely.

5. So Brown, "'Whatever Your Hand Finds to Do,'" 279.

6. The verb 'āmāl appears thirteen times in Ecclesiastes. Outside of Ecclesiastes, significantly, the term does not carry a sense of difficulty or burden. As a noun, it appears twenty-two times in Ecclesiastes and thirteen times in the Psalms. On its appearance and usage generally in the Old Testament, see Thompson, "'āmāl,'" 435.

7. This negative perception of work in part is an extension of the ancient—and to a large extent, medieval—distinction between "contemplative" and "active" (i.e., manual) labor, out of which—in its application—varied forms of slavery were justified. Manual labor, to many in our day, is undignified. While few people would admit to this attitude, it is broadly assumed in our cultural context.

8. In *Every Good Endeavor*, Keller and Alsdorf properly stress the "deep untapped

labor *is* "meaningless" only apart from a theocentric motivation and when or where it is undertaken as an end in itself. Our argument has been that *work as both a sign of contentment and a divine gift* is part of the writer's broader theme of enjoyment.

Moreover, the dual admonition central to the message of Ecclesiastes—fear God and enjoy the life he gives you—accords with the command given to Israel by Israel's God: "so that you, your children and their children after them may fear the Lord your God as long as you live . . . and so that you may enjoy long life" (Deut 6:2).[9] In fact, Ecclesiastes is the source of the *carpe diem* ("seize the day") admonition familiar to many readers: "Whatever your hand finds to do, do it with all your might!" (9:10).[10] Neither is this the language of divine determinism, nor is it a portrait of drudgery and toil, nor does it mirror a "harsh" and "distant" God, as many would suppose. It is, rather, a challenge to invest ourselves and make the most of our gifts and abilities as well as our opportunities—a challenge which, unlike the rest of life, knows *no (known) limits* and which is truly exhilarating. And indeed this seemingly stark incongruity invites our consideration: the very same treatise that, in the strongest terms, presents divine inscrutability also exhorts the reader to take great "risks" in sowing seed (11:1, 2, and 6) and maximizing opportunity (9:10). Providence and free will co-exist gloriously in some mysterious way.

While most people are familiar with the emphasis in Ecclesiastes on the "vanity" or "meaninglessness" of life, little attention in standard commentary has been given to these intermittent and juxtaposed "wisdom" observations about work as a "satisfying gift" or means of "seizing the day." What's more, the sad reality is that this perspective on work from Ecclesiastes is wholly absent from teaching and preaching found in the Christian church. And at the most basic level, one typically will not hear sermons and teaching that attempt to reconcile the realities of joy and the fear of God. One can only explain this phenomenon on the basis of theological illiteracy that inhabits the pulpit and the church's leadership.[11]

---

potential for cultivation" of all of creation (22). Would to God that this emphasis be found in standard Christian teaching and preaching and in our training of Christian leadership. In fact, based on standard teaching and preaching, one would never guess that the *marketplace* is a high and noble calling. A good part of the reason for this, of course, is due to our focus, the "spiritual life"—i.e., the "vertical" dimension of faith rather than the "horizontal."

9. NIV.

10. Most people will perhaps recognize this expression from the 1938 poem of the same name by Robert Frost, if not from the first-century-BCE Roman poet Horace.

11. And, as suggested throughout the present volume, professional scholars of the Old Testament have not served the pastorate—and hence the wider Christian

The writer's observations on satisfying work, it should be remembered, agree with another wisdom saying: "In all labor there is profit" (Prov 14:23a[12])—a "profit" that is measured not foremost in economic terms but in *contentment*. Note, once more, the "contradiction": human labor is declared "meaningless" (1:3, 10, 18-19; 4:4, 8; 5:12, 16; and 8:16), and it is portrayed as meaningful and satisfying (2:24; 3:13, 22; 5:18, 19; 8:15; and 9:10 [implied]). Both outlooks cannot be correct.

In the final analysis, I am not contending that pain and pessimism or toil and drudgery are absent from Ecclesiastes (and hence from the human experience); such is not my argument. It is only that pessimism is (a) one voice and (b) not the writer's own position and conclusion. Moreover, my interpretation assumes (c) a difference between despair or resignation and hardship or suffering. If pessimism, despair, and resignation were in fact *the* message of Ecclesiastes—"Everything is meaningless. Period."—then it would be reasonable both to assume and to argue that death would be portrayed as a *release* from the absurdity of human existence and that the book *per se* would have ultimately been excluded from the canon of Scripture. Neither, however, is the case. On the matter of death, it needs emphasizing that death is not portrayed in the book as a *release* from life's absurdity; it is portrayed as life's final arbiter.

Internal evidence, as we have attempted to argue, reveals in Ecclesiastes the presence of a "dialogue"—a dialogue between two competing frameworks for interpreting reality.[13] It is true that the reader is easily swayed—by means of the writer's comprehensive "All is meaningless" language, not only at beginning (1:2) and end (12:8) but intermittently throughout—to bypass a competing voice ("under heaven") that is intermittent yet, in my view, potent and decisive.[14] The text of Ecclesiastes itself, as it turns out, supplies its own rebuttal to the voice of "meaninglessness." And in this dialogue, we should note the final piece of advice given, in 11:9: *pursue a joy that is tempered with sobriety*. After all, hedonists, gluttons, and workaholics tend not to reflect on God's wisdom and his good gifts. And it is on that note that the dialogue in Ecclesiastes ends.

---

church—very well, either in seeing the great value of wisdom literature more generally or in gleaning insights from the book of Ecclesiastes in particular. I say this with sadness.

12. NASB.

13. Hereon see Perry, *Dialogues with Kohelet.*

14. Not many commentators seem prepared to wrestle adequately with this tension. Exceptions include Whybray, Ogden, and Lee.

Allowing Wisdom to Speak

There is a tendency among some Old Testament commentators to treat the writer of Ecclesiastes as a sort of foil for the Christian gospel, as if in Qoheleth the teacher we are witnesses to a defective person who is "in dire need of rehabilitation"[15] or as if he were confused, despairing, and resigned to life's misfortunes—a state or condition that is "resolved" in the New Covenant through Christ. But such a reading errs at several levels. Most significantly, it fails to recognize the universality, the enduring nature, and the function of wisdom literature and the wisdom perspective. When, for example, proverbs entreat us to eschew sloth and be diligent or seek wisdom or act justly or be good stewards or rescue the perishing, this is not some unique "Christian" insight that is only relevant (or newly relevant) to the "New Covenant"; it is a *human* insight, based on creation and applying to all people everywhere at all times. The wisdom perspective, *perennially* true and necessary for life, speaks to our humanity and our limitations, whether we are Christian or non-Christian, occupying history "before Christ" or "after Christ." The reality of divine providence, the goodness of creation, divine inscrutability, the fear of God, and the need for wisdom are *every bit as true* and valuable in the New Covenant era as they were prior. Alas, Ecclesiastes serves, in an *abiding* way, as an effective "apologetic." It presents a dialectic that *continually* informs people of the need for transcendent faith by presenting the grimness of the metaphysical alternative.[16]

Perhaps Ecclesiastes is consigned to neglect—in the past and in our day—because it confronts us with what we as autonomous, self-serving individuals fear the most. It is withering in its exposure of life's absurdity and nakedness when human existence has been bleached of an acknowledgment of God whose ways are inscrutable. At bottom, in its own unique way Ecclesiastes is a guide—an invaluable one at that—to living faithfully in a world or cultural context that at best is agnostic and at worst is hostile to the One who is creator, sustainer, and judge of all things. Perhaps, then, it is high time that Western societies be exposed for what they are. From the wisdom perspective, a "fool" is not merely some imbecile; rather, he is one who resists the witness of truth as it is on display in creation, in human nature, and in human activity. Particularly in our day, science[17] tends to

15. So Brown, *Ecclesiastes*, 121.

16. Helpful reminders of this can be found in Provan, "Fresh Perspectives on Ecclesiastes," and Fredericks, "Preaching Qohelet."

17. Because science (properly understood) has flourished most in cultural contexts in which faith in the Creator has flourished (hereon see, for example, Carroll and Shiflett, "Christianity and Science"), we should perhaps speak here of "scientism," which

replace the human need for wisdom. But science is incapable of producing wisdom. Wisdom cannot be manufactured; rather, it must *grow*. In the end, wisdom makes us aware of our limits.

A Recasting of Work and "Vocation": The Lutheran Breakthrough

While a secularist-materialist perspective strips life and life's vocation of its inherently religious meaning, "vocation" properly understood infuses mundane secular life—the "ordinary"—with meaning and significance. Such renewed understanding of the "ordinary" occurred in significant ways 500 years ago in Western history. One of the breakthroughs of early sixteenth-century Protestant reform was to recover a deeper understanding of the notion of *vocation*, given the Reformers' conviction that more than a millennium of the church's devaluing of human work, aside from a "calling" to the priesthood and the monastery, was at stake.

In Martin Luther's reaction to this devaluation, it is utterly fascinating to find that the book of Ecclesiastes played no small role in helping shape his thinking on human labor and *vocatio*.[18] In *Notes on Ecclesiastes*, Luther offers the following reflection:

> No less noxious for a proper understanding of this book [Ecclesiastes] has been the influence of many of the saintly and illustrious theologians in the church, who thought that in this book Solomon was teaching what they call "the contempt for the world" [*contemptus mundi*].[19]

Here Luther is citing Jerome as an example, who encourages fourth-century monastic life in the preface of his *Commentarius in Ecclesiastia*[20] and whose

---

conflates open-minded search for truth with militant secular-materialism that has little regard for whether "truth" exists. Helpfully distinguishing between the two is Lawler and Guerra, eds., *Science, Virtue, and the Future of Humanity*.

18. We know that Luther lectured on Ecclesiastes at the University of Wittenberg from July until November of 1526, based on the notes of a student. Luther had asked his colleague Philip Melanchthon to do a new translation from Hebrew to Latin, but Luther did not get around to a commentary. Someone who was influenced by him, however, did in 1528, to which Luther then would write a preface. Four years later Luther's lecture notes did in fact become a commentary of his own, which was translated into English in 1972 by Jaroslav Pelikan.

19. Luther, *Notes on Ecclesiastes*, 4.

20. For an English translation, see St. Jerome, *Commentary on Ecclesiastes*.

"contempt for the world" interpretation would be standard for most of the church for over a millennium.[21]

The first teaching to observe in Ecclesiastes's message, according to Luther, is that the book condemns not the realm of the created but "depraved affection and human striving." The second point made by Luther needing the reader's attention is that the Teacher is "clearly himself within the limits of human nature," that is, within "the efforts, the endeavors, and the desires" that are acceptable based on creation.[22] At the heart of the book's message is a human tendency: "the vanity of the human heart . . . is never content with the gifts of God that are present."[23]

It has been said that Jerome's interpretation of Ecclesiastes, against which Luther was reacting, was less an exegesis of the text than it was a *reinterpretation* in his own likeness.[24] On the other hand, the parallels between Jewish and Christian interpretation of the book are remarkable; both developed a spiritual/allegorical interpretation that would be standard for well over a millennium. In any event, Jerome's interpretation was enduring.[25] Given the opening salvo of the book—"Everything is vanity" [*Vanitas vanitatorum*]—there were good reasons, in Jerome's view, for being detached from this temporal world. If everything that God made is "good," then how can everything be not only *vanitas* but *vanitas vanitatorum?* he reasons.[26] Offering commentary on Eccl 1:3, Jerome observes that men sweat "in vain in the labor of this world"; "they carry nothing from all their labor with them" out of this life.[27] "All things pass away," he bemoans, and "the universe declines toward its own end."[28] Significantly, Jerome's interpretation of 1:2 is figurative: "If a living person is vanity, it follows that a dead person is the

21. The creation order for Jerome is not "good" in an ontological sense or in the sense that Reformed theologians would understand creation; rather, it is "vanity," based on Eccl 1:2 and 12:8. According to Kallas, "Ecclesiastes," whose definitive study explores Ecclesiastes interpretation from Jerome down to the sixteenth-century Protestant reformers, no medieval exegete challenged Jerome's interpretation of Ecclesiastes.

22. Luther, *Notes on Ecclesiastes*, 9.

23. Luther, *Notes on Ecclesiastes* , 10.

24. Provan, *Ecclesiastes, Song of Songs*, 25.

25. Kallas, "Ecclesiastes," 172, describes the influence of Jerome's allegorical interpretation of Ecclesiastes, until the Lutheran breakthrough, as a "stranglehold." In one of the few studies that examines medieval exegesis of Ecclesiastes, Eliason, "*Vanitas Vanitatum*," 18–19, observes that interest in the book of Ecclesiastes appears to have peaked in the early fourteenth century.

26. St. Jerome, *Commentary on Ecclesiastes* 1.2, 35.

27. St. Jerome, *Commentary on Ecclesiastes* 1.2, 36.

28. St. Jerome, *Commentary on Ecclesiastes* 1.2, 36.

vanity of vanities."[29] And with an allusion to 1 Cor 13:10, Jerome concludes that "all is vanity until the perfect comes."[30]

Contemptus mundi, then, was to be understood not merely as a relative "good" but as an *independent*, even *necessary*, "good." The world, as Jerome sees it, is *pro nihilo* and not "good." "Goodness" and "vanity," he reasons, can be neither equated nor reconciled. The implication, therefore, is clear: since *everything* in this world is *vanitas*, passing away, and subject to mutation, we are to live in a detached manner. Understandably, something of an apocalyptic tone informs and colors much of Jerome's commentary on Ecclesiastes, which, of course, is to be anticipated if one is writing from the standpoint of *contemptus mundi*.

It is important to understand attitudes toward work that surface in the early church, particularly among monastic writers. As it was, Jerome's *contemptus mundi* did not simply appear out of nowhere. It is an interpretive outlook that traces itself from earlier fathers as well as rabbinic commentary. In the late second century, Tertullian posed the famously provocative question "What does Jerusalem have to do with Athens?"[31] in his *Prescriptions against Heretics* (AD 198) in a way that would help define the thinking of many believers not only in the early church but for centuries to come in terms of their involvement in temporal affairs. Tertullian's question, of course, was rhetorical, and his answer, spelled out not only in *Prescriptions* but also in his well-known *On Idolatry* (written a few years later), was essentially this: "Little to nothing." It was a response rooted in a presumption of *contemptus mundi*.[32] By "Athens," Tertullian was referring primarily to intellectual culture and the life of the mind—whether the study of philosophy, language, history, literature, the arts, or the sciences. And, of course, by "Jerusalem" he meant the life of faith and redemption through Christ. Offering further context to his rhetorical question, Tertullian observes: "After Jesus Christ we have no need of speculation, after the Gospel no need of research. When we come to believe, we have no desire to believe anything else; for we begin by believing that there is nothing else which we have to believe."[33] Since we have Christ, who is the end of all things, he reasons,

---

29. St. Jerome, *Commentary on Ecclesiastes* 1.2, 35.

30. St. Jerome, *Commentary on Ecclesiastes* 1.2, 36.

31. While most attempts to cite Tertullian get the order wrong—usually the translation is rendered "What does Athens have to do with Jerusalem?"—we generally sense, correctly, the overall thrust of Tertullian's rhetorical question.

32. The earlier Tertullian, for example, as mirrored in his *Apology*, was far less isolationist than the later, sectarian Tertullian.

33. *Prescriptions against Heretics* 7; I am relying on the English translation of *Prescriptions* provided by and accessible at http://www.tertullian.org/articles/

why do we need "Athens"? After all, on the last day we will not be judged according to how much pagan wisdom we have assimilated. Consequently, does not our involvement in the temporal world then, at bottom, amount to "fiddling while Rome is burning"?

It is the tendency of the Tertullians of any age to remind us that we are *in* the world but not *of* it. They prefer, with not only Tertullian himself but a host of fathers including Jerome in some respects,[34] to emphasize the "not of it" part of the equation. Hence, not the goodness of creation and the related creation mandate of Genesis but *contemptus creatio* is to be accentuated. The ever-present Tertullian error, alas, fails to take seriously all of creation, which was declared intrinsically "good" (Gen 1:31). Thus, *contemptus mundi* downplays or ignores human culture and the temporal world in which we live and of which we are a part. As a consequence, it fails to appreciate the width and breadth of redemption—a doctrine which, as already noted, is properly understood as creation *restored*.[35]

The early monastic tradition, as one historian points out, appears to have inherited the attitude that those who chose to work for a living were second-rate Christians, with the consequence that

> work often came to be seen as a debasing and demeaning activity, best left to one's social—and spiritual—inferiors. If the social patricians of ancient Rome regarded work as below their status, it has to be said that a spiritual aristocracy appears to have developed within early Christianity with equally negative and dismissive attitudes towards manual labor. Such attitudes probably reached their height during the Middle Ages.[36]

Such attitudes, moreover, appear to have informed the church's reading of Ecclesiastes. Jerome's interpretation, as it happened, would dominate the church's reading of the book for well over a millennium. "There was very little disagreement," writes one medieval scholar, over what the Teacher taught in Ecclesiastes:

> His subject was contempt for the world. The . . . descriptions of the world in constant but unproductive change suggested to medieval readers very good reasons for withholding one's trust

---

greenslade_prae/greenslade_prae.htm).

34. This is not to deny Jerome's contributions in terms of Bible translation.

35. Consider, for example, Paul's teaching in his letter to the Christians in Colossae (Col 1:15–20): Christ, who created all things, is both the *goal* and the *agent* of redemption. That he is both creator and redeemer underscores the essential fact of the *goodness and value* of all of creation—both material and non-material, visible and invisible.

36. McGrath, "Calvin and the Christian Calling," 33.

in the *temporalia* which make up the world. As a result, the major enterprise in commenting on Ecclesiastes in the Middle Ages was the effort to distinguish between those things which last and those things which don't.[37]

The sheer influence of Jerome's interpretation can be seen almost 800 years later. One very popular and influential *contemptus mundi* reading in the Middle Ages was Pope Innocent III's *De miseria condicionis humane* ("On the Misery of the Human Condition"), published in 1195. Written by Innocent while he was still Cardinal Losario, the work survives to this day in almost 700 manuscripts and, remarkably, had undergone nearly fifty printed editions by Luther's day. The three principal sources of human moral failings identified by Losario in *De miseria* are riches, pleasures, and honors. The following brief extract illustrates contemporary medieval thinking about the world:

> There is nothing without labor under the sun, there is nothing without defect under the moon, there is nothing without vanity in time. For time is the period of motion of mutable things. "Vanity of vanities," says Ecclesiastes, and "all is vanity." O how various are the endeavors of men, how diverse are their efforts! Yet there is one end and the same consequence for all: labor and vexation of spirit.[38]

Consider for the moment that statement: "There is one end and the same consequence for all: *labor and vexation of spirit.*" Surely, these words resonate with every human being, or so it would seem.

Far more familiar to the average reader is another medieval tract, Thomas à Kempis's *The Imitation of Christ*, which mirrors in the early fifteenth century a similar attitude toward the temporal realm: "Strive to withdraw your heart from the love of visible things, and direct your affections to things invisible. For those who follow only their natural inclinations defile their conscience, and lose the grace of God."[39] Tellingly, the introductory section of *Imitation* is titled "Of the imitation of Christ, and of contempt of the world and all its vanities." Among those things condemned as "vanity" in *Imitation* are seeking after "riches that shall perish," coveting "honors," pride and "to lift ourselves on high," and "to desire a long life." The introduction to *Imitation* concludes with a citation of Ecclesiastes: "The eye is not satisfied with seeing, nor the ear with hearing.

---

37. Kallas, "Ecclesiastes," 51.

38. Losarío dei Segni (Pope Innocent III), *De miseria condicionis humane*, 108.

39. Thomas à Kempis, *The Imitation of Christ* 1.1.

Strive, therefore, to turn away thy heart from the love of things that are seen, and to set it upon the things that are not seen."[40]

During the medieval era there existed a remarkable fascination with the figure of Solomon and his persona.[41] Jerome, in his writing, had assumed not only Solomonic authorship but also that Solomon had repented of his sins. As it was, the virtues of repentance would figure ever more prominently in the medieval era. And by the late-medieval period, i.e., by the Protestant reformers' day, new forms of penitential piety were growing, whereby satisfaction or atonement for sins was understood to be achieved through elaborate, painstaking steps and *labor*—labor that often entailed physical discomfort and pain. By Luther's day it was commonly believed that to take monastic vows and therewith be subject to the external rigors of monastic life allowed one to accrue merit through divine favor. (Luther, of course, as an Augustinian monk had partaken of this ordeal of meritorious self-denial and doubt prior to his conversion.) If, then, Solomon truly repented, a confession of the *vanitas* of all his deeds would not only be expected but multiplied, so that the *inevitable* result is a *contempt for the world*. In this light, Ecclesiastes would have been read and understood by Luther's day as teaching a flight from this world (as a sign of true repentance) through its renouncing of all attachments to the world.

But, for Luther, a "contempt for the world" meant that Christians, among other things, would have to "forsake the household, the political order . . . [and more] to flee to the desert, to isolate oneself from human society, to live in stillness and silence; for it was [deemed] impossible to serve God in the world."[42] Luther is at pains to counter the long-standing tradition of ascetic monasticism and isolation from the world that had accrued over the centuries.[43] In his view, this outlook on "the world" was counter to a proper understanding—and acknowledgment—of creation's *essential*

40. Thomas à Kempis, *The Imitation of Christ*; cf. Eccl 1:8b. For a helpful summary of readings and interpretations of Ecclesiastes before Luther, see Christianson, "Ecclesiastes in Premodern Reading."

41. See Eliason, "*Vanitas Vanitatum*," 40–56.

42. Luther, *Notes on Ecclesiastes*, 4.

43. While it is true that that the monastic communities following the Benedictine Rule worked as well as prayed, as Hardy, *The Fabric of This World*, 50, points out, they worked with the goal of maintaining their own communities. Furthermore, by the late-medieval period, "the liturgical practices within the major orders had grown to the point that the monks no longer had time to work to support themselves at all. Instead they lived off of the gifts and endowments given by the aristocracy in exchange for a share of the spiritual benefits of the monastery." What is more, wandering monks (the "friars") also did not work for a living but were dependent on the charity of those whom they encountered.

and not merely *relative* "goodness" (Gen 1:31). Monks, however, were *disengaged*, which caused Luther to polemicize against the world-fleeing monastic tendency.[44] In reading Ecclesiastes, Luther laments that "it is almost a bigger job to purify and defend the author" from mistaken ideas "smuggled" in by the church.[45] "Some foolish men," he observes,

> have not understood this [i.e., what Ecclesiastes condemns] and have therefore taught absurd ideas about contempt for the world and flight from it, and they themselves have also done many absurd things . . . The proper contempt of the world is not that of the man who lives in solitude away from human society, nor is the proper contempt of gold that of the man who throws it away and who abstains from money, as the Franciscans do, but that of the man who lives his life *in the midst* of these things and yet is not carried away by his affection for them. This is the first thing that should be considered [by those reading Ecclesiastes].[46]

A Recasting of Work and "Vocation": The Lutheran Reading of Ecclesiastes

Luther's break with standard medieval interpretation of Ecclesiastes was both philological and theological in nature.[47] Luther turned the medieval reading on its head by affirming, rather than denying, the ordinary affairs of this life. The problem, as Luther saw it, is sin and *not* the lack of goodness in creation. His *Annotationes in Ecclesiastea* ("Notes on Ecclesiastes"), published in 1532, contain one comment that perhaps best summarizes his overall burden: "For God has made all things to be good and to be useful for human purpose."[48]

In his reading of Ecclesiastes, Luther believes that two priorities are to govern our interpretation: the author's purpose and the author's unique style. The author's aim, in this light, is thereby clarified: "to put us at peace and to

---

44. As a former monk who had entered the Order of Hermits of St. Augustine in 1505, Luther understandably railed against the "monkish" life, particularly in the early years following his conversion. In his 1521 treatise *De votis monasticis* ('On Monastic Vows'), he takes full aim at the monastic system of which he was a part, criticizing its tendency towards works righteousness, its negation of faith and Christian freedom, and its assumption that monastic works and withdrawal are of a superior or "holier" quality.

45. Luther, *Notes on Ecclesiastes*, 7.

46. Luther, *Notes on Ecclesiastes*, 9 (emphasis added).

47. Thus Wolters, "Ecclesiastes and the Reformers," 55–68.

48. Luther, *Notes Ecclesiastes*, 8.

give us a quiet mind in the everyday affairs and business of this life, so that we live contentedly in the present."[49] What Ecclesiastes condemns, Luther asserts, is not "creation or the created order" but rather "depraved affections" and a "lack of contentment."[50] The natural order is and remains "good." *Misuse* of the "good," not its *use*, is what leads to *vanitas*.[51] In this light, then, the expression "under the sun," Luther insists, should be understood not in cosmological or physical sense but religiously and philosophically, so that we do not exclude the works of God the Creator.[52]

In addition to the tendency of medieval exegesis to be anchored in a "contempt for the world," a second notable—albeit related—feature was inherited from the early Christian fathers since the days of Origen, extending through Jerome, Ambrose, Augustine, and down to the Protestant Reformation.[53] As suggested above (recall Jerome's rendering of Eccl 1:2), interpretation of Ecclesiastes was characterized by a conspicuous *spiritualizing* of the text. Above it was suggested that Jerome's opening salvo in his commentary on Ecclesiastes was to "afflict the comfortable"; that is, any person expecting or hoping to be "at home" in the temporal world is living under an illusion. Jerome seems to have Epicurean thinking—or reasonable facsimile thereof—in the back of his mind. For this reason, then, food and drink need to be allegorized. Hence, the allusions in Ecclesiastes to eating and drinking, which along with work are the practical expressions of God's gifts, are understood allegorically as references to the Lord's Table[54] and not to be interpreted in a literal manner.[55] In Jerome's treatment of Eccl 2:24–26, for example, he observes: "What is good is to take the true food and the true drink, which we

---

49. Luther, *Notes on Ecclesiastes*, 7.

50. Luther, *Notes on Ecclesiastes*, 8. Discontentment, according to Luther, is "always looking for something that is lacking" (11).

51. Luther, *Notes on Ecclesiastes*, 8–9, 16.

52. Luther, *Notes on Ecclesiastes*, 14.

53. The earliest surviving Christian comments on Ecclesiastes are found in Origen's prologue to his commentary on the Song of Songs, and it is not surprising that Origen allegorizes. Origen elsewhere—*On First Principles* 1.7.5, cited in J. Robert Wright, ed., *Ancient Christian Commentary on Scripture—Vol. IX: Proverbs, Ecclesiastes, Song of Songs*, 194—calls vanity "the possession of material bodies." For his part, Ambrose cites the circus, horse-racing, and the theater as examples of vanity; therefore, we are to seek the word of God and "flee from this world" (Ambrose, *Flight from the World* 1.4, cited in Wright, *Ancient Christian Commentary on Scripture*, 194).

54. St. Augustine, in *City of God* 17.20, employs the same line of interpretation.

55. The general sentiment among Christian historians and Old Testament scholars is that allegorizing ended up "rescuing" Ecclesiastes among the early fathers, insofar as it dulled perceived contradictions and heterodox statements.

find in the divine books concerning the body and blood of the Lamb."[56] Jerome will apply this sacramental, "bread and wine"/"body and blood" interpretation again to eating and drinking (in 3:12–13, 5:19, and 8:15). Similarly, "enjoyment" in these verses means for him *holiness*; Jerome cannot accept the conclusion of 2:24–26 and the subsequent enjoyment refrains that God sanctions material joy. Finally, behind the entire book's interpretation stands Christ, whom Jerome will make the "Preacher" who then is directing the words of Ecclesiastes to the church.[57]

But Luther rejects this allegorizing and spiritualizing of Scripture, foremost because of its disregard for the doctrine of creation and attendant world-fleeing, isolating tendency. As a good Augustinian, the reformer affirms the reality of the "two cities." And while it is uncontested that our ultimate allegiance is to the "city of God," this does not mean that we take our earthly citizenship lightly. Rather, we are stewards of various callings that have been given by the Lord of creation. We occupy various "stations" in life which have been "assigned" to us by the Lord, using those "outposts" and the attendant gifts and abilities that go with those callings to serve God and serve others. Ecclesiastes agrees with this outlook in its statements that our "portion" or "lot" (*heleq*) has been "assigned" by God (for example, 3:22; 5:18; 5:19; 9:6; and 9:9). If we flee to the desert or to the monastery, we are fleeing the created order, and it is *to* the created order that Christian believers—indeed *all believers*—are called. Luther is convinced that Ecclesiastes is not escapist, that it does not call the reader *out of the world*.[58] Properly read and understood, it does not breed a *contemptus mundi*.

This perspective is not only implicit in Ecclesiastes, it is strengthened, as Luther understands it, by the notion of *vocatio* ("calling"). And while vocation is a wholly biblical concept, it was perhaps most thoroughly—and practically—developed during the Reformation era by Luther. In medieval thinking, to have a "calling" (*vocatio*) was to become a monk or nun or enter the priesthood in the service of the church. Over against those "ordinary" occupations of the marketplace—for example, as a farmer, a tool-maker or craftsman, a maid, a miner, a cobbler, a soldier, or even a ruler—monastic or priestly life was understood to be *the* means by which to serve God fully.[59]

---

56. St. Jerome, *Commentary on Ecclesiastes* 2.24, 54.

57. St. Jerome, *Commentary on Ecclesiastes* 1.1; for a broader understanding of this spiritualized interpretation by Jerome, see the commentary's "Introduction," pp. 1–31.

58. Philip Melanchthon, Luther's colleague at the University of Wittenberg, will also publish a commentary on Ecclesiastes in 1550 (*Enarratio brevis concionum libri Salomoniscuius titulus est Ecclesiastes*), and like Luther, he emphasizes the goodness of creation—a goodness that is providentially preserved.

59. As it was, Luther came from a family of miners.

Having a "vocation," then, which required celibacy and a retreat from public life to constant daily "devotion" to God in and through the church, was reserved for the "sacred" realm. Among Luther's important innovations was his theological accent on the "priesthood of every believer," according to which every Christian is made holy, sanctified, and set apart unto God for service through Christ. Rather than point lay people back toward "vocation" through various monastic or priestly orders of the church, Luther reversed the process, emphasizing that *every type of work* was a *sacred* "calling"—and a "calling" every bit as noble as that of the priest.[60] Whereas monastic spirituality as conventionally understood interpreted *vocatio* as being called *out of* the world and to the desert or the convent or monastery, Luther (as would Calvin) recast *vocatio* as a calling *to* the everyday life of living in the world.

> Work was thus [newly] seen as an activity by which Christians could deepen their faith, leading it on to new qualities of commitment to God. Activity within the world, motivated, informed, and sanctioned by Christian faith, was the supreme means by which the believer could demonstrate his or her commitment and thankfulness to God. To do anything for God, and to do it well, was the fundamental hallmark of authentic Christian faith.[61]

Work, therefore, because of the Reformed emphasis on the "priesthood of the believer," had the effect of transforming the daily, the ordinary, the mundane, and the necessary.[62] It collapsed the long-standing distinction between "sacred" and "secular," demonstrating that *all of life,* based on the goodness of creation, is "sacred" and therefore a means by which both to serve God and serve our neighbor.[63] Hence, for Luther, vocation

60. In his open letter *"To the Christian Nobility of the German Nation Concerning the Reform of the Christian Estate"* (1520), Luther writes, "It is pure invention that pope, bishops, priests and monks are called the spiritual estate while princes, lords, artisans, and farmers are called the temporal estate. This is indeed a piece of lying and hypocrisy. Yet no one need be intimidated by it, and for this reason: all Christians are truly of the spiritual estate, and there is no difference among them except that of office." (Luther, *"To the Christian Nobility of the German Nation,"* in *L.W.* 44:127.)

61. McGrath, "Calvin and the Christian Calling," 34.

62. To illustrate, Luther wrote to a professional soldier who also served as a counselor to a duke who was sympathetic to the Reformation cause. Thereby Luther reminds the soldier, a man of Christian faith, "In the first place, we must distinguish between an occupation and the man who holds it, between a work and the man who does it. An occupation or a work can be good and right in itself and yet be bad and wrong if the man who does the work is evil or wrong or does not do his work properly." (Luther, *Whether Soldiers, Too, Can Be Saved,* in *L.W.* 46:94.)

63. One of the ways Luther describes vocation is to call it a "mask of God" (see

entails a call to love one's neighbor through the tasks and duties that are a part of one's "station" or social context in life.[64] The purpose of Christianity is not to abandon the world but to live in its midst, for people are in need of the Christian's good works.

The implications of Luther's teaching were felt not only in terms of viewing work as *vocation* but also as it concerned a proper view of wealth and the material realm. In his commentary on Eccl 5:18–20, Luther notes the contrast between the miser and the God-fearer. Luther is struck by the previous description of the plight of the miser: in vv. 12–14 he is depicted as poor "in the midst of his riches," and the more he has, the more he wants, which confirms the power of greed. Alas, in his misery the miser cannot sleep (v. 12).[65] The admonition to enjoyment that follows the critique of the miser is decisive; it constitutes for Luther, as did 2:24–26, "the conclusion of this entire book."[66] The "gifts" of God, reiterated in these verses as coming from the hand of God (cf. 2:24), are reassuring to Luther. That "God keeps him occupied with joy in his heart" (v. 20) is *the opposite of anxiety*, as Luther points out.[67] Anxiety—or shall we say, the freedom from anxiety—is very important to the reformer. In contrast to the miser, in these statements we see that the Teacher does not condemn riches, nor does he forbid that we acquire food and drink and riches. Rather, he calls these things "gifts" of God. For Luther, these are granted to us by God not for the purpose of rejecting or abstaining from them. What is more, the statement "Because God keeps him occupied with joy in the heart," for him, "shows that man has joy in his toil here."[68] In the reformer's thinking, joy given to the human heart suggests delight.[69]

Finally, the last of the "joy" refrains, 11:7–12:1, reminds Luther of the basic need to be cheerful yet sober. For "when the heart has been

---

Luther's *Exposition of Psalm 147* in *L.W.* 14:109–34). This is to say that God "hides" himself in the ordinary, in the family, and in the daily, which includes the marketplace and the "secular" realm. There God is present, even when he is "hidden," Luther wishes to instruct us. Doubtless in his day, as in ours, people sought God in the mystical and the miraculous. But for many, to come to the realization that God is actually *present* in the "ordinary," foremost in the workplace, is nothing short of revolutionary. It is a vision that can utterly change our lives. And to grasp the implications of the "enjoyment" refrains in Ecclesiastes, with their implications for work, is no less transformative.

64. That social context or "station" may or may not be paid employment or one's formal "occupation."

65. Luther, *Notes on Ecclesiastes*, 88–90.

66. Luther, *Notes on Ecclesiastes*, 93.

67. Luther, *Notes on Ecclesiastes*, 93.

68. Luther, *Notes on Ecclesiastes*, 93.

69. Luther, *Notes on Ecclesiastes*, 93.

correctly instructed," he notes, "no joy or happiness will harm it." What is more, these verses counter the attitude of the monks, who are legalistic, ascetic, and self-denying.[70]

In summarizing the message of Ecclesiastes, Luther notes that "the vanity of the human heart . . . is never content with the gifts of God that are present." Nevertheless, "with thanksgiving we may use the things that are present and . . . generously given to us and conferred upon us by the blessing of God." What is more, we should do so "without anxiety" about the future, seeking to have "a tranquil and quiet heart and mind filled with joy." Such will allow us to "be content with the Word and work of God."[71] Contentment, tranquility, and grateful acknowledgment of God's good gifts—these represent the teaching of Ecclesiastes, confirming for Luther the importance of work and *vocatio*.

While the primary focus of the present chapter is Luther, it should be remembered that about the same time that the reformer was preparing his *Notes on Ecclesiastes* John Calvin was reflecting and writing on work and vocation in his systematic theology, the *Institutes of the Christian Religion*.[72] In Book III of the *Institutes*, Calvin writes that the Lord asks us, in all of life's activity, to look to our "individual callings." This is especially important, he notes, given the restless tendency of the human heart. Therefore, to prevent confusion within the individual believer, God has "appointed" particular duties for every individual in different spheres of life. These appointed duties correspond to each person's vocational calling. Every person's vocation is a "post assigned" by the Lord, in order that he or she may not "wander around" in uncertainty throughout life.[73] Our awareness of the Lord's "calling" to particular spheres of living is, for Calvin, the "foundation" of our attempts at "well-doing." Otherwise, he believes, we will not hold true to a "straight path" in terms of our duties, and our lives will lack a "harmony." Where this awareness *is* present, by contrast, the believer will be able to endure all manner of challenges and trials, with the consequence that no job, task, or duty will fail to be "precious" in God's sight. For Calvin, as for Luther,

> The work of believers is thus seen to possess a significance that goes far beyond the visible results of that work. It is the person working, as much as the resulting work, that is significant to

70. Luther, *Notes on Ecclesiastes*, 177.

71. Luther, *Notes on Ecclesiastes*, 10–11.

72. Luther's *Notes* were published in 1532, while the first edition of Calvin's *Institutes* was published in 1536.

73. John Calvin, *Institutes of the Christian Religion* III.10.6; I am relying on the English translation provided by Ford Lewis Battles (Grand Rapids: Eerdmans, rev. 1986).

God. There is no distinction between spiritual and temporal, sacred and secular work. All human work, however lowly, is capable of glorifying God. Work is, quite simply, an act of praise—a potentially *productive* act of praise. Work glorifies God, it serves the common good, and it is something through which human creativity can express itself.[74]

For both Calvin and Luther, work is a heavenly vocation and divine gift to be received with joy.[75] With this line of thinking, Ecclesiastes stands in fundamental agreement.

The Renewal of "Vocation"

On occasion throughout its history, as in the sixteenth century, the Christian church is permitted to gain renewed insight into its "apologetic" mission in the world. Part of that mission entails rediscovering the meaning and purpose of neglected domains of social life—for example, in the arts or sciences or medicine, in language and linguistics, or in the study of history, literature, philosophy, politics and law, and human psychology. Not infrequently, those breakthroughs—as they did in the early sixteenth century—adjust our

74. McGrath, "Calvin and the Christian Calling," 34.

75. For a thorough yet accessible overview of the contributions made by Luther and Calvin to work and vocation against the backdrop of the late medieval church and society, see Hardy, *The Fabric of This World*, 44–67. With a renewed emphasis in some circles in recent years on work and vocation, it has become customary—perhaps even fashionable—to criticize the Reformed breakthrough of the early sixteenth century. Not infrequently this critique proceeds on a misconstrual of Luther's emphasis on "vocation" and "stations" in life and/or an ignoring of the accent, in both Luther and Calvin, on neighbor-love, mutual service, and the common good. Two such examples are Waalkes, "Rethinking Work as Vocation," and Rotman, "Vocation in Theology and Psychology." While Waalkes is sensitive to the danger of transforming "vocation" into egoistic "self-discovery" and denying the cross, his "gospel corrective" misreads Luther on the cross and Christian discipleship and reads generally like a Quaker or Anabaptist reaction to Reformed thought. Luther himself offers the needed corrective to the purported "corrective": "I ask you where our suffering is to be found. I shall tell you: Run through all the stations of life, from the lowest to the highest, and you will find what you are looking for ... [T]herefore do not worry where you can find suffering. That is not necessary. Simply live as an earnest Christian preacher, pastor, burgher, farmer, noble, lord, and fulfill your office faithfully and loyally" (*D. Martin Luthers Werke. Kritische Gesamtausgabe*, 51:404; Eng. trans., Hardy, *The Fabric of This World*, 53). Rotman's essay explores the "inadequacies" of the Protestant Reformation's emphasis of "work as vocation," arguing that "practicing the love command" and a restoration of "God's intentions for creation" best define vocation in biblical theology. In reality, at the very heart of *Luther's own* understanding *of* vocation were precisely these two components—neighbor-love and the goodness of creation—which are amply demonstrated in his writings.

views of the marketplace and culture as we grasp a deeper understanding of the concept of "vocation," and hence, the strategic value of our work. And during those seasons of "breakthrough," whether culturally or personally, we find God *sanctifying the mundane*, the ordinary, the daily. This means that he sanctifies our efforts *in the workplace*, giving us a sense of meaning, purpose, and satisfaction *in and through* our work. He reminds us, as he did Luther and the reformers, of the high calling to be butchers and bakers and candlestick-makers; nurses and doctors and drivers of hearses; psychologists and businessmen and information technologists. In short, he collapses—once *again*—the two-tiered "sacred-versus-secular" dichotomy that we (both Catholics and Protestants) are all too fond of continually erecting.[76] Since we are called *to* the world, we might even argue that everything that we undertake in life is "secular." Or, perhaps we might say, for the very same reason, that everything we undertake in life is "sacred"—where, that is, it is done in obedience and in faith.

While an examination of the reason for Christians' and churches' false dichotomizing of the "sacred" and the "secular" goes beyond the scope of this volume, much of the blame for this split-thinking resides with Christian leaders, and hence with pastoral and priestly training institutions (namely, divinity schools and seminaries).[77] Most pastors and priests would seem either indifferent to or intimidated by the fact that their congregants need to be equipped for the *workplace*. For example, in evangelically minded churches, the chief emphasis of most teaching and preaching is *private*—as opposed to *public*—faith, that is, what God does *in* me rather than what God wishes to do *through* me. And the fact of the matter is that most pastors and priests probably have never spent a significant season of their lives working in the marketplace; hence an inability to empathize with congregants, and therefore, the absence of regular teaching and preaching that would equip 99 percent of their congregations for the challenges of the workplace, to which that 99 percent is called by God.

Vocation properly understood has the effect of "recalibrating" our sense of duties and obligations within the larger ethical framework of God's providential care and purpose. Work, as it turns out, is perhaps the most significant element of the believer's vocational calling, even when it does not represent

---

76. Hereon see Knapp, *How the Church Fails Businesspeople*, which, in a wonderfully rich manner, captures the burden of viewing the marketplace, and our investment in "Monday through Friday," as sacred.

77. And where in theological education there *do* exist "faith and work" or "theology of work" components, these are typically adjunct in nature and part of an "institute" or a "center," without intentional and thoroughgoing integration into the seminary's or divinity school's broader curriculum in a manner that would be transformative.

the totality of that calling. Thus, when Ecclesiastes commends work as a "satisfying gift" and yet the believer's day-to-day experience at work is *neither* satisfying *nor* viewed as a gracious gift, theological recalibration is in order. Anything less is to fail to live in harmony with our Creator, or to fail to be fruitful and possess a strong sense of direction and purpose.

For what purpose, then, do our lives exist here "under the sun"? This, in a very practical sense, represents the real "end of the matter" in Ecclesiastes, to which we will turn in the final chapter. How are we to understand "vocation" and "calling"—or, in the language of the Teacher, the "portion" that has been "assigned" to us by the Lord—in their genuine religious sense? What are the practical and ethical implications of the admonition in Ecclesiastes "Whatever your hand finds to do, do it with all of your might!" (9:10)? Correlatively, what might be the implications, in each of our lives, of the "sow-give-sow" admonitions (11:1–6) that are part of the final hortatory section of the book?[78] And finally, why is it not merely optional but *requisite* for all believers to function in their individual vocational callings, regardless of the season of life in which they find themselves?

---

78. If one takes the time to meditate on the implication of Eccl 9:10 and 11:1, 2 and 6, the prospects are exhilarating. Much in contrast to the emphasis on human limitations which pervades much of Ecclesiastes, these remarkable statements suggest that there is literally *nothing* that restricts our vision and potential.

Rethinking the Message of Ecclesiastes

Second Thoughts on the Value of Work and the Importance of Vocation

The Intrinsic Value of Work

- "Human work proceeds directly from persons created in the image of God and called to prolong the work of creation by subduing the earth, both with and for one another."

- "Work honors the Creator's gifts and talents received from him."

- "[M]an collaborates in a certain fashion with the Son of God in his redemptive work."

- "Work can be a means of sanctification and a way of animating earthly realities with the Spirit of Christ."

- "In work, the person exercises and fulfills in part the potential inscribed in his nature. The primordial value of labor stems from man himself, the author and its beneficiary."

- "Work is for man, not man for work."[1]

OVER A HALF-CENTURY AGO, human labor was described by one thoughtful devotional writer as a "lost province" of Christian faith in the modern era.[2] Written in 1952, this lament was justified in the writer's thinking by the presence of communist totalitarianism worldwide. It illustrated why Christian *absence* from the realm of work, the worker, the workplace, and economics was so vitally important, and so utterly tragic. Is it possible, this writer wondered, that Christians' failure to articulate and demonstrate a

---

1. *Catechism of the Catholic Church* nos. 2427 and 2428.
2. Trueblood, *Your Other Vocation*, 15–41.

sturdy and honorable theology of work was a contributing factor in the emergence of the "Marxist gospel"?[3] Seventy years removed, we scarcely have reason to challenge his thesis. How much of the globe is subject to communist tyranny?[4] Might the writer, in truth, have been correct in his prognosis? What he was calling for, in the end however, was not resignation, but *reformation*—a new reformation. And, as it is, Christianity has demonstrated historically that it is able to reform itself *from within*. This, then, is our hope and our prayer.

The key to reform and a "new reformation" strategy, as the aforementioned writer envisioned it, was the role of the lay person. In keeping with reform movements of the past, the laity is "close to common life" of the surrounding culture and therefore the linchpin in terms of social-cultural change.[5] God's call to "secular" work, he noted, was a "holy enterprise."[6] In the marketplace, therefore, we the laity are both *stewards* of our talents and *donors* of those talents and our labor.[7] But this vision, he insisted, should excite rather than weary us; it should energize rather than exasperate us. For, in truth, "work which has no other incentive than the paycheck is closer to slavery than it is to freedom."[8] A large part of the modern workplace dilemma is that "boredom is our chief occupational disease"; hence, "deeper reasons" for our labors are required.[9] And because *our* world is *God's* world—i.e., the world of God's wondrous creation—our involvement therein is intrinsically and necessarily holy and life-giving.[10]

Chapter 5—"Wisdom and Human Labor in Ecclesiastes: A Closer Look"—was devoted to examining the "enjoyment" refrains that are recurring throughout the book. The first of these refrains, lodged in 2:24–26, represents a "response" to the writer's opening lament (recorded in 1:2–2:23)

3. Trueblood, *Your Other Vocation*, 25.

4. This, tragedy, of course, does not even begin to address the problem of Christian absence from the workplace in the relatively free world, which is the focus of the present volume.

5. My own view is not that the laity must *always or necessarily* lead reform movements; after all, throughout the present volume I have called for reform among those in Christian leadership positions. However, based on historical precedent (i.e., almost 2,000 years), it may well be the case that the laity is the primary vehicle through which true reform occurs and that the clergy are entrenched in their religious "calling" in such a way that often makes them either impervious to or unaware of the true nature of "vocation" as it applies to the Christian community.

6. Trueblood, *Your Other Vocation*, 58.

7. Trueblood, *Your Other Vocation*, 61.

8. Trueblood, *Your Other Vocation*, 62.

9. Trueblood, *Your Other Vocation*, 62.

10. Trueblood, *Your Other Vocation*, 63–64.

and serves as an introduction to the theological framework (beginning in 3:1) that undergirds the entirety of Ecclesiastes. The presentation of this theological framework begins with the didactic poem on "seasons" (3:1–8)—a memorable literary testament to the fact that everything, indeed *everything*, has meaning and purpose in life and that thereby serves as a counter-argument to the "everything is meaningless" adage (1:2, 14; 2:11, 17; 3:19; and 12:8). What follows the poem is a clarification of divine sovereignty and inscrutability (3:9–22). Various seasons of our lives can only have meaning and purpose *if* God the Creator is sovereign in his works and his working in the cosmos. Given our human limitations, this sovereign working—"everything that God does endures forever" (3:14a)—is designed not to frustrate but to encourage human beings, bringing them to a point of awe-inspired worship—"God does this so that humans will revere him" (3:14c); "Therefore stand in awe of God" (5:7b)—and dependence.[11]

Placed in the middle of this unit describing divine sovereignty and inscrutability is a noteworthy pronouncement that represents the second "enjoyment" refrain (3:12–13). The writer observes that "every man may eat and drink and *find satisfaction in his work*—this is a gift of God" (3:13).[12] He then concludes this particular unit of thought with the following words: "So I saw that there is nothing better for a man than to *enjoy his work*, because that is his portion" (3:22).[13]

This theistic conclusion, as noted earlier, is strengthened later in Ecclesiastes with the pronouncement that "when God gives any man wealth and possessions and enables him to enjoy them, to accept his lot and *be happy in his work*—this is a gift of God . . . because God keeps him occupied with gladness of heart" (5:18–20). What is more, the reader is informed later that "joy will accompany him *in his work* all the days of the life God has given him under the sun" (8:15), despite human inability to comprehend what God does. And if this were not enough, in what begins the final major unit of the book the reader is admonished in the strongest form of *carpe diem* yet by the writer: "Whatever your hand finds to do, do it with all your might" (9:10). Together, these refrains underscore the Teacher's own position on the value of human labor, as chapters 2–5 of the present volume have sought to clarify.

---

11. As has been noted several times throughout the present volume, the generally negative reading of Ecclesiastes by Old Testament scholars is an indication that they bring their own frustrations with divine sovereignty and inscrutability to the text themselves. This is not a criticism on my part; it is merely an observation.

12. Emphasis mine.

13. Emphasis mine.

That view, anchored in (a) human creation based on the image of God and (b) the fear of God, is that work has intrinsic value.[14]

Work is that for which we are created, and not even the fall itself—the hint of which appears in 7:29 (human creation followed by sin)—removes this fact.[15] The curse does not alter creation. Human beings were designed for work; therein they show themselves to "be like God."[16] And where work *is* a "curse," it is one of our own making. Properly viewed, work is "participation in God's activity" and thus has an intrinsic ethical value of its own.[17] The ancient world tended to make distinctions between "classes" of workers, chiefly differentiating between physical and mental-spiritual labor—a distinction that continued even through the medieval period. Historians describe this as a contrast between the *vita contemplativa* and the *vita activa*—a contrast that finds no biblical justification.[18] It is significant that the very Son of God and Creator of the universe incarnated himself not as a philosopher but as a carpenter and craftsman.[19]

Three generations ago the Christian apologist Dorothy Sayers, communicating against the backdrop of global upheaval (the early stages of the Second World War) and economic uncertainty, called for "a thoroughgoing revolution in our whole attitude toward work."[20] Sayers charged her audience to view work "not as drudgery to be undergone for the purpose of making

14. Note that the purpose clause "so that people will revere him" (3:14) follows immediately on the heels of the "enjoyment" refrain in 3:12–13.

15. As evidence of this reality, one need only consider the frequently devastating effects of unemployment when they visit an individual—psychologically, mentally, spiritually, and physically. Much of a person's sense of self-esteem consists in having his or her skills needed and used, and when these are not needed and go unused, the effects on the individual can be catastrophic. The truth is that few people wish to be out of work, even when the psychological and spiritual reasons for this escape them.

16. This theological reality negates much standard commentary on Ecclesiastes, which—as chapters 3 and 5 observed—proceeds on the assumption that (a) any joy or enjoyment being depicted in the book functions as a palliative, anesthetic, and duller of life's pain and (b) work is only of temporal benefit and an inherently fruitless activity that only passes the time ("the best that human beings can do"). This latter portrait, however, is neither the message of Ecclesiastes, nor the perspective of wisdom literature, nor the teaching of biblical theology.

17. In his 1981 encyclical letter *Laborem Exercens*, Pope John II develops this point quite helpfully; see esp. nos. 6 and 25.

18. An exceedingly helpful historical overview of contrasting views of work, from the ancient to the modern world, is to be found in Hardy, *The Fabric of This World*, 6–43. Hardy contrasts the views of the ancient world, the medieval era, the Renaissance and Reformation, and Marxism.

19. Jesus will even refer to his Father as a vinedresser (John 15).

20. Sayers, "Why Work?," 89. "Why Work?" was first presented as a speech in April of 1942.

money" but "as a way of life" in which human nature "should find its proper
exercise and delight and so fulfill itself to the glory of God."[21] Sayers's challenge remains every bit as relevant—indeed, imperative—two decades into
the twenty-first century as it was when it was issued several generations ago.
Consider, for a moment, these core elements in her charge:

- Work is not a form of drudgery
- The main purpose of work is not finances
- Work should be a way of life
- Work is a source of proper exercise and delight
- Work is a source of intrinsic human fulfillment
- Work is a means of glorifying God

These elements, as it turns out and to the surprise of many, find their
confirmation in the teaching of Ecclesiastes. As the present volume has
sought to demonstrate, a "double theme" is intended by the Teacher, which
juxtaposes two metaphysical outlooks on life, two "ways of life."[22] One outlook is materialistic and self-dependent in its constitution, receiving from
the Teacher a blistering critique—"Life is meaningless!" It defines itself by
living and working for temporal "gain" or "profit," seeking *self*-fulfillment,
and aiming at *self*-glorification. The alternative outlook—"Life is meaningful!"—emerges again and again throughout the book, both implicitly and
explicitly. Its emphasis, as we have observed, is joy in the simple, ordinary
things of life, including heart-felt satisfaction in one's work. It understands
that *all* of life is a gift, to be received from the hand of the Creator and Maker
of all things. This alternative outlook reaches an unmistakable crescendo
in 9:7–12:1, even to the extent of challenging the reader to unprecedented,
"risk"-laden applications of human freedom (11:1–6):

- Cast your bread upon the waters (v. 1a)
- Give portions to seven, even eight (v. 2a)
- Sow seed early (v. 6a)
- Don't grow idle in sowing (v. 6b)
- You just never know what will succeed (v. 6c)

21. Sayers, "Why Work?," 89.

22. This conclusion is supported by the sheer presence of contrasting and prominent keywords in the book: *hebel* ("meaningless"), which appears thirty-eight times;
the noun and verb forms *śimḥâ* ("enjoyment," "pleasure," "contentment") and *śāmaḥ*
("to enjoy," "to be content"), which together appear seventeen times; and *tôb* ("good"),
which appears fifty-two times.

"You just never know . . ." You never know what the weather will bring, what circumstances will befall you, or how life itself develops. In fact, "you just never know *what will succeed.*" The language here is not only evocative but demonstrably positive and vision-stretching, standing in diametric opposition to the "meaninglessness" of the alternative outlook being lamented from 1:2 onward. And once more it needs reiterating that the message of Ecclesiastes is not merely that "meaninglessness" and meaning are somehow blended or melded in life—a line of interpretation that characterizes much commentary on Ecclesiastes. At the same time, the argument being advanced in the present volume is *not* that hardship or suffering are absent from the God-fearing life; only that two clashing metaphysical outlooks are being juxtaposed, with the conventional view being exposed at its roots and utterly demolished.

Work, then, from the vantage-point of the God-fearer (3:14; 5:7; 7:18; 8:12–13; 9:1; 11:9; and 12:13), is recast, and utterly so in the "enjoyment" refrains. Whereas human labor performed "under the sun" becomes oppressive toil and a meaningless exercise, without "profit" or "gain" because of its materialistic self-promotion, it becomes a vehicle of satisfaction and joy, a meaningful expression of why we were created in God's image, when and where human beings receive all of life as a gift of God and seek to serve God (and serve others) through their gifts and abilities.[23]

In recent months, I stumbled quite accidently upon Viktor Frankl's classic and deceptively brief work *Man's Search for Meaning.* Frankl, it will be remembered, was a survivor of two of the Nazi's most notorious death camps—Auschwitz-Birkenau and Dachau.[24] His own family was sent to the gas ovens, with the exception of a sister. Yet despite the bestial conditions to which he was subjected, quite miraculously Frankl lived to reflect on these experiences and then, after the war, practice psychotherapy in Vienna (he was a student of Freud). Frankl notes that in his practice he would sometimes ask his patients who were suffering from various forms of torment why they did not simply commit suicide. From his patients' answers he would then derive a particular therapeutic strategy that best suited them in the consulting room. Frankl observed three general types of reasoning

23. This, of course, is a fulfilling of the "Great Commandment" taught in the Old Testament (e.g., Lev 19:18, 34; Deut 6:5; 10:19-20; 11:13, 22; 19:9; and 30:6) and reaffirmed by Jesus (Matt 22:37–39; Mark 12:30–31; and Luke 10:27). Work is the primary means by which we serve others and contribute to the common good.

24. Partial disclosure is here in order: my German father-in-law, during the Second World War, worked for the German railroad (*Bundesbahn*). All five years of the war found him stationed in Poland, where his job was being a railroad-car switcher. Only God knows what "Papa" witnessed during these years. This, if no other reason, causes me to reflect with utter sobriety on what went on in these camps.

among his patients. For some, love of one's family members prevented them from taking their lives; for others lingering memories of the past served as an obstacle. But for yet other patients there was a sense of responsibility to use their talents responsibly in this life. Frankl was especially intrigued by this third answer: life seemed to be worthwhile where hope, meaning, and purpose were identified in work.

Consider, for a moment, that outlook: *life is worthwhile where hope, meaning, and purpose are identified in our work.* Or, stated in the reverse as Ecclesiastes presents it, we find meaning and purpose—and satisfaction— in our work precisely *because* life itself has meaning and purpose. In this concluding chapter, my argument is quite simply this: finding satisfaction and contentment in and through our work is directly related to—indeed, the very fruit of—having clarity in our vocational calling. That is to say, life is either meaningful or meaningless to the extent that we are aware of that calling. Work and vocational calling are interlocking concepts, with both of these being foremost theological matters. Hence, the first order of business is to understand "vocation" in terms of Christian theology. This, in turn, will help us understand their connectedness.

After thirty years of teaching, doing public-policy research, probing the relationship between faith and society, and counseling multitudes of students (of differing ages), I have found one particular conversation to be recurring. It is a topic which often goes unanswered or unaddressed by our churches and most preaching, teaching, or training, and it is a topic which desperately needs to see the light of day. I refer to an awareness of our vocation or calling as it relates to our work, whether that work is paid or "volunteer" in nature. (For the sake of clarity, I am using "vocation" and "calling" interchangeably.)

Theology in the Service of Vocation: Rethinking the Doctrine of Divine Providence

The English words which derive from the Latin *vocatio* (from *vocare*: to call) show their root to be rich with meaning and ramification—"voice," "vocalize," "vocation," and by extension, "call," "summons," "bidding," and "invitation." Christianity is unique in its conviction that the "ordinary" in daily living is "holy" or "set apart," even when our experience may seem to deny it. It is also unique in its conviction that God's "calls" are discernible and to some degree "accessible." This is in accordance with God's fundamental nature: he speaks, communicates, reveals, initiates, prods, and confirms, even when we must concede that *how* he does this remains something of a mystery.

What is tragic is that in our day there exists little serious discourse on the topic of vocation. Where we *do* find it is usually among self-help gurus and business-motivation speakers and authors.[25] The Christian church and Christian leaders for the most part have not grasped the importance of the inherently Christian doctrine of vocation. We typically understand vocation in a bifurcated way that encourages the insidious, two-tiered "sacred"-versus-"secular" dichotomy which has plagued the church since time immemorial. When and where the language of "vocation" is employed in the wider culture, it has been denuded and typically is used in the sense of "vocational training"—that is, job assistance, vo-tech education, and employment enhancement. Once "calling" and "vocation" were stripped of their inherently religious meaning, they devolved into a "flabby pietism" or "vague moral idealism" as well as career and job training.[26] But sadly, where the Christian community *does* use the term "vocation," more often than not we presuppose a separation between "calling" and our work. Contemporary religious understandings of "vocation"—be they Catholic, Orthodox, or Protestant—unfortunately translate into varied forms of "Christian service," prayer and Bible study, week-long "mission" trips, and the like (not that there is anything inherently wrong with these).[27]

In my opinion, the disappearance of the notion of vocation—or, at least its misunderstanding—is tragically the result of *religious thinking* that has dominated *our own circles*. Thus, we are in desperate need of rediscovering the concept of vocation, rightly understood, given its centrality in Christian theology. A return of this biblical concept to its proper place will require several things. For one, it may require, at least in the Protestant context, that we repent of the idols of "church growth," "seeker-friendliness," numerical measurements of "success," and business as usual, which usually centers on a "personal" as opposed to a "public" faith. Among Catholics and Orthodox it may mean actively working against the clergy-laity distinction that for centuries has been a part of their churches. After all, a clergy-centered view of "ministry" has produced a widespread passivity among the laity as well

25. One thinks, for example, of Stephen Covey's *The Seven Habits of Highly Effective People*, as well as his sequel, *The Eighth Habit: From Effectiveness to Greatness*. Where "God" does enter the "self-help" genre is often in the role of a "guarantor for the authenticity of the self," as Scholes, "Vocation," 217, has astutely pointed out.

26. So Williams, "Protestantism and the Vocation of Higher Education," 162.

27. Veith, "Vocation," 119, writes that of the three major teachings characterizing the Protestant Reformation—justification by faith, scriptural authority, and vocation—the first two remain while the third has been lost. It is difficult to disagree.

as a "professionalization" of the clergy.[28] Where this recognition occurs, it will then need to be followed by a vision and willingness to train and equip our parishioners and congregants *for the marketplace*, in the awareness that our real work is *in the marketplace*, since most of us are in fact called *to the marketplace*. After all, that is where we spend most of our lives—at least most of our waking hours. Permit me to ask this question, in order to illustrate my point: *why not have commissioning services*—as we do for so-called "missionaries"—for businessmen, lawyers, I/T people, social workers, mental health professionals, government employees, medical professionals, economists, as well as all sorts of craftsmen who are serving *in the marketplace*?

The answer to *why we are not commissioning our congregants into the marketplace* surely lies in the way in which we view the marketplace and in a deficient theology of work and vocation.

The theological framework of the entire book of Ecclesiastes, as we have emphasized, is built around divine providence. Even when wisdom literature is not intended to be explicit theological discourse, few books of the Bible showcase this doctrine as does Ecclesiastes. And, sadly, few doctrines are more misunderstood than this foundational element of faith. The English word itself stems from the Latin *pro + videre*—literally, to see forward, and thus implying both foresight as well as provision. God's activities and works in the world, hence, are not arbitrary or *ad hoc* in nature but rather the result of an eternal perspective (Eccl 3:11, 14, 15) that facilitates God's seeing all possible outcomes. To "provide" for his creation is to sustain and govern that created world.

God initiates, God incarnates, God acts in the world, God "calls." Providence, hence, suggests purpose and meaning. It also implies redemption and restoration of the created order. It is a distortion—albeit a common one—to view "the hand of providence" as some rare intervention or interruption in human affairs. Rather, providence is a daily, even moment-by-moment presence of the Creator and Maker of all things (Eccl 3:11; 7:29; 11:5). It is accurate to say that God's governance of the created order operates by means of natural laws that were set in place at the time of creation; however, another way of expressing this governance is to view it as God's ongoing personal involvement in that created order. This daily, moment-by-moment presence of the Creator in human affairs means that God is "ceaselessly active" both *among* human beings and *within* the human person.[29] This itself renders

28. Pope John Paul II, however, contributed to an important "shift" through two major encyclicals during his pontificate—*Laborem Excercens* ("On Human Work") in 1981 and *Centesimus Annus* in 1991 on the 100th anniversary of *Rerum Novarum*.

29. So Blamires, *The Will and the Way*, 43–62.

daily life and the realm of the "ordinary" meaningful. And it implies that there is direction to our individual lives.

It follows, then, that human affairs—as well as my individual life—work toward a greater design. That design is both general (i.e., wider) and specific (i.e., to each human being) in its application. And it therefore follows that God wishes us "to experience, in full awareness, the joy of his service" and "to realize, in some measure at least, the part we are playing in his great design."[30] This is true even despite the "curse" (Eccl 1:2; 7:29; 12:8), which has distorted our view of work as a result of sin (Eccl 2:17–23).

It may well be that the circumstances of our own family life or upbringing and our individual life experiences have given us a distorted picture of God's nature, of serving God, of work, or of vocational calling. Perhaps failure, unwise decisions, disappointment, deep personal wounds, and/or even seemingly unanswered prayer have contributed to a wrong understanding of providence. It needs emphasizing that providence, properly understood, does not equate to fatalism. It is not a sort of predeterminism that somehow frustrates or torments us and to which we all must begrudgingly submit. Rather, it implies a purposefulness and, as noted above, it connotes God's *provision*. Providence is not meant to cause us to lament, "Such and such must be God's will, so unfortunately we'll just have to accept it." Providence, rather, should invoke within us the response, "Even in this adversity God's good purposes can be achieved, since there is a time and season for everything under heaven" (Eccl 3:1 and 7:14). And as chapter 4 of the present volume sought to make abundantly clear, providence does not cancel out that marvelous realm of free will and moral agency with which human beings are endowed. In fact, negatively viewed, even Judas's treachery did not negate God's redemptive purposes; mysteriously, it was used by God—though not *caused* by God—for our greater good.[31]

Ecclesiastes in particular, perhaps more than any biblical book, makes a case for God's inscrutability. However, the fact that the divine nature is "inscrutable" does not mean that it is necessarily an *utter* mystery. That is, God has revealed himself and his nature through both general and special forms of revelation.[32] The fact that God sustains the universe in a general way and prevents it from degenerating into a state of chaos demonstrates the centrality of "common grace" and the "natural law." Thus, for

30. Blamires, *The Will and the Way*, 44.

31. See Matt 26:24. Redemption is part of God's character, not an exception to it. Incarnation and redemption belong to the very nature of God himself.

32. This is essentially the argument that opens St. Paul's letter to the Christians living in the imperial seat of Rome; see 1:2—2:16.

example, God does not simply intervene directly to cause all of nature and the cosmos to continue and function.

The natural law, what St. Paul refers to as the law "written on the heart" (Rom 2:14–15 and implied in 1:19–20), makes human beings aware of basic moral reality that is woven into the fabric of creation and part of our design in the image of God. Human beings demonstrate this awareness when they make statements such as "People reap what they sow" or "What goes around comes around." The awareness of the natural law can be seen, for example, in the language of the founding fathers of the American "experiment in liberty." These individuals assumed—and frequently spoke in terms of—the "laws of nature and of nature's God." These laws, in turn, formed the basis for what they called "self-evident truths" and particular "inalienable rights." Even in the mid-first century, we find the Apostle Paul, in his work in Athens, utilizing general revelation and similar categories while addressing Epicureans and Stoics at the Areopagus for the purposes of bridge-building (Acts 16:22–34).

Where do these reflections on divine providence and inscrutability leave us? The realities of creation, providence, incarnation, and redemption lead us not to pronounce judgment on the world and flee from it but rather to *enter* it—with all of its sin, its anguish, and its meaninglessness (*hebel*) as people experience it. We do this with a view toward redeeming and restoring particular spheres of the created order as stewards of that order, and we do it through our lives and our God-given gifts in service to God and to others.[33] Each believer's self-offering opens doors that allow divine grace to express itself, shining into all of the created order. What is more, each individual's self-offering joins that of millions of others, permitting our presence in the world to have a leavening effect.[34]

Nowhere will this effect be felt in a cumulative way as it will in the marketplace.

A "Theology" of Vocation

Let us recall our prior assumption concerning providence: God is *ceaselessly*—not occasionally—operative in human affairs, even when this working is unseen or indiscernible; God's works, as all of Ecclesiastes reminds

33. John Paul II's encyclical letter of 1981, *Laborem Exercens*, states the matter quite well: "only through work" can human beings serve fellow human beings (no. 12).

34. Few have expressed this with greater clarity than Blamires, *The Will and the Way*, 62.

us, are inscrutable.[35] Recall as well that the divine will is not fatalistic. What sets human creatures apart from all of creation is the *imago Dei* and moral agency. We exercise the glorious realm of free will throughout our lives on a continual basis, even when many of our daily decisions are not freighted with moral implications. We can shop at Walmart or Aldi, walk on the left or right side of the street, drive a Ford or a Nissan, live in New York or Los Angeles, and tip at 15 percent or 20 percent. We can choose more education or less education, as well as where we wish to be educated. And, of course, we choose *the reason* for which we should be educated. We make decisions, we cultivate virtue or vice through those decisions, and we chart a course for our lives through our decisions in a way that ultimately is in accordance with or in denial of God's design. And it is for this reason that, in the end, every human being will be judged by the One who is creator, sustainer, and judge of all things (Eccl 3:15; 5:6c; 9:1–2; 11:9; 12:1a; and 12:14).

Among those of religious faith, vocation is a generally neglected topic. More often than not it is associated with "religious callings." As we observed in chapter 6, Luther's rupture with the church was fueled in no small part by the "sacred"-versus-"secular" dichotomy. In addition to a new, non-monastic perspective on "vocation," one of the theological factors that helped facilitate the early sixteenth-century Lutheran breakthrough was a new awareness of the linkage between providence and vocation; the two go hand in hand, with the latter issuing out of the former. While providence, as Luther came to understand it, underscores the ceaseless operation of God in human affairs— Luther understood farmers and cobblers and miners and woodworkers and princes and rulers to be occupying particular "stations" in life that were appointed by God—vocation defines the *mode* of that operation.[36] To every individual person God has apportioned or assigned particular and diverse gifts and abilities (Eccl 2:10; 3:22; 5:18–19; 9:9; and 11:2).

In describing the linkage between providence and vocation, someone has said that vocation is "what providence asks of us." Similarly, vocation has been called "the voice of Providence."[37] Thus, we may state categorically that the foundation of the doctrine of vocation, or "calling," is the active presence of God continually and ceaselessly in human history and in our individual lives. To believe, as some do, that life (in general terms) is purposeful but that work (or, at least, most work) is *not* purposeful (and

35. So, for example, 1:13; 3:11, 14; 7:13; and 11:5.

36. The Protestant reformational argument was not that any particular kind of work pleases God; rather, that God can be pleased by any kind of work, whereby work and ordinary life achieve a new sense of dignity. This insight needs restating in our own time and in the language of our day.

37. Blamires, *The Will and the Way*, 69.

gratifying), quite simply, is a contradiction. Purpose, at bottom, is to be our criterion and guide in judging and undertaking *any and all* human activity. This applies to all types of work, whether it is cleaning toilets, crunching data, raising crops, doing research, applying medicine, doing computer programming, writing op-ed columns, doing landscaping, studying human psychology, or building houses. Drudgery is inevitable and, at some point, accompanies all work and every human activity. What, however, is crucial is our sensing that this drudgery be "purposeful drudgery" and that the task contributes to the common good.[38]

It has been standard for much of the church's history to speak of two general types of calling—a calling to Christ and a calling to a specific task or service in the form of one's daily obligations. Out of the "general calling" to Christ and his lordship, specific avenues and types of service are assumed, suggested not only by New Testament texts such as Romans 12[39] but also by the Protestant Reformation context wherein Luther, for example, can speak of various life "stations,"[40] as noted above. "Vocation," properly understood, encompasses the totality of our lives, not merely our

38. "Purposeful drudgery" is the expression used by Blamires, *The Will and the Way*, 69–70.

39. In Romans 12, various attitudes are identified by St. Paul as befitting the Christian in terms of public witness—for example, moral integrity, service-orientation, continual transformation of the mind, the ability to discern, sober judgment, humility, and the awareness of gifts given graciously by God to every person. Cf. as well 1 Corinthians 12–14 and Ephesians 4.

40. The relevant literature is not agreed on either the meaning or the contemporary application of Luther's "stations," based on the reformer's treatment of 1 Corinthians 7. The relevant Pauline prescriptions in that text are v. 17—"each one should retain the place in life that the Lord has assigned to him and to which God has called him . . ."—and v. 20—"Each one should remain in the situation which he was in when God called him"—as well as v. 24—"each man, as responsible to God, should remain in the situation God called him to" (NIV). What frequently is ignored in much commentary is the immediate context, which suggests social setting more than "vocation": "Now concerning the matters about which you wrote . . ." (v. 1). The material that follows in Pauline thought, alas, concerns the question of being married, getting married, or remaining married, based on the individual's specific situation as a believer. What is invariably missed or ignored by much commentary on this text is the undergirding premise of Paul's response: namely, *contentedness* in the present. In Luther's day, contentedness corresponded to various "stations" in life. While it would be anachronistic to measure early sixteenth century life with today's standards, this did not necessarily mean an utter lack of mobility or unjust support of the status quo (as, for example, Volf, *Work in the Spirit*, 107–8, has argued). In fact, Luther and Melanchthon, the latter serving as the chief representative of the Reformation cause at the official level, encouraged others to pursue education, which meant mobility in sixteenth-century terms (as much, that is, as social structures of the time allowed).

career, occupation, present job, or so-called "retirement"—although vocation does encompass *all of those,* and more.[41]

Moreover, everyone has a "calling," even when many do not have a
clear sense of it or a clearly defined "career" or "occupation."[42] In other
words, my work, my job, or my career might come to an end or change, but
my calling (my *vocatio*), which is all-encompassing and broader, does not.
In addition, there might be different "seasons" within my calling, seasons
which seem to involve unrelated jobs, responsibilities, or duties, yet all of
this occurs within my wider calling.

Vocational questions, it needs emphasizing, follow us through various
stages of our lives. Not just when we head off to college. Not just when we
graduate from college and enter the workforce. But in middle adulthood
and later adulthood as well. In any case, the Christian wrestles with—and
keeps in tension—two basic vocational questions: *How is God calling me to
serve him at this time, in this season of life?* and *What is my wider calling in
life, for which I've been given particular gifts, abilities, capacities, and passions
or burdens?* Having a sense of the latter—i.e., an awareness of our wider
calling in life—will anchor us, giving meaning and purpose to the particular
season in which we presently find ourselves.

Perhaps at this point the reader is thinking, "Well and good, and
perhaps even interesting, but *what do we mean in practical terms* by 'vocation'?" "What does it mean for me to think vocationally?" For the sake of
some clarity, let us consider several descriptions or definitions of "vocation."
Properly understood,

- Vocation entails the basic awareness that based on the image of God
  (i.e., his likeness), we are created for work; hence, through vocation we
  respond to God's initiative, which itself is a form of worship.

- Vocation entails the awareness that we do not "choose" our calling;
  rather, it "chooses" us. Just as none of us choose our DNA, our families
  or our children, in the same way we *receive*—that is to say, we discover—our vocation from God. The term *discovery* is apt to the extent
  that the awareness of our calling is often a gradual process, coming to
  us over time in whispers rather than in supernatural manifestations.[43]

41. Perhaps the most helpful resource on vocation and calling remains Lee Hardy's
The Fabric of This World, published in 1990. Hardy attempts to flesh out the neglected
tradition of vocation, considering its history, its meaning, and its application.

42. To say that the entire Christian life is a "response" to God's "call" is true at a
certain level; however, this assertion does not really help us in terms of practically discerning the specific contours of our individual callings. More needs to be said.

43. In order to remove some of the unnecessary "mystery" that surrounds "calling,"

- Vocation entails the desire to meet genuine human need around us. While we cannot meet *every* surrounding need, we are individually equipped in such a way as to be able—through gifts and abilities, energy and influence—to meet *some* need around us in a strategic, specific, and practical sense.

- Vocation entails our recognition of skills, talents, and abilities that have been given to each of us by God and of which we are stewards; stewardship involves an intentional and guided development of those skills and abilities.[44]

- Vocation entails a willing desire to serve others and thereby serve the common good. What is the Great Commandment identified in the Old Testament and reiterated by Jesus in the New Testament? Serve God and serve your neighbor.[45] *That* is constitutive of our calling.

- Vocation entails the recognition that we are placed in particular social-cultural contexts. For most of those reading this book, the context of

---

it needs emphasizing that our basic posture is not to expect "blind-light" revelations, lay out fleeces, or require "signs" from God; rather, it is a *response*—a response to live in prayerful confidence and trust that God will guide our steps and bless the work of our hands, regardless of the particular season of life and where we happen to find ourselves. The "will of God," after all, is *relational*, not geographical or circumstantial. In our day, unlike previous generations, we need to be reconciled to the fact that most careers and work paths are not guaranteed or unchanging; moreover, our lives are marked by detours, dead-ends, unmarked intersections, and unexpected surprises. And it may be the case that working a job—*any* job—for a season is healthy, causing our desires and our goals to settle and take shape. While the topic of guidance takes us too far afield of the present discussion, elsewhere I have written briefly on its relationship to vocation. See Charles, "Take This Job and Shove It," esp. 136–39. Although somewhat dated, Joseph Bayly's edited volume *Essays on Guidance*, published in 1968, contains helpful wisdom that is a necessary corrective to the impatient and the mystical side of us.

44. Stewardship, of course, is the lesson of the "parable of the talents" (Matt 25:14–30; cf. Luke 19:12–27). Even when the context in which the parable is lodged is "messianic" and concerns Jerusalem and Israel's "calling," its application in terms of generic stewardship is timeless—for example: (1) various talents are given by the Master; (2) the stewards vary in terms of their responses to the Master and their willingness to "invest"; (3) the Master departs for an unspecified period ("a long time"), leaving his return unknown; (4) those stewards who are faithful ("wise") and who bring an increase are a cause of great joy to the Master, resulting in his affirmation and their increase; (5) the unfaithful ("unwise") steward has a distorted view of the Master (that is, he should have known better); and (6) the fact that the unfaithful steward does not use and invest his talents evokes a strong negative response by the Master. Elsewhere, we find Jesus teaching that faithfulness in the small is measurement of faithfulness in the larger (Luke 16:10–12). Calling, then, works by our response, i.e., "by affection rather than by coercion" (Trueblood, *Your Other Vocation*, 65).

45. Lev 19:18; Matt 22:36–40; Mark 12:28–34; and Luke 10:25–28.

that calling is *not* Kazakhstan or Kenya or Calcutta; it is here where God has placed us, likely between California and Connecticut.[46] Callings must be culture-specific and culturally relevant.[47]

- Finally, because vocation entails the recognition of work's intrinsic worth, dignity, and value, work therefore is its own reward in terms of a certain level of satisfaction. Work must not be our *identity*, but it does offer a measure of satisfaction, properly viewed, since it is that for which we have been created.[48]

All of these descriptions of vocation or calling have their foundation in theological truth. This foundation, as several chapters of the present volume have suggested, is supported by the doctrines of creation, providence, redemption, and incarnation, all of which are interlocking and inform one other.

The benefits of thinking vocationally, it needs emphasizing, are many; and they are both profound and quite practical. Thinking vocationally, for example, will prevent us from a sort of chaotic, day-to-day, meaningless lifestyle that can plague us when we have no sense of direction.[49] This sort of mode of living, of course, takes its toll on us both spiritually and mentally-psychologically. For some of us, it can even lead to despair. Relatedly, thinking vocationally liberates us from what someone has called the "tyranny of

---

46. My argument here is not that God does not or cannot call us to a form of service in other parts of the globe; it is only that we take seriously where we have been planted. Again, it bears repeating that work (in whatever form) is central to our calling, and therefore that the Christian community's chief social witness will be its witness in the *workplace*. It is there that we spend most of our waking hours serving God and others; it is there that we contribute most to the common good.

47. Years ago I responded to a "call" to leave North American culture and live in Europe. Although I had no idea how long that season of life would last, it ended up lasting several years. This meant, of course, that I had to "re-acclimate" myself and learn a new culture, which meant learning the language (which is basic to understanding any culture) and learning to adopt that particular culture's values. In hindsight, I can say (with great joy) that this season of life was by far the most formative for me and the most satisfying, even when it required a humbling and personally "breaking" process. Faith must clothe itself in ways that are meaningful to the specific culture to which we are called.

48. Biblically and theologically, vocation is anchored in a commitment to serve others and glorify God, not self-therapy or self-actualization. At the same time, we may expect that a measure of satisfaction and contentedness comes through our service to others (and hence to God). This satisfaction, after all, is a divine "gift," coming from "the hand of God" (Eccl 2:24; 3:13; 3:22a; 5:18–20; 8:15; and 9:7).

49. In this regard Calvin notes: "Therefore each individual has his own kind of living assigned to him by the Lord as a sort of sentry post so that he may not heedlessly wander about throughout life" (*Institutes of the Christian Religion* III.10.6).

the urgent"—a tyranny insofar as the lack of direction and purpose have the effect of paralyzing us when faced with competing priorities. In addition, thinking vocationally keeps us from a false sense of duty and conformity to the world and its standards, while also freeing us from comparing ourselves with others—i.e., becoming people-pleasers. Living in the reverential fear of God rather than in the fear of what others think is liberating, causing us to be at peace with ourselves and giving us a boldness and confidence. Finally, it liberates us from the common but insidious "sacred"-versus-"secular" view of work and calling that afflicts every generation of believers.[50]

Dorothy Sayers, already cited in the present chapter, possessed a sturdy understanding of vocation, asserting that "every worker is called to serve God in his [or her] profession or trade—not outside it."[51] But Sayers was attentive to the standard pious objection: *What about Acts 6 and the apostles' priority, which was that they not leave the ministry of the word and prayer in order to serve tables?* Her response bears repeating. The person whose vocation it is to prepare meals "might with equal justice protest" in the following manner: "It is not meet for us to leave the service of our tables to preach the word."[52] In fact, she insisted, the church "commits sacrilege" if it encourages its members to go into so-called "Christian work" rather than to the marketplace.[53] Her point is well-taken: calling cuts both ways, and the fact of the matter is that most all of us—over 99 percent of us—are vocationally called to the *marketplace*, not to church work. The overwhelming majority of Christians are not in "full-time Christian service" as it is commonly understood; nor are we meant to be! Hence, we continually need to tear down the false "sacred"-versus-"secular" dichotomy that arises in the thinking of many devoutly religious believers and extol the dignity of "secular" work.

Further (and Final) Reflections on Human Labor

Although the concept of work can turn into an "exaggerated mystique," as one papal encyclical warned us two generations ago, nevertheless "it is something willed and approved by God." Fashioned in the image of our Creator, we "cooperate" with God in "completing the work of creation and engraving on the earth the spiritual imprint" that we ourselves have received as God's

---

50. None has expressed the "benefits" of thinking vocationally more practically and usefully than Smith, *Courage and Calling*, 128–47.

51. Sayers, "Why Work?," 107.

52. Sayers, "Why Work?," 107–8.

53. Sayers, "Why Work?," 108.

image-bearers. "Every worker," therefore, "to some extent, is a creator," wheth-er "artist, craftsman, executive, labourer or farmer."[54]

Even when sin has marred the beauty of the created order, God's origi-nal intention was not "withdrawn or cancelled" due to the fall, since human creation was in God's image and according to his likeness. The consequence is that "dominion" is still "proper to him over the visible world."[55] That ap-plication of "dominion" or subduing of creation is, therefore, "good"—and good in multiple senses: (1) it is good in the sense that work possesses worth, value, and therefore dignity; (2) it is good in the sense of work's satisfaction or enjoyment both in and through one's labor; and, most importantly, (3) it is good in that our work contributes to the common good and the good of our neighbor in a social manner.[56]

The third of the aforementioned "goods," the common good, needs our thoughtful consideration, particularly among Protestants, for whom the language of the "common good" is not deeply embedded in our faith-life, given our more recent history and the emphasis on *personal* (as opposed to *public*) faith.[57] Work serves not only the purpose of providing for one's own needs but "above all, to elevating unceasingly the cultural and moral level of the society" whereby the individual lives "in community with those who belong to the same [human] family."[58] It is well worth pondering whether contemporary evangelically minded believers—and evangelically oriented churches—are capable of placing the needs of the broader "common good" above purely personal needs. That communal burden is perhaps best mea-sured not by social or political activism, as mainline Protestants would have it, but by the value that we place on our service in the workforce and the dignity that we ascribe to our daily tasks.

Relatedly, working for the common good underscores the fact that there are wide-ranging implications of the creation mandate. The "subduing" of

54. Pope Paul VI, *Populorum Progressio* no. 27.

55. Pope John Paul II, *Laborem Exercens* no. 9.

56. Pope John Paul II, *Laborem Exercens* no. 9.

57. In spite of the Catholic view of work and "calling" that crystallized during the Middle Ages, against which the Protestant reformers reacted, one can observe a shift—indeed, a "reformed shift," as Hardy, *The Fabric of This World*, 67, calls it—that has been occurring over the last 100 years. It began in the 1890s with Pope Leo XIII's encyclical *Rerum Novarum* (1891), which addressed the pressing "social question " of the day, and has continued particularly through the influence of John Paul II, who produced two major encyclicals on work: *Laborem Exercens* (1981) and *Centesimus Annus* (1991), the latter celebrating the one-hundredth anniversary of *Rerum Novarum*. In the early twenty-first century we are witnessing a convergence of Protestant reformed thought and Catholic social teaching that is extremely encouraging.

58. Pope John Paul II, *Centesimus Annus* no. 6.

creation—and the language of "subduing" is biblical, not reckless, language which automatically produces exploitation—is inter-generational in nature, even when at the same time it is inter- and intra-personal. At the macro level, the dominion mandate that extends to all of creation necessarily entails the cultivation of every conceivable aspect of cultural and economic development.[59] "Service" to others, then, will always be inherently *economic* in nature, inasmuch as it involves abilities, resources, and goods and aims at building the common good.

Biblical faith, as chapter 4 sought to demonstrate, describes God chiefly as *working*: he creates, makes covenant, redeems, justifies, sanctifies, cultivates, and transforms. From Genesis to Revelation, from creation to the new Jerusalem, "the biblical narratives overflow with work."[60] In the beginning of the creation narrative, as we have repeatedly stressed, work arises not because of the fall but because of the *imago Dei*.[61] According to Genesis 3 and countering the perception of not a few religious believers, the *ground* was cursed, not *work*. Human work is patterned after the divine model; therein we share in God's likeness. In Jesus' parabolic teaching, work or work-related themes predominate.[62] Building, fishing, investing, planning, administrating, and stewarding are at the heart of his illustrations. And even the apostle to the Gentiles does not abandon his trade after being called by God to take up the apostolic ministry; he still makes tents. Furthermore, we can assume that the disciples—*all* of them—continued in their professions. In the early church, there were no "clergy"; all were "laity." Fishermen still fished in the sea of Galilee, even when they were made "fishers of men." In fact, our Lord himself, before a mere three-year messianic stint, spent the better part of thirty years apprenticing and working as a carpenter. Does anyone think that the Son of God was getting impatient as he awaited the time of his revealing? Does anyone think that he did shoddy woodwork? Is it conceivable that he on occasion made bad furniture?

Earlier in this chapter we noted the "revolutionary" attitude toward work that was called for by Dorothy Sayers. Work, according to Sayers, is best

59. As observed earlier in the present volume, the *misuse* of creation's resources cannot be laid at the feet of Christians' vision to "subdue" and cultivate all of creation, which is an issue of stewardship and obedience.

60. Jensen, *Responsive Labor*, 22.

61. In the words of Plantinga, *Not the Way It's Supposed to Be*, 199, creation is stronger than sin, and grace is stronger still.

62. One finds over fifty occurrences in the Gospel accounts of Jesus resorting to parabolic discourse for the purposes of teaching, and most of these have work-related themes at their core.

understood as "a creative activity undertaken for the love of the work itself."[63] This understanding, it is safe to say, is far removed from how most people, even *many Christians*, would view their jobs and their day-to-day role in the marketplace. Several underlying convictions and baseline assumptions, as Sayers saw it, needed identifying—foremost among these: (1) human beings image the very nature of God; (2) because of this there exists an almost "sacramental" relationship between the human person and work; (3) in work the Christian should find spiritual, mental, and physical satisfaction; (4) work is a medium in which the human person offers himself/herself to God; and (5) the only truly "Christian" work is work that is well done.[64]

Permit me, upon concluding, to add yet another conviction to those of Sayers. The very notion of rewards presupposes the value of work when it is done with the proper motivation. The New Testament epistle of James, in fact, argues that "a person is justified [and therefore judged] by what he [or she] *does* and not by faith alone."[65] And on that final day, judgment will be according our works[66]—the very note on which the book of Ecclesiastes ends (12:14). The implication of this reality should strike us with force: our efforts here on earth in the present truly mean something, and their fruit will endure beyond this life. Even when the New Testament writers speak of "a new heaven and a new earth," there will be some continuity with the present life.[67] Our works and the created order will not simply be thrown on some cosmic ashheap; they will *remain* in some discernible form and fashion, even when that form is mysteriously *transformed*.[68]

63. Sayers, "Why Work?," 89.

64. Sayers, "Why Work?," 101, 108.

65. Jas 2:24 (emphasis mine); cf. 2:17. Perhaps there exists some correspondence between our difficulty with these statements in James and contemporary (Christian) views on work.

66. Ps 62:12; Prov 24:12; Eccl 12:14; 1 Cor 3:13–15; 2 Cor 5:10; and Rev 20:12; cf. 1 Pet 1:17.

67. Even the well-known text of Rom 8:19–22, which describes creation's "groaning," serves as evidence: redemption and "release" mean not obliteration in an absolute sense, but rather a transforming of the present state, and hence some form of *continuity* that will be distinguishable.

68. Full disclosure: it is this perspective on stewardship—i.e., that the fruits of our work will endure eternally—that has infused (and transformed) my own thinking about work and vocation in recent years. Fully aside from fatherhood, I have gladly worked in the realms of education, public policy, and ethics at the professional level, wholly invigorated by a sense that I have been investing my God-given gifts and abilities in the ongoing process of "creation regained" (irrespective of any so-called "success" in these efforts). And yet I am also well aware that the church, inclusive of the training institutions for Christian leadership (i.e., seminaries and divinity schools), has largely failed her constituents. We have not properly equipped our own—that 99 percent of

The Christian church has not always had a healthy view of work. For this reason the Lutheran breakthrough in the early sixteenth century was so important, for it addressed two primary—and abiding—distortions regarding work: (1) the notion of work as salvation or justification before God and (2) the "sacred"-versus-"secular" dichotomy, which existed—and continues to exist—because of the religious devaluation of earthly occupations, as personified in monastic orders and the priesthood. Work, for Luther, was a divine vocation. When people asked what they should do, the *last* thing Luther could recommend was to retreat into the desert or to a monastery. Rather, serve God and others *where you are*, he would have said. Every believer is a priest, serving God and society *through work*.

But we need not look solely to Luther and the sixteenth century, even when the Protestant breakthrough has much to teach us 500 years removed. Three generations ago, theologian Emil Brunner, writing about the same time as Dorothy Sayers was reflecting on the devaluation of work, stated the truth of the importance of work and vocation. As an idea, Brunner noted, vocation "has been degraded, so disgracefully, into something quite trivial." In his view, it "has been denuded of its daring and liberating religious meaning" to such an extent that "we might even ask whether it would not be better to renounce it altogether." On the other hand, he insisted, "it is a conception which in its Scriptural sense is so full of force and so pregnant in meaning" that "to renounce this expression would mean losing a central part of the Christian message."[69]

With both Brunner and Sayers, we stand in a period of noteworthy social and political upheaval. And with both, we might argue as well that to devalue the nature of work and to renounce (or misconstrue) the notion of vocation is to lose a central—if not *the* central—part of Christian witness to the world. Time will tell whether the Christian church, at least in the West, will regain the "daring and liberating" religious meaning of work and vocation.

Reading the book of Ecclesiastes, with new and open eyes, would be a good place to start in that recovery process.

---

our congregants—to understand the true nature of "vocation" and thus to view their "secular" callings to the marketplace as "holy," high, and noble, and central to God's intention.

69. Brunner, *The Divine Imperative*, 205–6.

Bibliography

Adams, Samuel L. *Wisdom in Transition: Act and Consequence in Second Temple Instructions.* Leiden: Brill, 2008.

Albright, W. F. "Canaanite Phoenician Sources of Hebrew Wisdom." In *Wisdom in Israel and the Ancient Near East,* edited by Martin Noth and David Winton Thomas, 1–15. VTSup 3. Leiden: Brill, 1969.

Alter, Robert. *The Art of Biblical Narrative.* Rev. ed. New York: Basic, 2011.

———. *The Wisdom Books: Job, Proverbs and Ecclesiastes.* New York: W. W. Norton, 2010.

Anderson, Bernard W. *Understanding the Old Testament.* 2d ed. Englewood Cliffs, NJ: Prentice-Hall, 1966.

Anderson, William H. U. "The Curse of Work in Qoheleth: An Exposé of Genesis 3:17–19 in Ecclesiastes." *EvQ* 70 (1998) 99–113.

———. *Qoheleth and Its Pessimistic Theology: Hermeneutical Struggles in Wisdom Literature.* MBPS 54. Lewiston, NY: Edwin Mellen, 1997.

Armstrong, James F. "Ecclesiastes in Old Testament Theology." *Princeton Seminary Bulletin* 4, no. 1 (1983) 16–25.

Atkinson, Tyler. *Singing at the Winepress: Ecclesiastes and the Ethics of Work.* London: Bloomsbury T. & T. Clark, 2015.

Balantine, Samuel E. *Wisdom Literature.* CBS. Nashville: Abingdon, 2018.

Barr, James. *Biblical Words for Time.* London: SCM, 1962.

Bartholomew, Craig. "Qoheleth in the Canon? Current Trends in the Interpretation of Ecclesiastes." *Them* 24, no. 3 (May 1999) 4–20.

Barton George A. "The Text and Interpretation of Ecclesiastes 5:19." *JBL* 27, no. 1 (1908) 65–66.

Barton, John. *Reading the Old Testament.* Philadelphia: Westminster, 1984.

Bayly, Joseph, ed. *Essays on Guidance.* Downers Grove, IL: InterVarsity, 1968.

Beckwith, Roger. *The Old Testament Canon of the New Testament Church.* Grand Rapids: Eerdmans, 1985.

Berger, Benjamin L. "Qohelet and the Exigencies of the Absurd." *Biblical Interpretation* 9, no. 2 (2001) 141–79.

Bickell, Gustav. *Der Prediger über den Wert des Daseins.* Innsbruck: Wagner, 1884.

Bickermann, Elias. *Four Strange Books of the Bible.* New York: Schocken, 1967.

Blamires, Harry. *The Will and the Way.* New York: Macmillan, 1957.

Blenkinsopp, Joseph. "Ecclesiastes 3.1–5: Another Interpretation." *JSOT* 66 (1995) 55–64.

———. *Wisdom and Law in the Old Testament: The Ordering of Life in Israel and Early Judaism.* Oxford: Oxford University Press, 1995.

Borgman, Brian. "Redeeming the 'Problem Child': Qoheleth's Message and Place in the Family of Scripture." *SBJTh* 15, no. 3 (Fall 2011) 62–71.

Braun, Rainer. *Kohelet und die frühhellenistische Populärphilosophie.* BZAW 130. Berlin: Walter de Gruyter, 1973.

Brown, William P. "Book of Ecclesiastes—I." In *Encyclopedia of the Bible and Its Reception—Vol. 7*, edited by Dale C. Allison, Jr., et al., 278–79. Berlin: Walter de Gruyter, 2013.

———. "Character Reconstructed: Ecclesiastes." In *Character in Crisis: A Fresh Approach to the Wisdom Literature of the Old Testament*, 120–50. Grand Rapids: Eerdmans, 1996.

———. *Ecclesiastes.* Interpretation: A Bible Commentary for Teaching and Preaching. Louisville, KY: John Knox, 2000.

———. "'Whatever Your Hand Finds to Do': Qoheleth's Work Ethic." *Interpretation* 55, no. 3 (2001) 271–84.

———. *Wisdom's Wonder: Character, Creation, and Crisis in the Bible's Wisdom Literature.* Grand Rapids: Eerdmans, 2014.

Broyde, Michael J. "Defilement of the Hands, Canonization of the Bible, and the Special Status of Esther, Ecclesiastes, and Song of Songs." *Judaism* 44, no. 1 (1995) 65–74.

Brunner, Emil. *The Divine Imperative: A Study of Christian Ethics.* Translated by Olive Wyon. London: Lutterworth, 1937.

Caneday, A. B. "'Everything is Vapor': Grasping for Meaning under the Sun." *SBJTh* 15, no. 3 (Fall 2011) 26–40.

Carasik, Michael. "Qoheleth's Twists and Turns." *JSOT* 28, no. 2 (2003) 192–209.

Carroll, Vincent, and David Shiflett. "Christianity and Science." In *Christianity on Trial: Arguments against Anti-Religious Bigotry*, 54–85. New York: Encounter, 2002.

Castellino, G. R. "Qohelet and His Wisdom." *CBQ* 30, no. 1 (1968) 15–28.

Catechism of the Catholic Church. Washington, DC: United States Catholic Conference, 1994.

Chang, Frances. "Suffering and Enjoyment/Hope in the Progress of Revelation: Qohelet and Romans 8:18–39." PhD diss., Dallas Theological Seminary, 2011.

Charles, J. Daryl. "Biblical Resources for Ethics: The Pauline Model." In *The Unformed Conscience of Evangelicalism: Recovering the Church's Moral Vision*, 144–57. Downers Grove, IL: InterVarsity, 2002 (repr. Fontes, 2020).

———. "Engaging the (Neo)Pagan Mind: Paul's Encounter with Athenian Culture as a Model for Cultural Apologetics (Acts 17:16–34)." *TJ* 16, no. 1 (Spring 1995) 47–62.

———. "Take This Job and Shove It: Theological Reflections on Vocation, Calling, and Work." In *Wisdom's Work: Essays on Ethics, Vocation, and Culture*, 121–39. Grand Rapids: Acton Institute, 2019.

———. "Wisdom and Work: Perspectives on Human Labor from Ecclesiastes." *JMM* 22, no. 1 (Spring 2019) 7–40.

Childs, Brevard. *Introduction to the Old Testament as Scripture.* London: Fortress, 1979.

Christianson, Eric S. "Ecclesiastes in Premodern Reading: Before 1500 CE." In *The Words of the Wise Are like Goads: Engaging Qohelet in the 21st Century*, edited by Mark J. Boda et al., 3–36. Winona Lake, IN: Eisenbrauns, 2013.

————. "Qoheleth and the Existential Legacy of the Holocaust." *HeyJ* 38, no. 1 (1997) 35–50.

————. *A Time to Tell: Narrative Strategies in Ecclesiastes.* JSOTSS 280. Sheffield: Sheffield Academic, 1998.

Clemens, David M. "The Law of Sin and Death: Ecclesiastes and Genesis 1–3." *Them* 19, no. 3 (1994) 5–8.

Clifford, Richard J. *The Wisdom Literature.* IBT. Nashville: Abingdon, 1998.

————, ed. *Wisdom Literature in Mesopotamia and Israel.* Atlanta: Society of Biblical Literature, 2007.

Crenshaw, James L. *Ecclesiastes: A Commentary.* OTL. Philadelphia: Westminster, 1987.

————. "Ecclesiastes (Qoheleth)." In *Urgent Advice and Probing Questions: Collected Writings on Old Testament Wisdom,* 499–519. Macon, GA: Mercer University Press, 1995.

————. *Old Testament Wisdom: An Introduction.* Rev. ed. Louisville: Westminster John Knox, 1998.

————, ed. *Studies in Ancient Israelite Wisdom.* New York: KTAV, 1976.

————. "Unresolved Issues in Wisdom Literature." In *An Introduction to Wisdom Literature and the Psalms,* edited by H. Wayne Ballard, Jr. and W. Dennis Tucker, Jr., 215–27. Macon, GA: Mercer University Press, 2000.

Crüsemann, Frank. "The Unchangeable World: The 'Crisis of Wisdom' in Koheleth." In *God of the Lowly: Socio-Historical Interpretations of the Bible,* edited by Willy Schottroff and Wolfgang Stegemann, 59–74. Translated by M. J. O'Connell. Maryknoll, NY: Orbis, 1984.

Curtis, Edward M. *Ecclesiastes and Song of Songs.* TTC. Grand Rapids: Baker, 2013.

Dahood, Mitchell J. "Canaanite-Phoenician Influence in Qoheleth." *Biblica* 33 (1952) 30–52.

Davidson, Robert. *The Courage to Doubt: Exploring an Old Testament Theme.* London: SCM, 1983.

Delitzsch, Franz. *Hoheslied und Koheleth.* BC 4. Leipzig: Dörfling und Franke, 1875.

Dell, Katharine J. *Interpreting Ecclesiastes: Readers Old and New.* Winona Lake, IN: Eisenbrauns, 2013.

Dell, Katharine, and Tora Forti. "Janus Sayings: A Linking Device in Qoheleth's Discourse." *ZAW* 128, no. 1 (2016) 115–28.

DeLoach, Albertus L. "The Concept of Work in Ecclesiastes." MST thesis, University of the South, 1972.

Dempster, Stephen G. "Ecclesiastes and the Canon." In *The Words of the Wise Are like Goads: Engaging Qohelet in the 21st Century,* edited by Mark J. Boda et al., 387–400. Winona Lake, IN: Eisenbrauns, 2013.

DeRouchie, Jason S. "Shepherding Wind and One Wise Shepherd: Grasping for Breath in Ecclesiastes." *SBJTh* 15, no. 3 (Fall 2011) 4–25.

Dillard, Raymond B., and Tremper Longman III. *An Introduction to the Old Testament.* Grand Rapids: Zondervan, 1994.

Douglas, Jerome N. *A Polemical Preacher of Joy: An Anti-Apocalyptic Genre for Qoheleth's Message of Joy.* Eugene, OR: Pickwick, 2014.

Duncan, Julie Ann. *Ecclesiastes.* AOTC. Nashville: Abingdon, 2017.

Eaton, Michael A. *Ecclesiastes: An Introduction and Commentary.* TOTC 16. Downers Grove, IL: InterVarsity, 1983.

Eichrodt, Walther. *Man in the Old Testament.* Translated by K. and R. Gregory Smith. SBT 4. London: SCM, 1951.

———. *Theology of the Old Testament—Volume 1.* Translated by J. A. Baker. OTL. Philadelphia: Westminster, 1961.

———. *Theology of the Old Testament—Volume 2.* Translated by J. A. Baker. OTL. Philadelphia: Westminster, 1967.

Eliason, Eric J. "*Vanitas Vanitatum*: 'Piers Lowman,' Ecclesiastes, and Contempt for the World." PhD diss., University of Virginia, 1989.

Ellis, Peter F. *The Men and the Message of the Old Testament.* Collegeville, MN: Liturgical, 1963.

Ellul, Jacques. *Reason for Being: A Meditation on Ecclesiastes.* Translated by Joyce M. Hanks. Grand Rapids: Eerdmans, 1990.

Enns, Peter. *Ecclesiastes.* THOTC. Grand Rapids: Eerdmans, 2011.

———. "Ecclesiastes according to the Gospel: Christian Reflections on Qohelet's Theology." *Scripture and Interpretation* 2, no. 1 (2008) 25–38.

Eswine, Zack. *Recovering Eden: The Gospel according to Ecclesiastes.* Phillipsburg, NJ: P&R, 2014.

Faulkner, R. O. "The Man Who Was Tired of Life." *JEA* 42, no. 1 (1956) 21–40.

Fee, Gordon D., and Douglas Stuart. *How to Read the Bible for All Its Worth.* Grand Rapids: Zondervan, 1982.

Finnegan, Ruth. "Proverbs." In *Oral Literature in Africa,* 379–412. Oxford: Oxford University Press, 1970.

Fisch, Harold. *Poetry with a Purpose.* Bloomington, IN: Indiana University Press, 1988.

Fletcher, Douglas K. "Ecclesiastes 5:1–7." *Interpretation* 55, no. 3 (2001) 296–98.

Fox, Michael V. *Ecclesiastes.* JPS Bible Commentary. Philadelphia: The Jewish Publication Society, 2004.

———. "Frame-Narrative and Composition in the Book of Qoheleth." *HUCA* 48 (1977) 83–106.

———. "The Inner-Structure of Qohelet's Thought." In *Qohelet in the Context of Wisdom,* edited by Anton Schoors, 225–38. BETL 136. Leuven: Peeters, 1998.

———. *Qohelet and His Contradictions.* JSOTSS 71. Sheffield: Sheffield Academic, 1989.

———. *A Time to Tear Down and a Time to Build Up.* Grand Rapids: Eerdmans, 1999.

———. "Wisdom in Qohelet." In *In Search of Wisdom,* edited by Leo G. Perdue et al., 115–31. Louisville: Westminster John Knox, 1993.

Fredericks, Daniel C. *Coping with Transcience: Ecclesiastes on Brevity in Life.* Biblical Seminar. Sheffield: JSOT Press, 1993.

———. "Preaching Qohelet." In *The Words of the Wise Are like Goads: Engaging Ecclesiastes in the 21st Century,* edited by Mark J. Boda et al., 417–42. Winona Lake, IN: Eisenbrauns, 2013.

———. *Qohelet's Language: Re-evaluating Its Nature and Date.* ANETS 3. Lewiston, NY: Edwin Mellen, 1988.

Fredericks, Daniel C., and Daniel J. Estes. *Ecclesiastes and the Song of Songs.* AOTC 16. Nottingham, UK: Apollos, 2010.

Frydrych, Tomás. *Living under the Sun: Examination of Proverbs and Qoheleth.* VTSup 90. Leiden: Brill, 2002.

Fuerst, Wesley J. *The Books of Ruth, Esther, Ecclesiastes, the Song of Songs, Lamentations* CBC. Cambridge: Cambridge University Press, 1975.

Galling, Kurt. "Kohelet-Studien." *ZAW* 50 (1932) 276–99.

Garrett, Duane A. *Proverbs, Ecclesiastes, Song of Songs.* NAC 14. Nashville: Broadman, 1993.

Genung, John Franklin. *Words of Koheleth.* Boston: Houghton, Mifflin and Co., 1904.

Gericke, J. W. "Axiological Assumptions in Qohelet: A Historical-Philosophical Clarification." *Verbum et Ecclesia* 33, no. 1 (2012) 1–6.

———. "Qohelet's Concept of Deity: A Comparative-Philosophical Perspective." *Verbum et Ecclesia* 34, no. 1 (2013) 1–8.

Gese, Helmut. "The Crisis of Wisdom in Koheleth." In *Theodicy in the Old Testament,* edited by James L. Crenshaw, 141–53. Philadelphia and London: Fortress and SPCK, 1983.

Gianto, Agustinus. "The Theme of Enjoyment in Qohelet." *Biblica* 73, no. 4 (1992) 528–32.

Gibson, David. *Living Life Backward: How Ecclesiastes Teaches Us to Live in Light of the End.* Wheaton, IL: Crossway, 2017.

Ginsberg, H. L. "The Structure and Contents of the Book of Koheleth." In *Wisdom in Israel and the Ancient Near East,* edited by Martin Noth and David Winton Thomas, 138–49. VTSup 3. Leiden: Brill, 1969.

Glasson, T. F. "'You Never Know': The Message of Ecclesiastes 11:1–6." *EvQ* 55, no. 1 (1983) 43–48.

Gordis, Robert. *Koheleth—The Man and His World: A Study of Ecclesiastes.* New York: Bloch, 1955.

———. "Quotations as a Literary Usage in Biblical, Oriental and Rabbinic Literature." *HUCA* 22 (1949) 157–75.

Greidanus, Sidney. *Preaching Christ from Ecclesiastes.* Grand Rapids: Eerdmans, 2010.

Gutridge, Coralie Ann. "Wisdom, Anti-Wisdom, and the Ethical Function of Uncertainty." PhD diss., University College London, 1998.

Hall, Stephen S. *Wisdom: From Philosophy to Neuroscience.* New York: Alfred A. Knopf, 2010.

Hardy, Lee. *The Fabric of This World: Inquiries into Calling, Career Choice, and the Design of Human Work.* Grand Rapids: Eerdmans, 1990.

Hayman, A. P. "Qohelet and the Book of Creation." *JSOT* 50 (1991) 93–111.

Hempel, Johannes. *Die althebräische Literatur.* Potsdam: Akademische Verlagsgesellschaft, 1930.

Hendry, G. S. "Ecclesiastes." In *New Bible Commentary,* edited by Donald Guthrie and J. A. Motyer, 570–71. Rev. ed. Grand Rapids: Eerdmans, 1970.

Hengel, Martin. *Judaism and Hellenism: Studies in Their Encounter in Palestine During the Early Hellenistic Period—Volume 1.* Translated by John Bowden. Philadelphia: Fortress, 1974.

Hill, R. Charles. *Wisdom's Many Faces.* Collegeville, MN: Liturgical, 1996.

Hinkle, Adrian E. *Pedagogical Theory of Wisdom Literature: An Application of Educational Theory to Biblical Texts.* Eugene, OR: Wipf and Stock, 2017.

Hirschman, Marc. "Qohelet's Reception and Interpretation in Early Rabbinic Literature." In *Studies in Ancient Midrash,* edited by James L. Kugel, 87–99. Cambridge, MA: Harvard University Press, 2001.

Hobbins, John F. "The Poetry of the Book of Qohelet." In *The Words of the Wise Are like Goads: Engaging Ecclesiastes in the 21st Century,* edited by Mark J. Boda et al., 163–93. Winona Lake, IN: Eisenbrauns, 2013.

Holm-Nielsen, S. "On the Interpretation of Qoheleth in Early Christianity." *VT* 24, no. 2 (1974) 168–77.

Holmstedt, Robert D., John A. Cook, and Phillip S. Marshall. *Qoheleth: A Handbook on the Hebrew Text*. BHHB. Waco, TX: Baylor University Press, 2017.

Horne, Milton P. *Proverbs-Ecclesiastes*. SHBC. Macon, GA: Smyth & Helwys, 2003.

Hubbard, David A. *Ecclesiastes, Song of Solomon*. CC. Dallas: Word, 1991.

Huwiler, Elizabeth. "Ecclesiastes." In *Proverbs, Ecclesiastes, Song of Songs*, by Roland E. Murphy and Elizabeth Huwiler, 159–218. NIBC. Peabody, MA: Hendrickson, 1999.

Ingram, Doug. *Ecclesiastes: A Peculiarly Postmodern Piece*. Cambridge, UK: Grove, 2004.

Jarick, John. "The Hebrew Book of Changes: Reflections on *Hakkōl Hebel* and *Lakkōl Zemān* in Ecclesiastes." *JSOT* 90 (2000) 79–99.

Jensen, David H. *Responsive Labor: A Theology of Work*. Louisville: Westminster John Knox, 2006.

Jerome, St. *Commentary on Ecclesiastes*. Edited by Richard J. Goodrich and David J. D. Miller. ACW. New York: Newman, 2012.

John Paul II. *Centesimus Annus*. Encyclical letter, May 1, 1991. http://www.vatican.va/content/paul-vi/en/encyclicals/documents/hf_p-vi_enc_26031967_populorum.html.

———. *Laborem Exercens*. Encyclical letter, September 14, 1981. http://www.vatican.va/content/john-paul-ii/en/encyclicals/documents/hf_jp-ii_enc_14091981_laborem-exercens.html.

Johnson, A. R. "Mashal." In *Wisdom in Israel and the Ancient Near East*, edited by Martin Noth and David Winton Thomas, 162–69. VTSup 3. Leiden: Brill, 1969.

Johnson, Ray E. "The Rhetorical Question as a Literary Device." PhD diss., The Southern Baptist Theological Seminary, 1986.

Jones, Scott C. "The Values and Limits of Qoheleth's Sub-Celestial Economy." *VT* 64, no. 1 (2014) 21–33.

Jong, Stephan de. "A Book of Labour: The Structuring Principles and the Main Theme of the Book of Qohelet." *JSOT* 54 (1992) 107–16.

Kaiser, Otto. "Die Sinnkrise bei Kohelet." In *Der Mensch unter dem Schicksal*, 91–109. BZAW 161. Berlin: Walter de Gruyter, 1985.

Kaiser, Water C., Jr. *Ecclesiastes: Total Life*. Chicago: Moody, 1979.

Kallas, Endel. "Ecclesiastes: Traditum et Fides Evangelica. The Ecclesiastes Commentaries of Martin Luther, Philip Melanchthon, and Johannes Brenz Considered within the History of Interpretation." PhD diss., Graduate Theological Union, 1979.

Keller, Timothy, and Katherine Leary Alsdorf. *Every Good Endeavor: Connecting Your Work to God's Work*. New York: Riverhead, 2012.

Kempis, Thomas à. *The Imitation of Christ*. Translated by William Benham. http://www.gutenberg.org/cache/epub/1653/pg1653-images.html.

Kidner, Derek. *A Time to Mourn, and a Time to Dance*. BST. Downers Grove, IL: InterVarsity, 1976.

———. *The Wisdom of Proverbs, Job & Ecclesiastes: An Introduction to Wisdom Literature*. Downers Grove, IL: InterVarsity, 1985.

Kim, Sang-Bae. "A Study of the Linguistic and Thematic Roots of Ecclesiastes." PhD diss., University of Pennsylvania, 2010.

Klein, Christian. *Kohelet und die Weisheit Israels*. BWANT 132. Stuttgart: Kohlhammer, 1994.

Knapp, John C. *How the Church Fails Businesspeople (and What Can Be Done about It)*. Grand Rapids: Eerdmans, 2012.

Knopf, Karl Sumner. "The Optimism of Koheleth." *JBL* 49, no. 2 (1930) 195–99.

Kreeft, Peter. *Three Philosophies of Life*. San Francisco: Ignatius, 1989.

Lauha, Aarre. *Kohelet*. BKAT 19. Neukirchen-Vluyn: Neukirchener Verlag, 1978.

———. "Die Krise des religiösen Glaubens bei Kohelet." In *Wisdom in Israel and in the Ancient Near East*, edited by Martin Noth and David Winton Thomas, 183–91. VTSup 3. Leiden: Brill, 1969.

Lawler, Peter Augustine, and Marc D. Guerra, eds. *Science, Virtue, and the Future of Humanity*. Lanham, MD: Lexington, 2015.

Lee, Eunny P. *The Vitality of Enjoyment in Qohelet's Theological Rhetoric*. BZAW 353. Berlin: Walter de Gruyter, 2005.

Leeuwen, Raymond van. "In Praise of Proverbs." In *Pledges of Jubilee: Essays on the Arts and Culture*, edited by Lambert Zuidervaart and Henry Luttikhuizen, 308–27. Grand Rapids: Eerdmans, 1995.

Leiman, Sid Z. *The Canonization of Hebrew Scripture: The Talmudic and Midrashic Evidence*. Hamden: ARCHON, 1976.

Lo, Alison. "Death in Qohelet." *JANES* 31, no. 1 (2009) 85–98.

Loader, J. A. *Ecclesiastes: A Practical Commentary*. Text and Interpretation. Grand Rapids: Eerdmans, 1986.

———. *Polar Structures in the Book of Qoheleth*. BZAW 152. Berlin: Walter de Gruyter, 1979.

Lohfink, Norbert. *Kohelet*. NEB. Wurzburg: Echter Verlag, 1980.

———. *Qoheleth*. Translated by Sean McEvenue. CC. Minneapolis: Augsburg Fortress, 2003.

———. "Qohelet 5:17–19—Revelation by Joy." *CBQ* 52, no. 4 (1990) 625–35.

Longman, Tremper, III. *The Book of Ecclesiastes*. NICOT. Grand Rapids: Eerdmans, 1998.

———. *The Fear of the Lord Is Wisdom: A Theological Introduction to Wisdom in Israel*. Grand Rapids: Baker, 2017.

Losarío dei Segni (Pope Innocent III). *De miseria condicionis humane*. Edited and translated by Robert E. Lewis. Athens, GA: University of Georgia Press, 1978.

Luther, Martin. *Exposition of Psalm 147*. In *Luther's Works—Volume 14*, edited by Jaroslav Pelikan, 109–34. St. Louis: Concordia, 1958.

———. *Notes on Ecclesiastes; Lectures on the Song of Solomon; Treatise on the Last Words of David*. In *Luther's Works—Volume 15*, edited by Jaroslav Pelikan, 3–187. St. Louis: Concordia, 1972.

———. "*To the Christian Nobility of the German Nation*." In *Luther's Works—Volume 44*, edited by James Atkinson, 123–217. Philadelphia: Fortress, 1966.

———. *Whether Soldiers, Too, Can Be Saved*. "To the Christian Nobility of the German Nation" in *Luther's Works—Volume 46*, edited by Jaroslav Pelikan and Helmut Lehmann, 91–129. Philadelphia: Fortress, 1967.

Lys, Daniel. *L'Ecclésiaste ou Que vaut la vie? Traduction; Introduction générale; Commentaire de 1/1 à 4/3*. Paris: Letouzey et Ané, 1977.

Magarik, Larry. "Darshanut: Bread on Water." *JBQ* 28, no. 4 (2000) 268–70.

Maltby, Arthur. "The Book of Ecclesiastes and the After-Life." *EvQ* 35, no. 1 (1963) 39–44.

McGrath, Alister. "Calvin and the Christian Calling." *FT* 94 (June/July 1999) 31–35.

McKane, William. *Tracts for the Times: Ruth, Esther, Lamentations, Ecclesiastes, Song of Songs*. London and Nashville: Lutterworth and Abingdon, 1965.

Michel, Diethelm. "'Unter der Sonne': Zur Immanenz bei Qohelet." In *Qohelet in the Context of Wisdom*, edited by Anton Schoors, 93–111. BETL 136. Leuven: Peeters, 1998.

———. *Untersuchungen zur Eigenart des Buches Kohelet*. BZAW 183. Berlin: Walter de Gruyter, 1989.

Miller, Douglas B. "What the Preacher Forgot: The Rhetoric of Ecclesiastes." *CBQ* 62, no. 2 (2000) 224–32.

Mitchell, H. G. T. "'Work' in Ecclesiastes." *JBL* 32, no. 2 (1913) 123–38.

Muilenberg, James. "A Qoheleth Scroll from Qumran." *BASOR* 135 (1954) 20–27.

Müller, Hans-Peter. "Wie Sprach Qohälät von Gott?" *VT* 18, no. 4 (1968) 507–21.

Murphy, Roland E. *Ecclesiastes*. WBC 23A. Dallas: Word, 1992.

———. "On Translating Ecclesiastes." *CBQ* 53, no. 4 (1991) 571–79.

———. "The Pensées of Qoheleth." *CBQ* 17 (1955) 184–94.

———. "Qoheleth and Theology?" *Biblical Theology Bulletin* 21 (1991) 30–33.

———. "The Sage in Ecclesiastes and Qohelet the Sage." In *The Sage in Israel and the Ancient Near East*, edited by John G. Gammie and Leo G. Perdue, 263–71. Winona Lake, IN: Eisenbrauns, 1990.

———. "The 'Thoughts' of Coheleth." In *Seven Books of Wisdom*, 87–103. Milwaukee, WI: Bruce, 1960.

———. *The Tree of Life: An Exploration of Biblical Wisdom Literature*. Rev. ed. Grand Rapids: Eerdmans, 2002.

———. *Wisdom Literature*. FOTL 13. Grand Rapids: Eerdmans, 1981.

Neriya-Cohen, Nava. "Rashbam's Understanding of the Carpe Diem Passages in Qohelet." *Revue des études juives* 175, no. 1–2 (2016) 27–46.

O'Donnell, Douglas S. *The Beginning and End of Wisdom: Preaching Christ from the First and Last Chapters of Proverbs, Ecclesiastes, and Job*. Wheaton, IL: Crossway, 2011.

O'Dowd, Ryan P. "Epistemology in Ecclesiastes." In *The Words of the Wise Are like Goads: Engaging Qohelet in the 21st Century*, edited by Mark J. Boda et al., 195–217. Winona Lake, IN: Eisenbrauns, 2013.

Ogden, Graham S. "The 'Better'-Proverb (*Tôb-Spruch*), Rhetorical Criticism and Qoheleth." *JBL* 96, no. 4 (1977) 489–505.

———. *Qoheleth*. Sheffield: JSOT Press, 1987.

———. "Qoheleth IX 1–16." *VT* 32, no. 2 (1998) 158–69.

———. "Qoheleth XI.7–XII.8: Qoheleth's Summons to Enjoyment and Reflection." *VT* 34, no. 1 (1984) 27–38.

———. "Qoheleth's Use of the 'Nothing Better'-Form." *JBL* 98, no. 3 (1979) 339–50.

———. "'Vanity' It Certainly Is Not." *The Bible Translator* 38, no. 3 (1987) 301–7.

Ogden, Graham S., and Lynell Zogbo. *A Handbook on Ecclesiastes*. UBSHHT. New York: United Bible Society, 1997.

Packer, J. I. *Knowing God*. Rev. ed. Downers Grove, IL: InterVarsity, 1993.

Paterson, John. *The Book That Is Alive*. New York: Charles Scribner's Sons, 1954.

Paul VI. *Populorum Progressio*. Encyclical, March 26, 1967. Accessible at http://www. vatican.va/content/paul-vi/en/encyclicals/documents/hf_p-vi_enc_26031967_populorum.html.

Perdue, Leo G. *Wisdom and Creation: The Theology of Wisdom Literature.* Nashville: Abingdon, 1994.

Perry, T. A. *Dialogues with Koheleth: The Book of Ecclesiastes.* University Park, PA: The Pennsylvania State University Press, 1993.

———. "Planning the Twilight Years: Qohelet's Advice on Aging and Death (Qoh. 12:1–8)." In *God's Twilight Zone: Wisdom in the Hebrew Bible,* 127–32. Peabody, MA: Hendrickson, 2008.

Plantinga, Cornelius, Jr. *Not the Way It's Supposed to Be: A Breviary of Sin.* Grand Rapids: Eerdmans, 1995.

Prince, Gerald. *Narratology: The Form and Functioning of Narrative.* Berlin: Mouton, 1982.

Pritchard, James B., ed. *Ancient Near Eastern Texts Relating to the Old Testament.* Princeton, NJ: Princeton University Press, 1950.

Provan, Iain. *Ecclesiastes, Song of Songs.* NIVACS. Grand Rapids: Zondervan, 2001.

———. "Fresh Perspectives on Ecclesiastes: 'Qohelet for Today.'" In *The Words of the Wise Are like Goads: Engaging Qohelet in the 21st Century,* edited by Mark J. Boda et al., 401–16. Winona Lake, IN: Eisenbrauns, 2013.

Rad, Gerhard von. *Old Testament Theology—Volume 1.* Translated by D. M. G. Stalker. San Francisco: HarperSanFrancisco, 1962.

———. *Old Testament Theology—Volume 2.* Translated by D. M. G. Stalker. San Francisco: HarperSanFrancisco, 1965.

———. *Wisdom in Israel.* Repr. Nashville: Abingdon, 1984.

Rankin, R. O. "The Book of Ecclesiastes." In *The Interpreter's Bible,* edited by George A. Buttrick, 1–88. New York: Abingdon, 1956.

Roper, Leon A., and Alphonso Groenewald. "Job and Ecclesiastes as (Postmodern) Wisdom in Revolt." *ThSt* 69, no. 1 (2013) 1–8.

Rotman, Marco. "Vocation in Theology and Psychology: Conflicting Approaches?" *JCHE* 16 (2017) 23–32.

Rudman, Dominic. *Determinism in the Book of Ecclesiastes.* JSOTSS 316. Sheffield: Sheffield Academic, 2001.

Ryken, Leland. "Ecclesiastes." In *A Complete Literary Guide to the Bible,* edited by Leland Ryken and Tremper Longman III, 268–80. Grand Rapids: Zondervan, 1993.

———. *Words of Delight: A Literary Introduction to the Bible.* Grand Rapids: Baker, 1992.

Rylaarsdam, J. Coert. *Revelation in Jewish Wisdom Literature.* Chicago: University of Chicago Press, 1946.

Samet, Nili. "How Deterministic Is Qohelet? A New Reading of the Appendix to the Catalogue of Times." *ZAW* 131, no. 4 (2019) 577–91.

Sayers, Dorothy L. "Why Work?" In *Creed or Chaos? Why Christians Must Choose Either Dogma or Disaster (Or, Why It Really Does Matter What You Believe),* 89–116. Manchester: Sophia Institute, 1974.

Shields, Martin A. *The End of Wisdom: A Reappraisal of the Historical and Canonical Function of Ecclesiastes.* Winona Lake, IN: Eisenbrauns, 2006.

Scholes, Jeffrey. "Vocation." *Religious Compass* 4, no. 4 (2010) 211–20.

Schoors, Anton. "Words Typical of Qohelet." In *Qohelet in the Context of Wisdom,* edited by Anton Schoors, 17–40. BETL 136. Leuven: Peeters, 1998.

Schultz, Richard L. "Unity or Diversity in Wisdom Theology? A Canonical and Covenantal Perspective." *TB* 48, no. 2 (1997) 271–306.

Schwienhorst-Schönberger, Ludger. "Via Media: Koh. 7,15–18 und die Griechisch-hellenistische Philosophie." In *Qohelet in the Context of Wisdom,* edited by Anton Schoors, 181–203. BETL 136. Leuven: Peeters, 1998.

Scott, R. B. Y. *Proverbs-Ecclesiastes.* AB. Garden City, NY: Doubleday, 1965.

————. "Wisdom in Revolt: Agur and Qoheleth." In *The Way of Wisdom in the Old Testament,* 165–89. New York: Macmillan, 1971.

Seow, C.-L. "'Beyond Them, My Son, Be Warned': The Epilogue of Qohelet Revisited." In *Wisdom, You Are My Sister,* edited by Michael L. Barre, 125–41. CBQMS 29. Washington, DC: The Catholic University of American Press, 1997.

————. *Ecclesiastes: A New Translation with Introduction and Commentary.* AB. New York: Doubleday, 1997.

Sharp, Carolyn J. *Irony and Meaning in the Hebrew Bible.* Bloomington, IN: Indiana University Press, 2009.

Shields, Martin A. *The End of Wisdom: A Reappraisal of the Historical and Canonical Function of Ecclesiastes.* Winona Lake, IN: Eisenbrauns, 2006.

Siegfried, Carl G. *Prediger und Hoheslied.* HAT II, 3. 2. Göttingen: Vandenhoeck & Ruprecht, 1898.

Smith, Gordon T. *Courage and Calling: Embracing Your God-Given Potential.* Rev. ed. Downers Grove, IL: InterVarsity, 2011.

Smothers, Thomas. "Biblical Wisdom in Its Ancient Middle Eastern Context." In *An Introduction to the Wisdom Literature and the Psalms,* edited by H. Wayne Ballard, Jr., and W. Dennis Tucker, Jr., 167–80. Macon, GA: Mercer University Press, 2000.

Sneed, Mark R. *The Politics of Pessimism in Ecclesiastes: A Social-Scientific Perspective.* Atlanta: Society of Biblical Literature, 2012.

————, ed. *Was There a Wisdom Tradition? New Prospects in Israelite Studies.* Atlanta: Society of Biblical Literature, 2015.

Spangenberg, Izak R. R. "Irony in the Book of Qohelet." *JSOT* 72 (1996) 57–69.

Staples, W. E. "'Profit' in Ecclesiastes." *JNES* 4, no. 2 (1945) 87–96.

Steele, Walter R. "Enjoying the Righteousness of Faith in Ecclesiastes." *CTQ* 74 (2010) 225–42.

Sternberg, Julius. "The Inner Coherence of the Four Wisdom Books." In *The Shape of the Writings,* edited by Julius Sternberg and Timothy J. Stone, 153–60. Winona Lake, IN: Eisenbrauns, 2015.

Tamez, Elsa. *When the Horizons Close: Rereading Ecclesiastes.* Translated by Margaret Wilde. Maryknoll, NY: Orbis, 2000.

Thompson, David. "'āmāl.'" In *New International Dictionary of Old Testament Theology—Volume 3,* edited by Willem A. VanGemeren, 435. Grand Rapids: Zondervan, 1997.

Towner, W. Sibley. "The Book of Ecclesiastes: Introduction, Commentary, and Reflections." In *The New Interpreter's Bible—Volume V,* edited by Leander Keck et al., 265–360. Nashville: Abingdon, 1997.

Troxel, Ronald L., et al., eds. *Seeking Out the Wisdom of the Ancients.* Winona Lake, IN: Eisenbrauns, 2005.

Trueblood, Elton. *Your Other Vocation.* New York: Harper & Bros., 1952.

Ullendorff, Edward. "The Meaning of *qhlt.*" *VT* 12, no. 2 (1962) 215.

Veith, Gene Edward. "Vocation: The Theology of the Christian Life." *JMM* 14, no. 1 (Spring 2011) 119–31.

Viviano, Pauline A. "The Book of Ecclesiastes: A Literary Approach." *The Bible Today* 22, no. 2 (1984) 79–84.

Volf, Miroslav. *Work in the Spirit: Toward a Theology of Work*. New York: Oxford University Press, 1991.

Waalkes, Scott. "Rethinking Work as Vocation: From Protestant Advice to Gospel Corrective." *CSR* 44, no. 2 (Winter 2015) 135–54.

Walsh, Jerome T. "Despair as a Theological Virtue in the Spirituality of Ecclesiastes." *BThB* 12 (1982) 46–49.

Watson, Francis. *Text, Church and World: Biblical Interpretation in Theological Perspective*. Edinburgh: T. & T. Clark, 1994.

Webb, Barry G. *Five Festal Garments: Christian Reflections on the Song of Songs, Ruth, Lamentations, Ecclesiastes and Esther*. NSBT. Leicester, UK: Apollos, 2000.

Weeks, Stuart. *Ecclesiastes and Scepticism*. New York: T. & T. Clark, 2012.

Westermann, Claus. *Roots of Wisdom: The Oldest Proverbs of Israel and Other Peoples*. Translated by J. Daryl Charles. Louisville: Westminster John Knox, 1995.

Whitley, Charles F. *Koheleth: His Language and Thought*. Berlin: Walter de Gruyter, 1979.

Whybray, R.N. *Ecclesiastes*. OTG. Sheffield: Sheffield Academic, rep. 1997.

———. *The Good Life in the Old Testament*. Edinburgh: T. & T. Clark, 2002.

———. *The Intellectual Tradition in the Old Testament*. BZAW 135. Berlin: Walter de Gruyter, 1974.

———. "Qoheleth the Immoralist? (Qoh. 7:16–17)." In *Israelite Wisdom: Theological and Literary Essays in Honor of Samuel Terrien*, edited by John G. Gammie et al., 191–204. Missoula, MT: Scholars, 1978.

———. "Qoheleth, Preacher of Joy." *JSOT* 23 (1982) 87–98.

Williams, D. H. "Protestantism and the Vocation of Higher Education." In *Revisiting the Idea of Vocation: Theological Explorations*, edited by John C. Haughey, 141–62. Washington, DC: The Catholic University of America Press, 2012.

Williams, James G. *Those Who Ponder Proverbs*. Sheffield, UK: Almond, 1981.

———. "What Does It Profit a Man? The Wisdom of Koheleth." In *Studies in Ancient Israelite Wisdom*, edited by James L. Crenshaw, 375–89. New York: KTAV, 1976.

Williams, Neal D. "A Biblical Theology of Ecclesiastes." ThD diss., Dallas Theological Seminary, 1984.

Wolters, Al. "Ecclesiastes and the Reformers." In *The Words of the Wise Are like Goads: Engaging Qohelet in the 21st Century*, edited by Mark J. Boda et al., 55–68. Winona Lake, IN: Eisenbrauns, 2013.

Wright, Addison G. "Additional Numerical Patterns in Qoheleth." *CBQ* 45, no. 1 (1983) 32–43.

———. "The Riddle of the Sphinx Revisited: Numerical Patterns in the Book of Qoheleth." *CBQ* 42, no. 1 (1980) 38–51.

Wright, J. Robert, ed. *Ancient Christian Commentary on Scripture—Vol. IX: Proverbs, Ecclesiastes, Song of Songs*. Downers Grove, IL: InterVarsity, 2005.

Wright, J. Stafford. "The Interpretation of Ecclesiastes." *EvQ* 18 (1946) 18–34.

Zimmerli, Walther. "Das Buch Kohelet-Traktat oder Sentenzensammlung?" *VT* 24 (1974) 221–30.

———. "The Place and Limit of the Wisdom in the Framework of the Old Testament." In *Studies in Ancient Israelite Wisdom*, edited by James L. Crenshaw, 314–26. New York: KTAV, 1976.

Zimmerman, Frank. *The Inner World of Qohelet*. New York: KTAV, 1973.

Zuck, Roy B. "God and Man in Ecclesiastes." *BibSac* 148 (1991) 46–56.

Subject Index

absurdity, 13, 82, 96, 134
achievements, death bearing on, 38
act-consequence principle, 24, 30, 31
admonitions
    "call to decision" following, 120
    on *carpe diem* ("seize the day"), 132
    in chapter 11, 122–23
    on considering works of God, 84
    on enjoyment of life, 11, 74, 92, 100,
        145
    to "fear God and keep his
        commandments," 31
    on God's gifts, 92
    in the New Testament, 115
    of Paul to Timothy, 105n27
    prudential, 26n49
    Walsh ignoring, 80n146
    on worship, 95
affections, directing to things invisible,
    139
African proverbs, considering, 39–40
age and life experience, associating
    "wisdom" with, 19–20
"agnosticism," 112n52
agreement, on Ecclesiastes as
    "unorthodox," 4–5
aim, of Ecclesiastes as clarified by
    Luther, 14
all human activity, "under the sun," 6
"All is *hebel*," as an exaggeration or
    metaphor, 63
"All is meaningless"
    comprehensive, 133

interpreting, 62–66
as true "under the sun," 8
allegorical interpretation of Ecclesiastes,
    influence of Jerome's, 136n25
allegorizing, "rescuing" Ecclesiastes,
    3n10, 142n55
alternative outlook, of Ecclesiastes, 103,
    107
Ambrose, citing examples of vanity,
    142n53
ancient Near Eastern literature, 35
ancient Near Eastern sources of
    wisdom, 17–18
ancient societies, views on work, 120
ancient wisdom literature, bleak and
    cynical strain, 35
Anderson, William H. U., 6n18
"animal theology" reading, of
    Ecclesiastes, 51
animals, man's fate as like that of, 54
Annotationes in Ecclesiastea ("Notes on
    Ecclesiastes") (Luther), 141
anthropocentric outlook, shifting to a
    theocentric, 108
anthropocentric wisdom, versus divine
    wisdom, 94
anthropological dilemma, "the
    knowledge of good and evil" at
    the heart of, 36
anthropology, wisdom perspective
    concerning itself with, 37
"anti-apocalyptic" classification, of
    Ecclesiastes, 25n47

Scripture Index